Sexual Violence and the Law in Japan

This book provides a detailed examinaton of judicial decision-making in Japanese cases involving sexual violence. It describes both the culture of 'eroticised violence' in Japan, which locates culpability in the feminine body, and the legal system which encourages homogeneity and conformity in decision-making. It details the significant legal constraints confronting women claiming sexual assaults through an analysis of specific case studies and provides a discussion of recent moves to address the problems.

Catherine Burns lectures at Griffith University, Australia. Her research interests include law and popular culture in Japan, gender studies and feminist jurisprudence.

Asian Studies Association of Australia
Women in Asia Series
Editor: Louise Edwards (Australian National University)

Mukkuvar Women: Gender, Hegemony and Capitalist Transformation in a South Indian Fishing Community
Kalpana Ram 1991

A World of Difference: Islam and Gender Hierarchy in Turkey
Julie Marcus 1992

Purity and Communal Boundaries: Women and Social Change in a Bangladeshi Village
Santi Rozario 1992

Madonnas and Martyrs: Militarism and Violence in the Philippines
Anne-Marie Hilsdon 1995

Masters and Managers: A Study of Gender Relations in Urban Java
Norma Sullivan 1995

Matriliny and Modernity: Sexual Politics and Social Change in Rural Malaysia
Maila Stivens 1995

Intimate Knowledge: Women and their Health in North-East Thailand
Andrea Whittaker 2000

Women in Asia: Tradition, Modernity and Globalisation
Louise Edwards and Mina Roces (eds) 2000

Violence against Women in Asian Societies: Gender Inequality and Technologies of Violence
Lenore Manderson and Linda Rae Bennett (eds) 2003

Women's Employment in Japan: The Experience of Part-time Workers
Kaye Broadbent 2003

Chinese Women Living and Working
Anne McLaren (ed.) 2004

Gender and Nation in a New Democracy: Indonesian Women's Organisations in the 1950s
Elizabeth Martyn 2004

Abortion, Sin and the State in Thailand
Andrea Whittaker 2004

Sexual Violence and the Law in Japan
Catherine Burns 2005

Sexual Violence and the Law in Japan

Catherine Burns

RoutledgeCurzon
Taylor & Francis Group
LONDON AND NEW YORK

First published 2005
by RoutledgeCurzon
2 Park Square, Milton Park, Abingdon, Oxon OX14 4RN

Simultaneously published in the USA and Canada
by RoutledgeCurzon
270 Madison Avenue, New York, NY 10016

RoutledgeCurzon is an imprint of the Taylor & Francis Group

Typeset in Times New Roman by
Florence Production Ltd, Stoodleigh, Devon
Printed and bound in Great Britain by
Antony Rowe Ltd, Chippenham, Wiltshire

British Library Cataloguing in Publication Data
A catalogue record for this book is available from the British Library

Library of Congress Cataloging in Publication Data
A catalog record for this book has been requested

ISBN 0–415–33651–1

**For Gully
with love**

Contents

Tables

Series editor's foreword

The contributions of women to the social, political and economic transformations occurring in the Asian region are legion. Women have served as leaders of nations, communities, workplaces, activist groups and families. Asian women have joined with others to participate in fomenting change at the micro and macro levels. They have been both agents and targets of national and international interventions in social policy at the level of the household and family. In the performance of these myriad roles women have forged new and modern gendered identities that are recognisably global and local. Their life experiences are rich, diverse and instructive. The books in this series testify to the central role women play in creating the new Asia and re-creating Asian womanhood. Moreover, these books attest to the resilience and inventiveness of women around the Asian region in the face of entrenched and evolving patriarchal social norms.

Scholars publishing in this series demonstrate a commitment to promoting the productive conversation between Women's Studies and Asian Studies. The need to understand the diversity of experiences of femininity and womanhood around the world increases inexorably as globalisation proceeds apace. Lessons from the experiences of Asian women present us with fresh opportunities for building new possibilities for women's progress the world over.

The Asian Studies Association of Australia (ASAA) sponsors this publication series as part of its on-going commitment to promoting knowledge about women in Asia. In particular, the ASAA women's caucus provides the intellectual vigour and enthusiasm that maintains the Women in Asia Series (WIAS). The aim of the series, since its inception in 1992, is to promote knowledge about women in Asia to both the academic and general audiences. To this end, WIAS books draw on a wide range of disciplines including anthropology, sociology, political science, cultural studies and history. The series could not function without the generous professional advice provided by many anonymous readers. WIAS, its authors and the ASAA are very grateful to these people for their expert work.

Louise Edwards (Australian National University)
Series Editor

Acknowledgements

I am deeply indebted to many people who have assisted me in various ways along what now seems like a very long journey. Even before the project began, Chilla Bulbeck's guidance was instrumental in shaping the direction of this path. For her surprising 'return' at the end with predictably incisive comments on an earlier draft I am very grateful. In the early years of this project, Reiko Atsumi and David Schak offered support when I was 'at sea' and Sandra Buckley led me into a new world of words. Particular thanks are owed to Mark Finnane and Kathy Daly for undertaking supervision of the project half way through. Their support and careful comments on earlier drafts were invaluable and significantly helped to sustain my momentum. I would also like to thank Veronica Taylor, Bronwyn Naylor and Vera Mackie for their constructive comments on an earlier draft. For her help, humour and encouragement in the final stages of this book, I thank Louise Edwards.

My fieldwork in Japan was enriched by the assistance of numerous friends, activists and professionals. I am particularly grateful for the encouragement, professional insights and introductions provided by Tsunoda Yukiko, Matsuda Tōru, Noda Aiko, Hayashi Yoko, Ogura Kyoko, Kinjō Kyoko and Kikuchi Yuriko. I also gained much from the insights and stories of activists and writers on the 'front-line', particularly Yunomae Tomoko, Miya Yoshiko, Kikuchi Kiyomi, Ikeda Richiko, Koichi Hikaru and Hamada Kazuko. For all kinds of nourishment during this time I thank Katalin Ferber. I also owe special thanks to Yuyama Yōko whose friendship, diligence and patience enabled me to continue my research in the direction I chose and to 'Endō-san' whose assistance, and determination enriched and grounded my approach to the study.

I would also like to acknowledge the financial assistance provided by the (former) Australian Vice-Chancellor's Asian Research Council and the (former) School of Modern Asian Studies, Griffith University. This support greatly facilitated my field research in Japan. I would also like to thank Seikei University and particularly Kato Takashi and Fukaya Kumiko for their assistance during this time. The provision of study space, access to resources, academic advice and the general atmosphere of warmth and interest in my work contributed significantly to my research and well-being while I was in Japan.

Finally, I am especially grateful for the humour, care and challenges of family, friends and colleagues. In particular, I want to thank Bernadette Sebar for her uncompromising standards and criticisms which helped me refine earlier drafts of chapters and for her companionship which has always been invaluable; Anne Cullen for her exceptional wit, confidence and comments on early drafts; Stacey Bush for her methodical eye and encouragement; and Maureen Todhunter, Kaye Broadbent and Sue Trevaskes for the Friday night laughs, good counsel and intellectual stimulation. Most importantly, I want to thank those at the centre of the project – to my mother Judy, siblings Helen and Jason, and son Gully for their support, endurance and love, and to Ujang Tinggi for his myriad forms of assistance, patience and serenity.

Prelude

Rape v. murder – or (excessive) self defence?

My narrative concerning the ways Japanese judges consider cases of sexual violence begins with the telling of a variety of stories that circulated in and around the trial of a woman who killed. The woman is not a 'victim' in the legalistic sense, yet, as a prostitute on trial, she has much in common with women who have been sexually victimised. The links begin to emerge from the questions that are raised when we ask how the judges made the sorts of decisions that they did in this case.

In 1987 a Japanese call girl was charged with the murder of her client in a hotel room in Ikebukuro, Tokyo. When she went to meet her client he was waiting for her in the hotel room equipped with a large pointed knife, a vibrator, hairdressing scissors, a screwdriver, masking tape, pegs, various types of rope, a douche, rubber gloves, a video camera, a polaroid camera and a 35 mm camera; paraphernalia familiar to the repertoire of sadomasochism (S&M). The woman was unaware that he might want a sadomasochistic service – for which plenty of specialised agencies exist.

Immediately after she telephoned her escort agency to let them know that all was well he punched her in the stomach, pushed her onto the bed, pinned her down and threatened to kill her if she struggled. He tied her ankles and wrists and with a knife to her face threatened to cut her if she tried to resist. He set the video camera on a tripod and turned it on. For one hour and twenty minutes he filmed and photographed while he ripped and cut off her clothing, harassed and humiliated her, and coerced her into what the court described as 'abnormal' sexual acts.

In her testimony, the woman explained her terror and confusion and her decision not to struggle so that she might avoid further violence, seize the knife, stab him in the stomach and then, presuming he would double over, run out of the door. So, in order to distract his attention, she began a performance of sexual pleasure that enabled her to untie herself and grab the knife.

She stabbed him in the stomach, but he did not double over and he chased her to the door. He grabbed and twisted her hand, which was holding the knife, and in so doing cut her thigh, which later required 13 stitches. Nevertheless, the woman managed to keep hold of the knife and get away from him. However, he caught her, bit her face, grabbed hold of her hair and smashed her forehead into the wall. Again she managed to break free but again he pursued her and blocked her way to the locked door. Finally, he fainted and she telephoned the hotel reception desk saying that the man was dying and needed an ambulance. The client had sustained 33 wounds including small ones and he died from loss of blood approximately one hour after fainting. The woman consistently stated that she had no memory of when she was cut or when she had stabbed her client, with the exception of one stab to the stomach and another to the chest. Two weeks later she was arrested for murder. She was convicted of the less serious charge of excessive self-defence and sentenced to three years' imprisonment. On appeal, her conviction was upheld, but her sentence was suspended.

S&M narratives constructed in the media

In an article published in a popular bi-weekly magazine a professor of psychiatry claimed that the incident occurred because women are ignorant of unusual sex and that if the prostitute had understood there would have been no need to go to the extent of killing her client. The magazine asked why such a man ('honest', 'graduate of a top university' and 'elite businessman') became involved in 'unusual sexual affection' (*ijōseiai*). Their explanation was that such behaviour is a product of intellect and civilisation, noting that 'unusual sex' is more common among men of high intelligence and that it is absent from the animal kingdom (Anon. 1987: 52–53). This narrative complicates simple phallocentric constructions of sex and male (hetero)sexuality centring on erection, penetration and ejaculation by positioning sadism within the range of acceptable expressions of male sexuality and, additionally, by incorporating this aspect as part of a class-based elite male's prerogative; ironically, something that confirms the separation of man from beast. Sadism is thus constructed as a meaningful, albeit unusual, form of masculine sexual expression.

The professor's understanding of sadomasochism as one aspect of normal male sexuality is important not only because it suggests that this construction is normative, but also because this idea, although not directly articulated, was central to the prosecutor's case and the initial decision to imprison the woman. The sadomasochistic sub-text may have appealed to the judge's familiarity with the themes and codes of popular Japanese representations of S&M or pornography.[1] Put another way, the images and narratives constructed in this case may have triggered familiar codes, making it difficult for the judges to read the events, including the video, in any way other than in the context of a pornographic story; that is, a script actors willingly consent to act out.

The prosecutor's narratives

The public prosecutor's case rested on two arguments. First, it was argued that the prostitute–client contract indicated implicit consent to 'abnormal indecent acts' (*hentai teki waisetsu koi*), and that the woman had thus relinquished her right to sexual and physical freedom. Second, the prosecutor argued that the situation was not dangerous and therefore the woman was not really afraid because up to the point when she stabbed him there had been no serious threat to her life. Moreover, at the point when she stabbed him he was unarmed and she was not tied up. According to this construction of events, the client's main goal was merely to get back the knife, and even if he had managed to do so, the prostitute would not have been in any great danger.

The prosecutor called for a degree of empathy for the man: his behaviour constituted a recognisable performance in which his actions and his threats to kill her were just part of the S&M script, and therefore not really serious or malicious. According to this narrative, the plot went wrong when the woman took up the knife, when she appropriated the power of the blade. At this moment she transgressed the boundaries appropriate to any of her possible roles: masochist, prostitute, or woman. As a prostitute, she lay outside the boundaries of socially appropriate female behaviour; as a woman fighting back, she transgressed normative constructions of passive femininity and female sexuality; and, as a masochist, she broke the rules of the sex play.

The defence narratives

The defence counsel's counter-story was that the woman's actions constituted proper self defence: the man had constrained the woman against her will, seriously injured her body, had been a danger to her life. Initially this argument gained only limited acceptance by the judges, possibly because there was little understanding of the woman's psychological state at the time – an aspect of the case barely mentioned in the first trial.

In contrast, a support group for the woman paid particular attention to the woman's psychological state arguing that, 'it is only natural to think that if he had taken the knife by force then he might have killed her' (Yunomae 1989: 48). This argument became one of the main points of the appeal, to some extent due to this group of women who enlisted the help of feminist lawyer Tsunoda Yukiko.[2] Tsunoda, in turn, enlisted the help of eminent psychologist Professor Fukushima Akira and together they constructed a story of a woman wielding a knife primarily as an instinctive reflex stemming from her extreme fear. This new version of events, a woman not playing sex games but genuinely frightened, succeeded in challenging the prosecutor's sub-text of S&M.

Judicial narratives

At the first trial the judges found that the woman's initial act of stabbing constituted legitimate self-defence, but subsequent stabs were unnecessary. The reasons for the sentence rested on the following five points:

1 The woman consented or gave a reasonable impression of consent

> [A]lthough at the beginning [the woman] was injured, threatened and abused by the victim, during the long time that this continued not once did she try to persuade the victim to stop. On the contrary, in the latter half, even if it was pretence, she indicated to the victim an attitude of consent to the indecent acts.

2 She could have escaped without stabbing the client

> Even after she had hold of the knife, and pointing this at the victim was her means to escape, suddenly with a knife which had a sharp, pointed 8 cm wide blade she stabbed him *with all her strength* in a vulnerable part of the body . . . this was exceedingly dangerous. In addition to this, she stabbed him again *with all her strength* into another vulnerable part of the body . . . it is impossible to argue that it was necessary to go to the extent of killing the said person (emphasis added).

3 The woman was partly to blame for the situation because she was a prostitute

> It can be said that one can personally invite danger, and . . . in this case . . . the defendant is partially to blame. Firstly, the fact that she was a prostitute is a cause. That is, hers is a dangerous occupation because prostitutes deal with unknown men alone in hotel rooms and . . . there is an accompanying danger depending on the man's character, and tragically this was the case for the defendant.[3]

4 Prostitutes are entitled to less freedom than 'ordinary women and children'

> Because the defendant was engaged as a prostitute by [her client] she had to consent to normal sexual intercourse and its accompanying sexual behaviour . . . According to the original judgment, it cannot be said that she had given up her personal and sexual freedom completely, but the extent of injury to her personal and sexual freedom is diminished compared to that of ordinary women and children.[4]

5 The woman offered no apology or compensation[5] to the man's family

> We must give consideration to the great emotional shock received by the victim's bereaved family and wife and the fact that the defendant has not offered an apology or any act of compensation.[6]

Leading questions

Could the judges not hear the woman's story of sexual intimidation and abuse? Why is that story so difficult to tell in the courtroom? This case raises far more questions than the judgment seems to answer, questions I attempt to address in this book. My focus is two-fold. First, I am interested in the role of Japanese cultural and socio-legal or extra-legal factors on judicial decision-making. Second, I am interested in what judgments in cases of sexual violence can tell us about dominant understandings of gender, sex and sexuality in Japan.[7]

It might appear odd or 'misleading', as Henshall (1999: 42) asserts, to focus on cases involving sexual violence in order to examine conventional understandings of gender, sex and sexuality, especially as sexual violence could arguably be defined as the very opposite of 'normal' gender and sexual relations. However, ideas about normative sexual relations are at the very core of the way sexual offences are defined. They are defined as crimes because they extend beyond or transgress the norms of heterosexuality – that is the standard against which they are compared. Judgments in these cases, therefore, reveal dominant (masculinist) understandings of gender and heterosexual relations (Naffine 1997: 99) and they simultaneously construct boundaries between normal and abnormal, natural and unnatural, acceptable and unacceptable, the terms coalescing in Japanese as *tsūjō* and *fushizen*. In judgments of sexual offences *tsūjō* (normal, natural, acceptable) and *fushizen* (abnormal, unnatural, unacceptable) are the most commonly used terms to convey these meanings. However, unlike the English terms, these two Japanese words are not binary opposites.

This book is therefore based on the assumption that law does not merely echo socially dominant values and conventions. Law, itself, is a powerful social discourse that produces particular kinds of knowledge and particular kinds of gendered sexual subjects. In so doing, legal discourse excludes and silences stories that do not conform to dominant narratives. What are the dominant narratives produced in Japanese judgments of cases involving sexual violence, what stories are excluded, and how might alternative narratives find a voice in the courtroom?

1 Legal storytelling and sexual violence

> If there were no punishment for rape, we would all be rapists. We do not become (rapists) because there is the deterrent of punishment.
>
> (Nishimura Shingo, quoted in *The Japan Times*, 20 Oct. 1999: 1)

This statement, made in 1999 by then Vice Defence Minister Nishimura Shingo, provoked strong protests in Japan and among neighbouring countries not because the reference to all men being potential rapists was offensive but because he was drawing an analogy with nuclear weapons, arguing that Japan should consider possessing them for their deterrence value. Of more critical concern to this book are Nishimura's assumptions regarding masculinity, the nature of male sexuality and the power of law.

Nishimura is not the only prominent figure in Japan to have drawn public analogies between masculinity and rape. In 1984 Miura Shumon, former Director-General of Japan's Agency for Cultural Affairs, observed that: 'although it is shameful for a gentleman to rape a woman, it is also shameful for a man not to have the physical strength necessary to rape a woman' (Miura Shumon, quoted in Brickman 1986: 38).

The following year, in another interview Miura stated:

> It would be better if rapists would choose unchaste women as their victims. Those women would probably take such incidents as lightly as tumbling down in a puddle . . . They might even be proud of themselves, believing they were raped because of their charm.
>
> (Miura Shumon, quoted in Brickman 1986: 38)

In June 2003 at a population seminar, Ota Seiichi, Liberal Democratic Party (LDP) Diet member and former head of the Management and Coordination Agency, stated that men who gang rape are more virile and therefore more 'normal' than weak men who lack the courage to marry. His comment was made as news was beginning to break on a story of gang rapes organised by elite university students' social clubs (see *The Australian*, 26 November 2003: 30–31). One week later Chief Cabinet Secretary Fukuda Yasuo commented to reporters that 'because men are like black panthers a degree of leniency should be accorded to a rapist if the woman dressed provocatively (*The Japan Times*, 4 July 2003). These 'political gaffes' suggest that rape discursively inscribes the appropriately masculine body with physical strength, aggression and an instinctive natural sexuality that demands release. The very public 'gaffes' also suggest that images of the violent sexual domination of women signal ideals of masculine sexuality and constitute a 'story' that displaces alternative images of rape as injury – how else could such public proclamations be explained? This 'story' resonates with a discursive construction of rape as a sexual attack by a man, overwhelmed by his instinctive sexual urges, on a woman who is guilty of arousing those urges unless or until she can prove her innocence – a narrative so familiar it is generally relegated to the categories of myth and fantasy. Yet, it is sustained in the courtroom and beyond; circulating within and partially constituting a broad culture of eroticised violence that is produced or facilitated by the perception that rape might be a mere 'tumble down in a puddle' – silencing conceptions of rape as unambiguous harm to women.

In Tokyo and other large urban centres, images of naked female bodies abound on the covers of magazines and comics sold in bookstores, kiosks and vending machines, on billboards, late night television shows and on the flyers advertising specialised sexual services which are hand-delivered daily into letterboxes and posted onto telegraph poles, telephone boxes and other available space. There is a highly visible mass culture of commodified female bodies, often eroticising their violation and degradation and this is augmented by a constantly changing array of cafés, clubs and services catering to predominantly masculine sexual pleasures. The conventions contained within this culture construct sex, gender and (hetero)sexuality in particular ways, privileging particular forms of male heterosexuality and denying female subjectivity. In other words, the culture of eroticised violence institutionalises a system of 'compulsory heterosexuality' (Rich 1980), which imposes sexual difference, locating the male as active desiring subject and female as passive object of that desire. The very pervasiveness of this culture normalises the images and practices of sexual violence (see Yunomae 1990: 137; Funabashi 1995: 255–263; Kinjō 1991: 256; Buckley 1991: 181–182).

However, this culture is not, as is often assumed, entirely tolerated. The caretaker of the central Tokyo apartment block in which I lived included in his morning ritual the removal of all flyers advertising sexual services from each of the mailboxes (with what appeared to be little regard for issues of privacy). I also observed like-minded citizens, men and women, similarly incorporating into their daily routine, the tearing down of 'offensive' posters from telegraph poles, phone boxes and so forth. The nightly replacement of these materials was, however, predictable. Japanese feminists have also contested what many refer to as the 'pornographic culture' or 'pornographic society' (Funabashi 1995: 255–263; Yunomae 1990; Miya, interview in Buckley 1997: 168). Political action and protests have targeted particular sexist materials, behaviours and advertising campaigns. Protests, telephone hotlines and surveys, aimed at identifying, naming, and raising public awareness of sexual assault, have served to begin the process of 'breaking the silence' surrounding sexual violence against women. Generating community support and attracting media attention to particular trials has also been an effective yet often overlooked strategy in shifting public awareness.[1]

Sexual harassment cases, in particular, are attracting broad public interest and it is evident that social attitudes are changing. Laura Miller (1998: 45) notes that this is reflected in various recent articles published in two popular magazines for young women (*Can Cam* and *Say*), which indicate that it is no longer 'cool' or acceptable to respond to sexual harassment by giggling or acting flattered. When the word 'sexual harassment' (*sekushuaru harasumento*) entered Japan in 1988 the subject took the popular media by storm. The word was shortened to *sekuhara* and voted the most popular new word in 1989. However, rather than acknowledging a specific and pervasive harm done to women, the term was used in popular discourse to trivialise and undermine the significance of this new challenge to what had been perceived as inevitable practices or effects of masculine sexuality. The first cases of sexual harassment entering the courts[2] received mixed responses. There were some successes, but other decisions were clearly influenced by rape myths. A decade later, however, there are clear indications of a shift in the pattern of judicial decision-making. The amount of damages being awarded to each plaintiff is gradually increasing as is the number of cases being found in favour of the plaintiff.[3] Moreover, the first legislation on sexual harassment (in the amended Equal Employment Opportunity Law) went into effect in April 1999. It is possible that the evident re-thinking of gendered power relations and the harm of sexual assault, which appears to be taking place in civil sexual harassment cases, will have an impact on future criminal rape and indecent assault cases. A central question in this book concerns the extent to which judicial decision-making responds to these competing social discourses concerning sexual violence, or rather, how the law might incorporate alternative stories of sexual violence that are largely excluded from the dominant discourse of rape.

In all cases that come before the courts, experiences and understandings of 'what actually happened' are reduced to simplified 'facts' in the ritualistic processing of criminal and civil trials. Institutional and administrative procedures are bound by legal principles and rules, which in the courtroom pertain to areas such as admissibility of evidence, relevance and so forth. These legal requirements inevitably constrain and shape the articulation of human experiences and perceptions of 'reality' and this inevitably impacts on judicial decision-making. Moreover, given the context of limited time and financial resources, the process of adjudication is essentially less concerned with 'reality' than it is with the efficient determination of 'facts' and a single version of 'truth'. The law, therefore, is limited in its capacity to recognise the full complexity of individual experience.

In cases involving sexual violence these broad limitations of legal procedure take on a more specific character. The determination of 'facts' and 'truth' at the centre of legal rules, principles and the process of adjudication produces sex, gender and sexuality as natural systems. As Judith Butler (1990: 140) argues, these forms that appear natural are an effect of norms produced over time by multiple discourses. The norms produced by the legal discourse of rape achieve their dominance at least in part from a particular narrative device. This device, mobilised in Japanese courtrooms (and elsewhere), incorporates a suggested link to particular theories of a natural world, of sexual drives, of a basic state of social organisation and behaviour. These 'theories' however, are never made explicit in the narrative, but the presumption and authority of verifiability as a theory is used as the basis or rationale for developing opinions and judicial decisions (see Amsterdam and Bruner 2000: 29–30). The implicit link to the theory strengthens the appeal of the narrative by concealing the choices that have been made in mobilising one argument or theory rather than another. Moreover, association with 'the natural order of things' suggests commonsense understandings that require no further explanation. And the most convincing arguments are those that go without saying. My goal is to explore that which goes without saying, or more specifically, to highlight the assumptions and normative standards that constitute persuasive narratives of sexual assault and to articulate the ways in which the Japanese legal discourse on rape produces and regulates the intelligibility of sex, gender and sexuality.

By offering an interpretive analysis of how judges come to their conclusions in particular sorts of cases, I suggest that the overwhelmingly positive evaluations of the Japanese criminal justice system are troubling for women claiming sexual assault. The cases analysed in this study indicate that there are two types of rape: *tsūjō* and *fushizen*. Only *tsūjō* rape cases (those conforming to stereotypic rape scenarios) are granted credibility in the courts. Women's alternative perceptions and experiences of *fushizen* rape (those which complicate the stereotypic rape scenario) are consistently distrusted, dismissed or not heard at all. This patterning effect is produced not by the establishment of legal rules and principles, but by the deployment of extra-legal factors that shape the interpretation of 'facts' in the adjudication process. Of central significance is the culture of eroticised violence in Japan that sustains and perpetuates a 'rape script' or dominant narrative of rape that frames judicial perceptions of sexual violence. The limited biological understandings of sex, sexuality and gender that inform this 'rape script' are therefore reproduced and reinforced through legal discourse. The 'rape script' also inscribes the feminine body as culpable and as such facilitates the notion of victim precipitation in cases that do not conform to dominant narratives of rape, a notion that diminishes the perceived harm of rape. While this study highlights the repressive effects of law's discursive construction of rape on women's ability to relate their experiences of sexual assault in court, I also follow Judith Butler's (1993: 22) assertion that '"repression" operates as a modality of productive power'. While Butler is concerned more specifically with theoretical questions regarding the explanatory potential of psychoanalytic vocabulary, her point is also applicable to empirical studies of law. I suggest that contrary to some feminists' rejection of law as a productive site for struggle, possibilities for feminist intervention emerge precisely out of the oppressive effects of law.

Emerging stories of sexual violence in Japan

Linkages between law, violence against women, and constructions of sex, gender and sexuality have received much academic attention in Anglophone countries, and increasing attention in Asian countries (e.g. Manderson and Bennett 2003 for a range of Asian countries; Idrus 2001: 43–56 for Indonesia; Goodstein 1996: 275–286 for Vietnam; Hilsdon 1995 for the Philippines; Rastam 2002 for Malaysia). In Japan this is still relatively unexplored territory, certainly in the English-language material. However, the growing number of Japanese-language texts, articles and newsletters on sexual violence and the recent implementation of new laws in this area (see Chapter 3) are indicative of Japanese feminists' increasing interest in this subject. In 1984 Miya Yoshiko published one of the first books on the topic, documenting the difficulties facing victims[4] of sexual assault in Japan, including their experiences of legal trials. The October 1990 edition of the legal journal *Hōgaku Seminā* contained six articles by feminist lawyers. The following year, two books by feminist lawyers Tsunoda Yukiko (1991) and Kinjō Kiyoko (1991) examined the institutionalisation of marriage, prostitution, heterosexuality and male violence, focusing on the ways that Japanese law reflects and reproduces patriarchal social structures. Tsunoda, in particular, concludes with a warning that legal and state intervention in the area of 'private relations' needs to be approached with great caution. These insights are further developed in a book by leading feminist lawyer and Diet member (elected in 1998), Fukushima Mizuho (1997). Fukushima highlights women's various subject positions as battered wives, single mothers, prostitutes, rape victims and sexually harassed workers, to challenge the supposed neutrality of judges and to document social and judicial constructions of marriage, sex, sexuality and the category of 'woman' in Japan.

Miya, Tsunoda, Kinjō and Fukushima share a concern in understanding how legal knowledge excludes women's experiences of sexual violence and how these problems can most effectively be challenged and remedied.

While legal reform in some areas is suggested, these authors appear reluctant to embark on this course. Tsunoda (1991) and Kinjō (cited in Miya 1984: 220), for example, argue that problems often lie in the interpretation of the law rather than the letter of the law itself. These works have made a primary contribution to the emerging body of literature documenting the sexual abuse of women in Japan and particularly to legal responses in this area. They play a critical role in retrieving and telling the stories of women who have been targets of sexual abuse – stories frequently silenced in both the courtroom and society at large. It is also clear from their work that the conventional explanation that adjudication is the result of a process of the application of objective rules, principles and facts does not adequately explain the process of selecting between conflicting stories.

Japanese approaches to judicial decision-making

Itoh Hiroshi (1970: 775–804) identifies two main approaches to judicial decision-making in post-war Japan: '*Minshohō*' and 'Experimentalist'. Both identify three stages of the judicial decision-making process: (1) fact-finding, (2) legal interpretation, and (3) application of law to ascertained facts. The two schools differ primarily in terms of the degree of emphasis that should be placed on the various stages and the progression of the stages. According to the *Minshohō* school, the process of judicial decision-making follows a progression: fact → rule of law → decision. While it is acknowledged that the ideology or value-orientation of judges influences fact-finding, a case is ultimately decided on the basis of objective and predictable legal norms rather than subjective value judgements. The analysis of judicial decisions should therefore focus on the causal relationship between the decision and the facts. The outcome of a case, according to the *Minshohō* school, is best explained by analysing the judicial reasoning contained in the written text of the judgment, because this contains the underlying legal norms that link facts with the final decision.

In contrast, the Experimentalists conceptualise the process of judicial decision-making in terms of a progression from: facts → conclusion → rationalisation. They argue that the judicial reasoning in a written judgment does not accurately reflect the actual decision-making process. Rather, a process of feedback takes place between ascertainable facts and tentative conclusions and then the final decision is rationalised in such a way as to *appear* to accurately reflect the actual decision-making process. Judges are obliged to do this because they are bound by rules of law and the concept of *stare decisis* (judicial precedent). Although Japan follows a civil law rather than a common law tradition, precedents are important. While prior decisions are rarely cited in the written judgments of particular cases, influential decisions are regularly discussed in legal publications. Within the Experimentalist school the most extreme position is put forward by Katō Ichirō who argues that: 'judges use their hunches first to decide the solution of conflicting interests and only after that try to justify their conclusion by the inductive process in a convincing and persuasive manner' (Katō, cited in Itoh 1970: 794).

According to the Experimentalists, the most influential factors in judicial decision-making are the judges' value systems and their obligation to harmonise their decisions in terms of existing legal norms – not the rule of law, as the *Minshohō* school advocates. The written judgment is therefore, essentially, the justification of a decision rather than an explanation of the innate logic of the process of arriving at that decision. The rule of law exists as a 'framework' to guide or regulate decisions, to ensure lawful interpretations of legal acts. However, Experimentalists argue that meaning is not fixed and legal language is frequently broad and ambiguous, which provides the judge with substantial powers of interpretation. It is up to the judge to choose or highlight one of several meanings of legal acts to correspond with the desired outcome, which the judge evaluates as the most appropriate, based on the 'facts'.[5] For example, Japan's legal definition of rape as 'a person who by violence or threat, obtains carnal knowledge [*seikō*] of a female person' (see Appendix 1) encompasses rape in marriage. Under the rule of law the relationship between the offender and the victim is irrelevant. However, it is clear that judges do not support this view and attempt to represent 'appropriate social values' by privileging instead the 'right' to sex with a spouse (see Chapter 3).

Itoh argues that the Experimentalists' approach is more useful in terms of its ability to describe, explain and predict judicial decision-making. He argues that the *Minshohō* school has failed to substantiate the assertion of a high degree of rationality in judicial decision-making based on the logic of the rule of law or legal reasoning, while the Experimentalists more reasonably claim a high degree of rationality in judicial decisions due to the consistency in the value judgements of individual judges (Itoh 1970: 803).

Itoh's evaluation of the two schools of thought provides a useful base from which to approach judicial decision-making in Japan although there are limitations. One of the problems is that both schools assume the judiciary is a neutral body, governed in its decisions by dominant community values. This orientation towards community-based standards reflects the Ministry of Justice's emphasis on maintaining a judiciary independent from political processes, reinforced by bans on judges' participation in, or membership of, political organisations. One consequence of this orientation towards community rather than overtly political-based standards is the tendency to neglect questions regarding the appropriateness of community standards (possibly sexist, racist or homophobic) as a standard for adjudication.

Another problem with both schools of thought is their over-determination of the rule of law as a constraint on judicial decision-making. Deconstructionist literary and legal scholar Stanley Fish (1980), for example, argues that the key constraint on judicial interpretation is the legal 'interpretive community'. Fish explains that judges are tacitly aware that their decisions must satisfy the legal 'interpretive community' and thus be seen to conform to existing legal norms and standards. Hunter (2003) makes a similar point regarding the culture of barristers in Australia, conceptualised following Benedict Anderson, as an 'imagined community'. This community reproduces a culture of hegemonic masculinity through the performance of particular practices and 'invented traditions'. The Experimentalists would agree that the legal community has an influence on decision-making, but they would probably differ on the degree of that influence and, unlike Fish and Hunter, insist on the fundamental rationality of existing legal norms and standards.

It is now widely accepted among legal theorists that if we are to understand judicial decision-making, the role of interpretation is what needs to be scrutinised. However, critical legal scholar Kim Lane Scheppele (1991) argues that while it is commonly understood that the law/fact distinction is not a matter of logic but an institutional convention, many theorists ignore the question of fact and focus primarily on the interpretation of law. Facts are still frequently regarded as being essentially transparent or given, simply true or false. Scheppele argues that legal interpretation constructs accounts of law and fact simultaneously and she demonstrates the degree of interpretive flexibility judges have in the construction of facts, that is, in the process of giving them meaning, which is derived primarily from the perspective or framework of the broader narrative (see also Green 1997).

Legal storytelling and tales of rape

The legal storytelling or narrative approach to law emerged from the Critical Legal Studies movement in the early 1980s and has been developed by feminist and critical race theorists in particular, who are concerned with Foucault's (1980) insight that what counts as 'knowledge' or 'truth' is determined by relations of power and materialised through the 'subjugation' of alternative accounts or experiences. The legal trial is imbued with stories that take a variety of forms. Not only must witnesses and their legal representatives construct stories that, like all stories, aim to persuade, but the legal storytelling approach argues that stories are central to judicial decision-making. The most convincing story format is the script, which 'provide[s] walk-through models of a culture's canonical expectations' (Amsterdam and Bruner 2000: 45). A script encapsulates ideas that virtually go without saying. What I refer to as the rape script, for example, is the conventional story of a violent sexual attack by a man on a woman who is guilty of arousing his sexual drives unless or until she can prove her innocence.[6] This script essentially serves as template against which all cases of sexual assault are measured. In contrast, Amsterdam and Bruner (2000: 5) define narratives as 'stories that illustrate what happens when a script is thrown off track or threatened with derailment'.[7] These are the stories that are mobilised to rationalise or explain events and behaviours that disrupt norms or expectations.

Richard Delgado (1989) usefully divides narratives into two types of stories: stock stories and counter-stories. Those in a position of dominance, or 'insiders', tend to produce stock stories, which often affirm in-group identity and normalise established power relations and hierarchies. An example of a stock story of rape is that 'real' victims resist the attack with all their strength. The power exercised in the construction of stock stories is all the more forceful when endorsed by the authority of the law. However, the very construction of these stories is partially constituted and circumscribed by the exclusion of alternative accounts of social reality, that is, counter-stories. Legal narrative scholars generally aim to retrieve the counter-stories (e.g. some women respond to fear by freezing), stories of marginalised groups or 'outsiders', whose consciousness is other than that of the dominant group at least partly due to experiences of oppression and devaluation by dominant discourses. Counter-stories may be subversive to the extent that they reconstitute a set of social relations to disclose new meanings.

Departing from conventional or positivist legal approaches, legal storytelling rejects claims of absolute meanings and objective truth. The feminist critique of objectivity and neutrality as scientific method is well argued by radical feminist Catharine MacKinnon (1987: 54–55). She notes that in the legal arena the objective standpoint, which is privileged because of its assumed 'point-of-viewlessness', can only be assumed by an embodied subject and traditionally it has been men who have been in a position to claim this subject position, the position of 'knower'. The fundamental feminist contention that sex/gender is one of the primary organising principles of how we come to know about and experience the world and construct our sense of reality means that within the patriarchal context the gender of the knower makes a difference. The male subject who has masqueraded as neutral has been in a position to construct what counts as knowledge, disavowing inherently masculine perspectives by positing objectivity and, in so doing, validating that knowledge as 'truth'. Experiences and perspectives that do not conform to dominant discourses are thereby disqualified or silenced.

Dispelling the myth of law's claim to objective neutral fact-finding, McBarnet (1981) highlights the constructedness of the legal trial as opposed to the notion of a trial as the search for truth. She explains that the trial is not merely based on distinguishing between lies and true accounts of 'what happened'. Witnesses may perceive and make sense of events differently and their varying self-believed descriptions of 'what happened' may all correspond with reality. Furthermore, the trial involves their recollections of what happened, that is, *how* the event is remembered, often long after the incident occurred. In addition, the rules of proof such as admissibility and relevance regulate and limit the evidence that can be shown and the stories that can be told and how they may be told, where they start and where they finish. All these factors have very real legal consequences, which will be explored in subsequent chapters of this book. McBarnet argues that,

> Just as the concept of the legal subject abstracts him from his real social being, so the case abstracts from the complexity of experience . . . Conceptions of reality are multifaceted and unbounded; cases are 'the facts' as abstracted from this broad amorphous raw material. The good advocate grasps at complex confused reality and constructs a simple clear-cut account of it. A case is thus very much an edited version. But it is not just edited into a minimal account – a microcosm of the incident – it is an account edited with vested interests in mind . . . Far from being 'the truth, the whole truth and nothing but the truth' a case is a biased construct, manipulating and editing the raw material of the witnesses' perceptions of the incident into not so much an exhaustively accurate version of what happened as one which is advantageous to one side. In relation to an incident, then, a case is partial in both senses – partisan and incomplete.
>
> (McBarnet 1981: 17)

How do judges make sense of and choose between these conflicting versions of 'what actually happened'? It is clear that judges do not make decisions arbitrarily, but it is also clear that we can no longer rely on law's 'rhetoric of objective fact-finding, truth discovery, scientific proof and conclusive evidence [which mask] a series of choices . . . informed not by "objective" considerations but subjective factors, which, because they accord with the dominant ideology, are frequently considered neutral' (Kaspiew 1995: 354). Legal storytelling aims to identify and analyse the reasons some stories (stock stories) are consistently found to be more persuasive than alternative accounts. For example, this study of Japanese judgments in cases of sexual violence reveals patterns consistent with similar studies in other countries that have found a particular configuration in the types of cases or stories accepted and rejected in the courtroom: cases in which the offender is a stranger and the woman cannot be construed as blameworthy do not require the same degree of force by the offender and resistance by the victim-survivor in order to secure a conviction. A conviction is less likely when the victim-survivor either knows her attacker or her behaviour can be construed as provocative (Estrich 1987; Lees 1997; Adler 1987; Sterling 1995: 87–132).

A story is recognised as persuasive when it adheres to and makes sense in accordance with the particular experiences and ideas that contribute to our perceptions of 'the way things are' (Scheppele 1987, 1989). The implicit standards for descriptions of reality tend to correspond to culturally specific normative conventions and understandings of the world and the way it operates. However, different perceptions of the way things are do emerge, particularly when differently situated people (e.g. class, gender, sexuality, ethnicity, ability/mobility) experience and come to see the world in distinctly different ways. Differing perceptions between differently situated social groups also tend to emerge and become reinforced during periods of significant social change and particularly when a lawsuit is at issue. This situation solidifies the competition between different perceptions of events. For example, there has been an evident shift in thinking about sexual violence and gender relations in Japan, particularly since the mid-1980s, and this has been partly due to legal battles regarding sexual harassment. As a result, with the increasing social recognition of women's experiences and perceptions of 'unwanted sexual attention', the same behaviour that once cast a man as 'appropriately masculine' is increasingly casting him as 'perpetrator' or 'criminal' (Ikeda 1995: 5).

Different descriptions of events or divergent stories may be an indication of existing gaps in perception, what Scheppele refers to as 'perceptual fault lines', rather than an indication that one party is telling the truth and another lying. In the legal context, these 'perceptual fault lines' are frequently greatest between insiders' stock stories and the counter-stories told by marginalised outsiders. Although a particular story may be an accurate interpretation of events, it may be rejected or excluded by the law because the story is based on experiences that differ from the experiences of those who sit in judgement. Scheppele (1989: 2082) goes so far as to argue that:

> In law, the adoption of some stories rather than others, the acceptance of some accounts as fact and others as falsehood, cannot *ever* be the result of matching evidence against the real world to figure out which story is true.

Legal storytelling scholarship generally aims to contribute, at the very least, to slow and incremental social change by detailing the ambiguity and contradictions contained within dominant narratives and the ways in which legal discourses disqualify and exclude alternative accounts of the social world. The subversive potential of legal storytelling lies in both the possible disruption of dominant ideologies and the empowerment of marginalised groups through the sense of 'community building' that the identification of common experiences and perceptions within a group can achieve. A notable example is that of the 'consciousness raising' collectivities that emerged through the 'women's movement' in the 1960s in Anglo-European countries and in Japan from the 1970s (see Tanaka, K. 1995: 345). Women gained strength and found political purchase in identifying common experiences of discrimination and abuse, particularly sexual abuse, which they previously had thought were solitary experiences unique to their own lives.

One of the most comprehensive studies of sexual violence using the legal storytelling approach is Susan Estrich's (1987) study of US rape trials. Focusing on both her own experience in reporting a rape and the hegemonic stories produced in the courtroom, Estrich clearly identifies two conflicting accounts of the way rape is regarded by law and legal personnel. On one hand, rape is regarded as a heinous offence and thus carries stiff penalties. Police, prosecutors and judges are likely to comment on the gravity of the offence or the viciousness of the attack and women who come before them may be treated with sympathy. On the other hand, there is evidence to suggest that the majority of sexual assault allegations will be trivialised and dismissed from further legal proceedings. An abundance of feminist research has revealed that in cases of sexual assault the majority of women are unlikely to file a formal complaint, at least partially because they believe they will receive little sympathy from the courts or from society in general. A concise summary of major studies across a range of countries is provided by Susan Edwards (1996: 331–332).

Estrich explains this seeming paradox in terms of two types of rape stories: 'real' rape and 'simple' rape. The law has no trouble identifying and treating seriously 'real' rape scenarios where a woman who could not be construed to have provoked an attack is physically beaten with a considerable degree of force, possibly threatened with a weapon, by at least one stranger in a public place. In such cases the law has no hesitation in condemning the act and the rapist. In contrast, 'simple rapes' are those cases where the woman and rapist were acquainted, where there is little evidence of physical force and where the woman's action could be construed as provocative. These are the cases most likely not to be reported or, if reported, they are most likely to be dismissed at some stage of the legal proceedings. In these cases it is more likely that perceptions of what happened are likely to diverge. This is not to suggest that all perceptions are equally relevant or valid. Rather, the point is that in such circumstances it is more likely that the woman's explanation of events will not be accepted at face value and the defendant's perceptions of what happened may differ to a considerable degree from that of the woman.

For example, in a 1987 Australian trial that could be classified as a 'simple' rape case, the woman argued that she was afraid of the defendant, was locked in a room with him and she was sure he intended to attack her. She therefore watched him very closely. The defendant argued, '[s]he kept looking at me, giving me the eye, and that's how I thought that she wanted to go to bed with me' (quoted in Nina Puren 1995: 19). Scheppele (1987: 1109) notes that social psychological research indicates significant gendered differences in perceptions of sexual intentions, with men more likely to sexualise their descriptions of women and social situations. For example, the same 'friendly' behaviour is more likely to be interpreted as mere politeness by women but seductive and provocative by men. Such research also indicates that men often make mistakes about what the woman thinks is going on. A woman may experience rape by a man who, in contrast, thought he was playing the role of seducer and used what he thought was the normal or appropriate degree of aggression needed to overcome what he perceived to be the 'no' that meant 'yes'. A survey of over 6,000 students in the US conducted by Mary Koss (1998) found significant discrepancies between the way men and women interpret women's consent to sex. The survey found that women who have been targets of sexual assault perceive their resistance and the degree of force and coercion used to attain sexual intercourse as much more extreme than did offenders. This type of research suggests that the perceptual fault lines occurring between men and women in the area of sexuality are 'deep, enduring, and of enormous consequence in daily life' (Scheppele 1987: 1110–1111).

Judges, prosecutors and police – those in the legal position of choosing between divergent accounts of events – are thus faced with these perceptual fault lines and must decide and accord validity to one side. But in law, the established legal standards on which this adjudication process is based serve to hide or disqualify one set of perceptions. It is, therefore, the telling of women's counter-stories and the exposure of the 'subjugated knowledges' (Foucault 1980) they entail that is the focus and political force of feminist legal storytelling.

However, many scholars argue that the telling of alternative or counter-stories is inherently limited in its aim to produce social change. Such arguments frequently draw attention to the lack of evidence in Australia, Britain, the US and Canada of substantial positive gains for women despite the implementation of numerous legal reforms intended to address the 'newfound' knowledge of the victimisation of female complainants in sexual assault trials (Graycar 1996: 297–316; Kaspiew 1995: 350–382). Responding to such criticisms of postmodernist discourses in general, Margaret Davies (1994: 169) argues that definitions of what constitutes social change are often too narrowly conceptualised. Whatever contributes to the production of the conditions in which change can occur, including theoretical or narrative works that generate alternative ways of viewing the world, can make significant contributions to the process of change. However, it is understandable that many feminists and other social reformers have not only grown impatient and frustrated with the slow and incremental changes to legal policies but have also recognised the need to deepen our understandings of the complexities involved in social and legal transformations. Some feminists have more recently begun to argue that although it remains important to continue to give voice to women's experiences of gendered violence, which are otherwise discounted in the legal system, it is also important to examine the constraints involved in telling these stories – that is, to move beyond mere storytelling and analyse the legal categories and frameworks that structure what can and cannot be said (Graycar 1996: 297–316; Ehrlich 2001).

How applicable are these questions and insights, developed in the Anglophone legal arena, to the Japanese judicial context? In order to examine this question it was necessary to gain access to judicial decisions in Japanese cases of sexual violence.

Locating legal cases

This study is based on 41 cases (listed in Appendix 2)[8] that went to trial from 1969 to 1997: 20 rape, 10 indecent assault and 11 sexual harassment cases (approximately one quarter of all sexual harassment cases which had gone to trial by 1997).[9] The sample includes eight full or partial trial transcripts (most are unpaginated): six transcripts of sexual harassment judgments, one transcript of a sexual harassment case not including the judgment because after 6 years the case was settled out of court,[10] and one full trial transcript of a compensation claim involving rape.[11] The remaining 33 cases were published in the two main commercial, fast-service case reporters *Hanrei Jihō* (*The Case Review*, three publications per month) and *Hanrei Taimuzu* (*The Case Times*, published monthly). Of these, 28 cases were located by a CD-Rom search of criminal cases from 1986 to 1996, and five cases from 1969 to 1985 were identified as significant by Japanese feminist legal scholars.

In the case reporters, the judgment (*hanketsu*)[12] is usually preceded by a very brief statement about why the case is noteworthy, followed by a short commentary or summary of the main issues in dispute, usually up to half a page in length. The judgment sums up the admitted facts, provides the reasoning behind the judgment, the judgment itself, the applicable laws and regulations, the verdict, and the sentence or any other penalty imposed. The length and detail of the judgment is largely dependent on the perceived complexity of the case and whether the charge was contested, in which case supplementary notes are provided. The length of each case in my sample ranged from 1 to 43 pages with the majority around 3 to 5 pages.

While the case reporters generally select for publication novel cases that raise questions of specific legal interest, many of these cases were of little relevance to my particular interest in how judges construct rape, sexuality and gender. On this basis, an additional 28 cases involving a sexual assault were eliminated from the study because the judgment focused entirely on issues such as DNA testing and the legality of unsigned documents, or on additional serious charges such as murder and robbery. When judgments are used for purposes other than that for which they were originally written, their usefulness is often limited in terms of alternative research questions. Information relevant to my study such as discussions of the character and behaviour of the complainant and defendant were often omitted from the judgments in my primary sample.

Both ‘good’ and ‘bad’ judgments in terms of awareness and sensitivity to feminist analyses of sexual abuse are found before and during the

1986–1996 period. While it is impossible to accurately gauge whether a shift has, in fact, taken place on the basis of the existing literature and my sample of cases, the implementation of new laws (e.g. anti-stalking law in 2000 and domestic violence law in 2001) and judicial decisions in recent sexual harassment cases (discussed in Chapter 7) certainly do suggest a re-thinking of the nature and harm of sexual abuse. However, this observation needs to be tempered by the legal fact that the standard of proof in criminal and civil cases is different. Similar to other legal systems, a criminal case demands proof beyond reasonable doubt while civil cases accept proof on the basis of reasonable probability. The 11 sexual harassment cases, two rape cases and one indecent assault case were heard in civil courts because they involved a claim for compensation.

The focus of this study is on the 20 rape cases (cases 1–9 are summarised in Chapter 4 and cases 10–20 in Chapter 5), however, where relevant this is supplemented by judicial comments in sexual harassment and indecent assault cases. More extensive incorporation of the indecent assault cases is complicated by the fact that five cases involved girls 13 years and under, one of whom was intellectually disabled, and another case involved a physically disabled woman. These sorts of cases rarely invoke judicial comment on questions central to this study, such as the degree of force and resistance used in an attack and 'victim precipitation'.[13]

I also observed 44 hearings at Tokyo District and High Courts and Utsunomiya District Court during June and July 1997, in order to understand the broader context in which the archival texts are generated. There is no system of trial by jury in Japan. Although a jury system existed from 1928–1943, it was abandoned primarily because the vast majority of accused persons waived their right to a jury trial believing that an untrained ordinary citizen was incapable of making a just decision. The re-introduction of a form of jury system to increase lay participation in court decision-making is currently under official review. At present, trials are heard by a single judge or a panel of three judges for particularly important, complex, or criminal cases where the penalty is imprisonment for one year or more.[14] The presiding judge is usually aged 45 to 50 and has had approximately 20 years' experience. The assistant judge seated on the right of the presiding judge is around 35–45 years old with approximately 10 years' experience and the assistant judge on the left of the presiding judge is generally younger and has had less than 10 years' experience. The courtroom is dominated by men, particularly when a tape recorder is used instead of a typist, who is invariably female. However, it is not uncommon to find that one of the assistant judges, the prosecutor, a lawyer (of the hearings I observed this was the case only in sexual harassment trials) or a trainee is a woman. While the number of women working in the criminal justice system remains quite small, the number has been steadily increasing in all areas over the past decade. In April 1999 there were 308 female judges (10.4 per cent of the total), 122 female prosecutors (5.5 per cent) and 1,532 female lawyers (8.9 per cent), while 287 women passed the bar examination (28.7 per cent) (Office for Gender Equality 2000). In December 1996 there were 1,194 female police officers in Japan engaged in sexual crime investigations (Office for Gender Equality 1997: 6).

In addition to archival research and courtroom observations I conducted interviews in Tokyo with a range of professional workers in the area, including legal personnel, academics, counsellors and bureaucrats. The most important interview in Tokyo, on 10 December 1996, was with Endō (a pseudonym), a woman raped by her boss at work who had the courage and tenacity to survive not only the rape but the rejection of her case from the Prosecutor's Office right through to the Supreme Court. In an environment encouraging silence, Endō's insistence on talking about her experience is unusual: she spoke not only with me but with quite a number of writers and journalists in addition to pursuing all legal channels of redress. The details of her story, however, are 'ordinary'.

Overview and organisation of the book

This book focuses particularly on the stock stories or 'hegemonic tales'[15] judges produce in cases concerning sexual assaults – and the counter-stories contained within them. The organisation is framed by Ewick and Silbey's description of the three scholarly forms of narrative research: narrative as research object, as method and as product of inquiry. In terms of narrative as object of analysis, I examine the stories judges construct to explain the events of specific cases that come before them – to make sense of and resolve the confusion created by multiple versions of truth, ambiguity and conflicting evidence. This process involves the selection and rejection of particular aspects of the stories told in court and particular pieces of evidence in order to form a satisfactory narrative that conforms to their understandings of the world and provides an explanation for the specific events entailed in the case. A critical reading of the judgments thus reveals the assumptions and normative standards that constitute appropriate or persuasive narratives of sexual assault in the legal context.

Narrative is also employed as the method of inquiry. Ewick and Silbey (1995: 202) note that 'scholars may collect and examine narratives as a way of accessing or revealing some other aspect of social life'. This method is based on the assumption that narratives can be approached as a window through which social life can be analysed. The aspect of social life in Japan that is central to this book is the intersection between gendered power relations and sexuality. Judicial narratives of rape and sexual assault are used to analyse and illustrate the way in which gender, sex and sexuality are produced through Japanese legal discourses. I suggest that particular gendered assumptions and conventions that have achieved considerable social currency in Japan constitute the pool of 'common sense' from which judges draw in order to interpret 'facts', come to their conclusions and construct their 'hegemonic tales'. These assumptions and conventions structure, contain and constrain what can be said and how. Nevertheless, an alternative reading of the stock stories of sexual assault produced in legal discourses also provides an opportunity to draw out and at least vicariously articulate the 'subjugated knowledges' of women whose experiences of sexual assault in Japan were not believed, were rejected or not heard at all. In other words, stock stories are never completely fixed or stable and from them can be retrieved counter-stories of sexual assault – albeit perhaps to a limited extent given their contained form within official versions of 'what happened'.

The third narrative approach involves the production of a narrative in the shape of this book. It constitutes my representation of judicial stories, based on the selective processes of research data collection, the configuration and interpretation of various materials and ideas which, as Ewick and Silbey (1995: 203) point out, may be as much imaginary as real. Nevertheless, I aim to produce a narrative that provides a sense of coherence and clarity and thus leads to a greater understanding of the intersections between gender relations, sexuality and Japanese criminal justice approaches to gendered violence.

Chapter 2 lays the groundwork necessary to develop the argument that the dominant culture of eroticised violence frames judicial decision-making in cases of sexual violence against women. I focus on how the commodification of eroticised violence normalises a culturally specific discursive construction of masculine sexuality as a system of natural drives. I argue that the productive effects of this discourse silences and obscures the harm of sexual violence by allocating responsibility for that violation to the woman. The chapter concludes with a discussion of how women, discursively constructed as blameworthy, respond to the courtroom environment as witnesses. This section highlights the extent to which these women are active participants in the trial. In contrast to the main focus of this book on judgments, the women are, in this discussion, removed from the perceptual lens of judges – although the distinction is somewhat artificial. A witness is always cognisant of the judge's presence and the presentation of an appropriate victim persona is constructed accordingly.

In Chapter 3, I examine aspects of the criminal justice system in Japan that provide a context for how judges make the types of decisions that they do. I argue that the assumed effectiveness and efficiency of the Japanese criminal justice system needs to be reconsidered in light of emerging evidence of sexual violence which has, until recently, remained relatively hidden. I focus on the principles and practices of the criminal justice system that perpetuate the silence surrounding sexual violence and which obstruct cases from proceeding to court.

Aspects of the legal definition of rape also constitute a significant barrier both to bringing a case to trial and achieving a conviction. In Chapter 4, I examine the black letter law of rape and Japanese legal arguments concerning its interpretation. These scholarly arguments are then considered in the light of nine cases that resulted in a conviction for rape. The examination of these particular judicial narratives of rape clarify these arguments by demonstrating what constitutes legal rape in contemporary Japanese courts. These cases illuminate the stock stories of 'normal' (*tsūjō*) rape in the Japanese context.

Chapters 5 and 6 further examine what criteria must be satisfied in order for an act to qualify and be legally verified as rape. This question is explored through an analysis of 11 cases in which the woman's testimony was subject to considerable scrutiny, most but not all failing to achieve a conviction. These cases constitute the stock stories of the 'unnatural' (*fushizen*) rape. I attempt to move beyond the empirical enterprise of describing what constitutes rape as a legal category. I aim to analyse both the ways in which gender and sexuality are produced in legal discourse and the discursive effects that constrain the telling of women's alternative accounts of their sexual abuse.

These constraints are enormous and, while the stock stories of rape appear to be hegemonic, there is space for resistance. In Chapter 7, I explore feminist legal strategies that attempt to highlight and exploit the inconsistencies contained within the dominant interpretations of rape. Recent decisions in sexual harassment cases are included in this discussion because they appear to offer an opportunity for the creative efforts of feminist intervention and the decisions may have possible consequences for the interpretation of rape law in the future.

In the Conclusion, I tie the various arguments together and discuss the future direction and possibilities for feminist intervention in the Japanese legal arena. In particular, I highlight the legal changes resulting from sexual harassment cases and consider the impact that these apparent shifts in thinking might have on criminal cases involving sexual violence.

2 Hegemonic masculinity and guilty feminine bodies

The discursive production of sex, gender and heterosexuality as interlinking natural biologically based systems is rarely called into question either inside the Japanese courtroom (Hata 1990: 50; Hayashi 1990: 31) or beyond feminist circles. Similarly, Anne Allison notes that in academic circles there is resistance to thinking about sexuality outside medical and physiological discourse. Despite great popularity, the world of sexuality as it is configured and played out in entertainment industries associated with sexual services (*mizu shōbai*) is overwhelmingly regarded as trivial and meaningless, not a significant aspect of Japanese culture and, therefore, not an appropriate field for research (Allison 1994: 145–148). However, social constructionist theorists argue that, on the contrary, sexuality can only be understood as socially constructed meanings and, indeed, can only be 'performed' once these meanings are learnt.

This chapter explores aspects of the historic and culturally specific discursive constructions of sexuality and gender in Japan in order to shed light on the societal silence surrounding the subject of sexual violence, and to suggest that these constructions shape and structure judges' 'hunches' (see Experimentalists' arguments in Chapter 1). Prostitution constitutes a common thread through much of this discussion, partly because it has played a central role in consolidating constructions of 'natural' male sexuality and partly because the prostitute and the woman who has been raped have much in common. They are both ascribed a sexuality, or sexualised in a way that sets them apart from 'ordinary' women. As Carol Smart (1989: 39) notes, when a woman makes a claim of rape she confesses to a sexual experience that sounds very much like a 'soft-porn' script. Her body, through the telling, is imagined in this framework and each body part becomes explicitly sexualised. The story, as it is described in minute detail to police, to lawyers and to judges, can be imagined as pornographic fantasy, about pleasure, and thus, like the prostitute, she becomes suspect. Like the prostitute, she is at least temporarily disqualified from the category of women who can be protected – who are protected precisely because they do not 'look like' prostitutes.

Disrupting the discourse of 'natural' sexuality

In the nineteenth century, biological understandings of sexuality that reduce sexual activity to natural instinctive sexual drives, constrained or repressed only by social and cultural conventions, came to dominate in Japan as in other, Anglo-European, countries. This was partly due to the rapid developments in biological science at this time and the increasing exchanges of scientific knowledge taking place between doctors in Japan, North America and Europe (Pflugfelder 1999: 242–244).

The first significant sociological challenge to biological explanations of sexuality developed in the US in the early 1970s. Sociologists John Gagnon and William Simon argued that sexuality is not a fixed biological 'fact' but, rather, it is produced through socially constructed meanings. They argued that the 'sexual script' has two dimensions: internal or intrapsychic states that relate to the motivational aspects informing arousal, and external or interpersonal states that organise actors' participation in sexual activity. Individual actors must learn and understand these states before sexual activity can take place: the script 'defines the situation, names the actors, and plots the behaviour' without which a sexual experience is unlikely to occur (Gagnon and Simon 1973: 19).

This challenge to biological assumptions of a 'natural' sexuality contributed to the fundamental feminist challenge to the assumption that 'biology is destiny'. However, there are a number of problems with Gagnon and Simon's argument. They assume that a 'neutral' body pre-exists the 'sexual script' and because the individual is the locus of theoretical attention, the role of power relations in producing meaning, subjectivity and the body is obscured. This gap is partially addressed by Foucault (1978) who used a wider framework to understand how meaning is produced. Foucault's analytical focus on the production of knowledge and power illuminates the ways in which meaning is produced through discourse and practice. According to discourse theory there can be no pre-existing individual situated outside discourse but, rather, both the body and the subject acquire meaning only through their location in social contexts and through cultural practices. They are constituted in and through the power relations that produce meaning. Biological discourses ignore the social history of sex and our understandings of nature and, therefore, also temporal and cultural variations.

Feminist scholars have extended these ideas further in their examination of the gendered power relationship that regulates the sexed bodies who 'perform' the 'sexual script', normalising particular forms of sexual activity. Some scholars have drawn on psychoanalytic theories to examine the construction of sexuality at the level of individual subjectivity, focusing on the question of how we become gendered sexual subjects (see Whitford 1991; Allison 1996). Other feminists have drawn on Foucault's work more directly to highlight the variability and plasticity of sexuality and to link this with structural analyses of inequality (see Duncan 1995: 326–352; Smart 1989: 90–113; Shibata 1999: 48–86). Judith Butler has argued that much of this work leaves the body untheorised. She is concerned with how gender and the body, or sex, come to be constituted through regulatory norms, and argues that the materialisation of sex (like gender) are the effects of repetitive ritual practice or 'reiteration'. Discourses construct the body/sex, but this does not imply originary, exhaustive or causal claims. Rather, 'it is to claim that there is no reference to a pure body which is not at the same time a further formation of that body' (Butler 1993: 10). Butler (1990) disrupts essentialist or biological arguments, arguing that gender is an ideal identity that comes into being in approximated forms through sustained 'performance'. Thus, gender is not an attribute that subjects have but, rather, something that they do. However, this performance does not provide the subject with unrestrained agency. Rather, as Ehrlich (2001) notes and develops in her own work, Butler (1990: 33) acknowledges that gendered sexual subjects are produced within a 'rigid regulatory frame' which, over time, produces the impression of a natural state. Ehrlich's detailed linguistic analysis of one rape trial highlights the significance of legal discourse as one element in this 'rigid regulatory frame' that shapes and constrains the enactment of gender.

Radical feminists have focused on sexual violence as a clear manifestation of male power, paying particular attention to the institutionalisation and normalisation of heterosexuality through which masculine power is reproduced as dominance and submission (see MacKinnon 1987; Kelly and Radford 1996; Tsunoda 1991; Fukushima 1997). Heterosexuality is, therefore, regarded as central to the creation of the gendered categories of 'men' and 'women', socially produced as unequal (Connell 1995; Jackson 1996; Chalmers 2002). A number of feminist theorists since the 1980s have emphasised that gender is not arbitrarily connected to the body. They use the term 'sexed bodies' to convey the idea that the meanings and significance of the ways in which masculinity and femininity are experienced by the individual is fundamentally based on ideas about male and female bodies (Gatens 1996; Pringle 1992). Attention has also turned to analysing the ways in which discourses and practices mark the body as masculine or feminine (Bartky 1988; Cahill 2000: 43–63). This work, as will be discussed further on in this chapter, highlights the gendering effects of sexual violence.

Normalising *sukebei* masculinity and prostitution

At various times and in varying contexts, the Japanese state has constructed prostitution as a means to prevent rape, maintain social control, and regulate public morals and hygiene – all of which reproduce ideas of instinctive male sexual drives requiring an outlet. Providing an appropriate sexual outlet for men was a premium concern in the early years of Meiji (1868–1912).

ation demanded 'new types of men' to work in urban factories release was regarded as central to the maintenance of healthy rkers. However, due to low wages and conditions of poverty, quently had to delay marriage and prostitution was, therefore, as a necessary means to sustain men's 'vital energies'. Consequently, prostitution was seen by some leading officials as an essential means of maintaining the socio-economic order and, therefore, a contributing factor in Japan's economic rise (Garon 1997: 101).

Similarly, prostitution was seen as vital to maintaining the type of masculine body required by the military. Justifying the establishment of *ianjo*, popularly known as 'comfort stations' or, more appropriately, 'rape camps', in which local women were forced to provide sexual services for Japanese military personnel in China, Korea and Southeast Asian countries from the late 1930s to 1945, author Naoi Masatake argues that:

> On a battlefield, in order for a man to be 'useful', it is necessary to maintain a healthy body and an aggressive mind. Managing sexual desire harmonizes body and mind, and lubricates war operations. It is natural and necessary for military leaders to establish comfort stations.
> (quoted in Shibata 1999: 62)

State-regulated prostitution, thus, functioned to regulate the sexuality of, and to obtain obedience from, male workers and military personnel (Shibata 1999; Chung 1997: 2230; see also Stetz and Oh 2001). Similarly, the fear of uncontrollable male sexuality prompted the government's immediate institutionalisation of Recreation and Amusement Association (RAA) brothels for the occupying forces at the end of the Second World War to protect 'respectable' Japanese women from rape and the purity of 'the Japanese family' from mixed race children.[1] Sexual service providers for the forces were sought from circles of women deemed less worthy of protection. All the major newspapers ran employment advertisements directed specifically at those who could be sacrificed: geisha, prostitutes, barmaids and waitresses. However, the RAA was far from successful in achieving its goal of preventing rape. Historian, Fujime Yuki notes that police statistics reveal that in 1946 there were 30 reported cases of Japanese women and girls raped by American soldiers, 283 cases in 1947, 265 cases in 1948 and 312 cases in 1949. Moreover, it is likely that many victim-survivors did not file a report due to feelings of shame or fear. Alternative sources estimate that cases were as high as 3,500 in the first month of the occupation forces landing in Japan (Fujime 1997a: 326). Yuki Tanaka (1995: 40) similarly notes that in the first 10 days of the occupation there were 1,336 cases of rape in the prefecture encompassing the two major ports near Tokyo.

In 1946, the system of licensed prostitution was abolished; however, tacit endorsement of prostitution continued for the next decade under a system of special zones for various types of prostitution and entertainment businesses, which were regulated by police. According to the government's National Public Opinion Survey Office, in 1949 the policy had popular support: 70 per cent of respondents justified the practice in terms of safeguarding ordinary girls and limiting the spread of venereal disease. In addition, a Labour Ministry commission on women's affairs stated in 1952 that 'in these days of marital problems, it is a necessary evil that satisfies the instincts of males' (Report by the Women's and Minor's Problems Commission, Labour Ministry, 27 December 1952, cited in Garon 1997: 199).

The shifting rationale for ensuring that male workers and military have access to sexual services indicates that while prostitution has been an area of contestation, the state has consistently seen its regulation as useful. One result of the sustained official regulation of prostitution has been the institutionalisation of the biological discourse on sexuality. This has contributed to the production of compulsory heterosexuality and the normalisation of a particular construction of Japanese masculinity and sexuality – the *sukebei*. As Anne Allison notes, *sukebei* loosely translates as a harmless, perverted, lecherous or 'dirty old man' framework of sexual desires and practiccs which, permeating class and status boundaries, is regarded as the fundamental nature of the (hetero)sexual male. It is the core of 'hegemonic masculinity' (Connell 1995) in Japan. Allison observed of upper- and middle-class male clients in hostess bars:

> Men will identify themselves as *sukebei*, refer to the others at the table as *sukebei*, question who in their party is the biggest *sukebei*, and explain their behaviour out at night as that of a *sukebei*. Obviously there is a strong desire to see oneself and other men as *sukebei* in this setting.
> (Allison 1994: 60)

The performance of *sukebei* underlies institutions such as prostitution and hostess bars, and practices (*sukebei na koto*) such as *chikan* (sexually molesting women on trains), voyeurism, the purchase of women's used underwear and a whole range of fads in the realm of sexual fantasy produced and consumed at a staggering rate. *Sukebei*-ness institutionalises compulsory heterosexuality, signalling the power to take or possess the female body. Consequently, rape is a common theme in *ero manga* (erotic comic books) and *sukebei*-ness is often expressed by exercising the 'right' to touch women's breasts in hostess bars (and elsewhere, although outside these bars this 'right' is being challenged through redefinition as *chikan* and sexual harassment).[2] *Sukebei* masculinity thus pivots around the expression of gendered power. This is highlighted in the familiar social narrative of the emasculated impotent salary man who has, through total devotion and sacrifice to his company, lost his sense of self and manhood symbolised by his inability to achieve an erection. The narrative is essentially a critique of the social expectation of loyalty and self-sacrifice to the company and nation, but the flaccid penis signifies the centrality of sexuality and power to constructions of masculinity.

Japanese men are not inherently or uniquely 'perverted'. The 'technologies' and pervasiveness of *sukebei* practices and the commodification of eroticised violence are derived primarily from the strength of the Japanese economy, sophisticated marketing techniques, the high level of discretionary capital and the consequent growth of a formidable consumer culture. The high levels of consumption and huge profits generated by sex-related industries, make these industries anything but culturally or economically marginal – although discursively peripheral to family and work.[3] One marketing technique of the sex industries (from 'hard-core' pornographic magazines and videos to 'late night television' shows known as '*sukebei terebi*') is to construct, package and sell particular objects or practices as 'perverse' to increase their economic value (e.g. used women's underpants on the *sukebei* market sell for at least three times their original unused price because the purchase is regarded as 'perverse'). While a 'perversion' is generally regarded as a form of mental illness, in this case, a 'perversion' is defined as normal but peripheral to dominant practices (Shigematsu 1996: 161–162).

The *sukebei* discourse is strengthened by its normalisation. This is achieved by incorporating *sukebei* practices into mainstream culture through the market processes of commodification. Shigematsu (1996: 161) discusses the example of a magazine on *chikan*, offering information such as train timetables and platforms where large numbers of schoolgirls and young women can be located, 'how to attack' articles, and mock interviews with women who relish being attacked. The mass circulation of this magazine normalises *chikan* by suggesting that it is a common practice (substantiated by several surveys)[4] and naturalises *chikan* by suggesting that the practice is so pervasive because men 'cannot help themselves', cannot restrain their sexual 'instincts'. S*ukebei* practices are thus constructed as natural and therefore inevitable, even though they may not constitute dominant practices of male sexuality. Dominant and 'perverted' aspects of male sexuality are, therefore, both regarded as expressions of 'healthy' masculinity, but the former receives greater social legitimacy through the institutionalisation of marriage while the latter is regarded as peripheral and of little if any social consequence (Allison 1996: 47). Moreover, coupled with narratives of low crime rates and safe cities, s*ukebei* behaviour as part-fantasy is rendered essentially harmless and as such provides a form of sexual licence to women's bodies.

The argument that the culture of eroticised violence is essentially harmless is sustained only as long as masculine sexuality is constrained by the vigilance of some women while sexual accessibility is guaranteed through the availability of Others, sacrificed women. Of course, the division of women into prostitutes and non-prostitutes facilitates male sexual access to women's bodies while maintaining a pool of chaste potential marriage partners, but on what basis are women divided and how does this division impact on constructions of gender? The explanation is not as simple as a few women merely choosing to become prostitutes while the majority do not. The recent social outrage and consequent legal measures to stop the phenomenon of *enjo kōsai* (compensated dating)[5] clearly demonstrates the social unacceptability of 'ordinary' middle-class girls engaging in practices associated with prostitution. However, the biological discourse on sexuality facilitates the idea that certain types of women can be sacrificed (*ikenie*) and this is critical to understanding the regulation of prostitution in imperial Japan and, more broadly, the context in which sexual violence is interpreted. The ideology of sacrifice alleviates the tensions between ideas of uncontrollable male sexual desire, the ideal of female chastity and the ideal of maintaining a 'safe' and harmonious society. In order to develop this argument it is necessary to first briefly explain the shifts in gender ideologies in the Meiji period, how these intersect with the demarcation of culturally specific private and public spheres, and the implication that these have for the ideology and practice of non-intervention.

Imperial constructions of sexual subjects and sites

With the overthrow of the Tokugawa shogunate in 1868 the new Meiji elites embarked on a programme of 'modernisation' and 'civilisation', which were seen as the necessary prerequisites to establishing a competitive nation-state in a new international environment. By the end of the nineteenth century, Japan had abolished feudal privileges, established industrial and military frameworks, systems of policing and compulsory education, and promulgated a Constitution and new civil and criminal codes. The new institutional arrangements produced a significant shift in social relations, constructions of gender and the regulation of sexuality (Mackie 1997).

For leading educationists Mori Arinori and Fukuzawa Yukichi, and some officials of the new government, 'civilisation' was symbolised by monogamy. In line with this view, several laws were passed. In 1883 a ban was placed on concubines for all except the emperor although conflicting laws and legal silences on the subject left their status ambiguous (see Hayakawa 1995: 31–40). The 1872 Ordinance Liberating Prostitutes (*Shōgi kaihōrei*), which released indentured prostitutes from brothel owners, appeared on the surface to abolish the formal sanctioning of licensed prostitution, however, a legal loophole allowed women to engage in prostitution on the basis of 'voluntary contracts'. This frequently involved an advance loan by the brothel owner, often paid to the women's families, which would then be worked off over several years. The local governments took control of the regulatory system, levying licensing fees on brothel owners and prostitutes, which provided prefectural administrations with valuable revenue. Similarly motivated by economic gain, particularly given the increasing demands of industrialisation, in 1900 the central government took formal control of the regulation of prostitution.[6] Also, in the late 1860s and early 1870s bans were placed on mixed bathhouses, public urination, public nudity, and on the sale of erotic images (*shunga*) and phallic objects. As Pflugfelder (1999: 147) notes, these legal changes were not merely the result of pressure to conform to the 'Western' sense of morality. Many of the laws had legal precedents in the Edo period (1600–1868), although they may not have been subject to serious enforcement. The introduction of a centralised policing system in Meiji reinvigorated the state's moral or civilising approach to sexuality.

For the first time, the new legal codes bound all Japanese regardless of class or region to national standards of morality. Lawmakers had to extract and/or combine codes from a range of domestic laws and negotiate imported European ideas. For women this resulted in a far more pervasive and restrictive legal standard, codifying, regulating and extending restrictions previously limited to women from the samurai class. The majority of women in Edo Japan were not bound by rigid gender and sexual codes emphasising chastity, largely because village life was beyond the reach of state control. Consequently, virginity was not socially valued among commoners and divorce rates were high (Ueno 1987a: 78, 1987b: 133). Moreover, until the late Edo period there was no single uniform marriage or family structure; laws varied across different domains, and actual practices were influenced by class, wealth and region. Despite attempts to introduce provisions based on European family structures into the Civil Code such as those relating to marriage, divorce, family headship and inheritance,[7] the 1898 Civil Code (*Minpō*) constructed a patriarchal family structure based on the samurai ideal of a stem family household known as the *ie* system.[8] This family structure and ideology, grounded in conservative Confucian ethics and values such as hierarchy, obedience, loyalty and filial piety, supported the Meiji elite's vision of a Confucian family-state suited to the needs of establishing a 'modern' and prosperous nation.

Under the new law, the wife's position in the family was unambiguously codified as inferior. According to Tanaka (1980: 642), '[h]er legal capacity was restricted to almost the same degree as that of a "feeble-minded" person. . . . Without her husband's consent, she could not borrow money, guarantee another person's obligations, sue, make or receive a gift, or enter an employment contract'. Under the new divorce law women gained the right to sue for divorce, but the conditions and grounds for divorce remained discriminatory. For example, while a wife's adultery was grounds for divorce, a husband's adultery with an unmarried woman was not. While the criminal code stipulated that wives who committed adultery were to receive a prison sentence, it was silent on the question of punishment for husbands' adultery (Garon 1997: 99). Although divorce by mutual consent was permitted (justified in terms of enabling couples to avoid 'shaming the family'), as both Mackie (1997: 37) and Tanaka (1980: 624–625) point out, women were frequently coerced into 'agreement' and there were no provisions for alimony or maintenance, and the father usually retained custody of any children.

Women's lives were further curtailed by the increased regulation of gender. For example, while samurai men were encouraged to cut their topknot, in 1872 officials in Tokyo and elsewhere banned women from cutting their hair short. Pflugfelder (1999: 151) notes that if a woman had been apprehended for the offence she was required to carry a special certificate until it grew back. Cross-dressing was also outlawed in the early 1870s and although this provision was superseded by the 1880 Penal Code (*Keihō*) which made no mention of the practice, it continued to be policed (Pflugfelder 1999: 152). The overt concern for regulating gender divisions was perhaps linked to the fact that discursively gender was firmly tied to sex. Pflugfelder notes that early twentieth-century medical knowledge in Japan constructed heterosexuality as the norm of sexual desire and conceived of 'male' (*dansei*) and 'female' (*josei*) accordingly in complementary terms. The categories comprised both physical attributes of sex and also gendered behavioural and personality characteristics. These included passivity in women and aggression in men, thereby 'cementing' the attributes as biological 'fact' (Pflugfelder 1999: 253).

The restrictions placed on women's lives were reinforced by the limited construction of rights (*kenri*), outlined in the Meiji Constitution. Rights were bestowed on the people as subjects of the emperor in contrast to the idea of citizens with 'natural' rights. In Europe, the concept of rights emerged from an environment of rising capitalism, protestantism and free market ideologies. Mackie (1997: 30) argues that under such conditions the concept of natural rights came to incorporate ideas of fundamental equality and universal values, which made it difficult to deny the logic in extending these rights to women. In contrast, women in Japan were discursively positioned as imperial subjects, 'as gendered subjects whose service to the Empire was mainly discussed in terms of service to home and family', encapsulated in the ideology of *ryōsai kenbo* (good wife, wise mother).

Initially, the *ryōsai kenbo* ideology was most clearly promulgated by the Ministry of Education and it was, therefore, primarily aimed at middle-class high-school girls because few working-class families could afford the luxury of sending girls to high school.[9] High-school education was extended to girls in 1899 to teach them how to become 'good wives and wise mothers'. Girls' education was, thus, quite distinct from the academic training received by boys. Donald Roden (1990: 43) notes that Meiji secondary schools focused on inculcating in girls 'the virtues of chastity, modesty, and submissiveness' and in boys 'the countervailing values of performance, unyielding determination, and fortitude'. Thus, two distinct and hierarchical gendered identities, 'feminine domesticity and masculine performance' were constructed to serve the nation's interests through discourses of nationalism, modernisation and 'civilisation'.

Clear class distinctions regarding appropriate female roles (middle-class women oriented inside the home and working-class women oriented towards employment outside the home) began to break down during the Russo-Japanese War (1904–1905). Expectations regarding women's contribution to the war effort extended the ideology of *ryōsai kenbo* to include activities both inside and outside the home, within the boundaries of feminine virtues and responsibilities (e.g. caring for family members and the sick, hard work, education, frugality and endurance). Thus, Nolte and Hastings (1991: 171) argue that by the end of the Meiji period gender replaced class as the fundamental social distinction.

The *ryōsai kenbo* ideology contributed to the production of a particular arrangement of the 'private' and 'public' spheres in Japan. In Europe, rationalist secularism provided the grounds for the emergence of modern nation-states in which the family was constructed as a private space. The division between the public and the private developed as the primary site of economic production shifted out of the home. Men began to engage in paid labour outside the home and the primary responsibility of middle-class women increasingly focused on the maintenance of the family's needs inside the home. Mackie (1997: 40–41) notes that: 'The ideological construction of the private sphere rendered aspects of gender relations "invisible" in political terms, and naturalised the gendered hierarchy in the family'.

Different configurations of 'public' and 'private' emerged in Japan as the state embarked on its modernisation programme. Under the ideology of the family-state or 'emperor system' the primary responsibility of the family became the production of loyal subjects. Mackie explains:

> According to Confucian ideology, power relations in the family were articulated directly into the power relations of the state. . . . In Japan, under the Constitutional system, notions of gendered hierarchy within the family were made explicit, and the family itself was politicized, rather than being seen as private haven.
>
> (Mackie 1997: 40–41)

Women as imperial subjects, denied a public political voice, were seen as contributing to the country's national interests from their designated social position located in the home and, in so doing, the Meiji state 'claimed the home as a public place' (Nolte and Hastings 1991: 173). At the same time, the family can be characterised as a 'desexualised public space', that is, primarily a place for producing subjects (Chungmoo 1997: v–xiv). It was not the primary site for the expression of male sexuality and, for women, this space entailed dedication to reproduction, nursing and child rearing rather than sexual pleasure. This construction was not without historical precedent:

> During the Edo period, sexual women such as geisha, courtesans, and whores, who sold their sexual services to more than one man, were excluded from motherhood in the family system. Sexual women . . . carried a physical mark, clothing, make-up, hair styles, perfumes, and distinct manners, delineating them as sexual beings. . . . Their bodies carried every trace of their status as service women used for pleasure and not for motherhood.
>
> According to this picture, women's sexuality and motherhood should not go hand in hand. Sexual women should not be mothers and mothers should not be sexual women.
>
> (Ariga 1992: 576–577)

In contrast, Japan's geographic containment of prostitution in licensed quarters, 'rape camps' or 'red line' zones, explicitly designated for male sexual pleasure and inhabited by explicitly sexualised women, suggests a sexualised and thus privatised 'public' space.[10] Thus, there are two clearly separated spheres for the expression of male sexuality: an explicitly sexualised sphere for sex play or recreation and a desexualised sphere for marriage and procreation (Allison 1996: 45–47). This culturally specific configuration of public and private pivoting on the particular constructions of male sexuality renders both spheres, in a sense, 'private'. In terms of intervention, the state is explicitly involved in very central aspects of the family; however, areas involving masculine sexuality are regarded as 'private' and non-intervention by the law has been the standard practice except in extreme cases of physical violence.[11] Thus, it is masculine sexuality and not the family as such that structures practices of non-intervention. This cultural complex partially accounts for the trivialisation of many issues involving sexual violence and the reluctance to address sexual harassment, *chikan*, domestic violence, stalking and so forth.

Sacrificed women

Another central aspect of the culturally specific silence surrounding sexuality is the ideology of sacrifice. The discussion so far, on women as imperial subjects, has indicated the significance of the Confucian-style chain of loyalty from the people to the emperor. Tomo Shibata (1999) convincingly argues that the ideology of sacrifice was central to this duty of loyalty to the emperor, the nation, 'common good', the family, household head and husband. This notion of sacrifice also links the various forms of prostitution from the Edo period to the early post-Second World War years and has served as a rationalisation of sexual violence arising from, and taking place within, the institutionalisation of prostitution. Shibata's analysis also offers a more nuanced reading of the frequent argument that a historical toleration of prostitution has always existed in Japan.

Once banned, the practice of selling daughters into licensed prostitution in the Edo and early Meiji periods was followed by women's 'voluntary' work as licensed prostitutes in Japan while others worked as prostitutes overseas. Their remuneration was frequently sent back to families struggling with poverty.[12] These women were explicitly constructed in official discourse as 'filial' daughters sacrificing themselves for their families. In 1896, Prime Minister Itō Hirobumi explained to a London *Daily News* reporter that a woman engaged in licensed prostitution 'does so often from a lofty desire to help her poor parents or relations; and, when she forsakes the life, by good conduct she is readmitted to society' (quoted in Garon 1997: 102).[13] This construction eased the tension between the state's need for women as both tightly monitored sexual servicers and moral guardians of the family. Nevertheless, according to Fujime (1997a: 154–156) all women working as prostitutes were stigmatised, largely as a result of imported 'Western values' condemning sex outside marriage. The distinction between prostitutes and 'ordinary' women, therefore, remained significant.

Similarly, the ideology of sacrifice was central to the rationale justifying the forced use of local women in 'mass-rape camps' during the period of imperialism in East Asia – to maintain an efficient military force and social order. It was also central to the rounding up of 'appropriate' women to work in the RAA brothels – to protect 'ordinary' Japanese women and ethnic purity. The discursive dominance of the idea that it is necessary to sacrifice specific women for the 'common good' was stated quite explicitly by a group defending prostitution in the 1920s as the abolition movement strengthened: 'The State's objectives are to maintain order and improve the welfare of the greatest number, and if the interests of a few [women] must be sacrificed, this is truly inevitable in terms of the existence of the State' (quoted in Garon 1997: 103).

The ideology of sacrifice is more difficult to sustain in the post-war period, given significant legal changes. The implementation of the 1947 Constitution positioned women as citizens with fundamental human rights rather than as subjects, and the Civil Code was revised to bring it into line with the Constitution.[14] Nevertheless, Shibata (1999: 60–61) argues that the ideology of sacrifice still plays a role in maintaining the silence around child sexual abuse: the child is sacrificed in order to avoid shaming the family by making the offence public through the pursuit of legal or counselling channels. Similar arguments could be made in relation to rape. The ideas that prostitution prevents the contamination of 'pure Japanese blood' by outsiders or rape, or that it saves marriages by providing husbands with an acceptable outlet for their sexual desires, suggest that the sacrifice of other women – more recently Southeast Asian women working as prostitutes in Japan – is still perceived as necessary for the protection of 'ordinary' Japanese women, girls, the family and nation.

At the same time, increasing intolerance towards prostitution generally, reinforces constructions of the prostitute as responsible causal agent or provoker of social/moral harm rather than as victim or sacrificed filial daughter, as was the case in Meiji Japan. Thus, with a different inflection on sacrifice, prostitutes may be seen as deserving of punishment rather than given up for the 'common good'. In 1955, lobbying for the Prostitution Prevention Law implemented the following year, socialist Diet member Kamichika Ichiko argued that prostitutes undermined the dignity of middle-class women and commented, 'we must punish the estimated five hundred thousand prostitutes to protect the life styles of forty million housewives' (quoted in Garon 1997: 203; see also Fujime 1997b: 386–390; Tsunoda 1990: 153–159). This clear class-based division of women into elite/ordinary and prostitute/others continues to function as an illusory buffer that protects 'good' women.

Sukebei's women and the body marked as feminine

The discourse on *sukebei* constructs two types of women: appropriate and inappropriate targets. *Sukebei* behaviour is not supposed to be directed towards 'ordinary'/'good' women (mothers, wives and daughters), but towards 'Others' (prostitutes, hostesses, and possibly ethnically 'other' women).[15] One very significant consequence is the assumption that 'ordinary' women are not targets of sexual assault and that they are to some extent protected by the sex industries' vast array of 'accepted' outlets and 'Other' bodies. Therefore, those who have been targeted must have provoked their attacker, 'asked for it' or in some way approximated the *mizu shōbai* woman. This makes the 'blame the victim' narrative in Japan particularly pervasive and salient.

Contrary to the familiar argument that prostitution threatens the family system because wives fear losing their husbands' interest and money to prostitutes (see Shigematsu 1996: 157), the discursive production of two sites of expression for male sexuality in Japan does not position the women contained within these sites in competition. The construction of two spheres for male sexuality and the two distinct 'types' of women who inhabit those spheres strengthens rather than threatens the family by providing husbands with a safely contained outlet for their sexual desires, thus keeping the family intact. Prostitutes do not threaten the institutions of marriage or family while marriage is conceived of as primarily a site of reproduction rather than an enduring site of romance, and while sex play with *mizu shōbai* women is 'tolerated'. Wives of middle-class businessmen may assume their husbands spend time with prostitutes, but generally prefer not to 'know' (Allison 1994: 148). 'Toleration', therefore, does not mean endorsement of prostitution or their husbands' activities, but rather a resignation to what is perceived as inevitable. The rules of sex play with *mizu shōbai* women are clearly defined and understood as short-term and recreational. Unlike mistresses or lovers, for whom a husband might contemplate leaving his wife, *mizu shōbai* women are not regarded as appropriate marriage or long-term relationship partners (see Tsunoda 1990: 160).

A man of significant wealth and power may support a mistress and his ability to do so signals healthy masculinity and status, but such relationships tend to be contiguous rather than threatening to the family. Hence, far from being seen as a 'menace to society' *mizu shōbai* women continue to be commonly regarded as providing a necessary service to society, albeit one that is accompanied by stigma and lack of social status.

Shigematsu argues that this distinction between women is the effect of a culturally pervasive discourse she calls 'moralistic essentialism', which is disseminated through the process of commodifying women's bodies and sexual violence. This concept refers to the evaluation of women and female identity using a 'madonna–whore' scale of sexual purity-impurity. However, by oversimplifying the construction of masculine sexuality and ignoring its power dimension she overdraws the sexual component to argue that 'moralistic essentialism':

> actually functions to structure and dictate men's sexuality. According to the modern paradigm of heterosexuality, a man is supposed to sexually desire a woman in inverse proportion to how much contact she has had with other men's body parts. . . . The virgin (*shojo* or *shoko*) . . . would thus be highly valued – an evaluation that can be said to engender to some degree the Lolita fetishism that is widely marketed for men in contemporary Japan.
>
> (Shigematsu 1996: 156)

Because dominant discourses on male sexuality in Japan do not limit the expression of male sexuality to marriage, 'moralistic essentialism' has little relevance as a standard for male sexual desire. However, it does, perhaps, have more significance as a standard for selecting an appropriate wife (in conjunction with considerations of ethnicity, class/social status, attitudes towards gender roles etc.).

Moreover, while the value of 'the virgin' is a familiar trope in discussions of male sexual desire, the Lolita phenomenon (*rorikon*, literally Lolita Complex) incorporates a more complicated range of ideas and practices. It can suggest paedophilia, or it might suggest, as noted by Japanese film director Harada Masato, a form of 'backlash' or reaction by 'weak' Japanese men intimidated by the growing power of feminism who 'have developed sexual preferences for "somebody minor and more obedient"' (interview in Barber 1998: 15).[16] Similarly, commenting on the allure of the sexually immature adolescent girl in Japanese mainstream (not pornographic) men's magazines, John Clammer (1995: 212) notes that the girls' sexuality is imagined as existing almost in spite of themselves; as merely a response to active masculine sexuality. Similar dynamics operate in the pornographic genre's images of young girls and, thus, the sexual desirability of virgins/young girls is not simply a question of their 'lack of contact with male body parts'. What is significant is the way in which the images inscribe sexuality onto the (virginal) feminine body and generate a gendered power dimension in the construction of male desire.[17]

The question of how female sexuality is configured and inscribed on the feminine body is crucial to an understanding of sexual violence and its commodification. The objectification of female bodies packaged for consumption refuses the notion of an autonomous female subjectivity and sexuality. This process of commodification inscribes sexuality onto female bodies, but the subject of this sexuality is male. While the female body is sexualised, it is not her sexuality but, rather, a 'mirroring' of male desire.[18] This idea is best illustrated by looking at the dominant themes within *ero manga*. Women are overwhelmingly scripted as vulnerable, passive objects of male conquest and abuse. Narratives of raped 'innocent virgins' who are 'betrayed by their bodies' are prolific (Buruma 1984: 54–60). Women are rarely depicted as achieving sexual pleasure and if they are then it is almost always derived from the rape of their bodies or some other form of violation. This degradation, Allison argues, is integral to the meaning of the sex itself (Allison 1996: 62).

Also of central significance is the fact that the body marked as feminine is inscribed as rapable, that is vulnerable and passive, and this facilitates the elaboration of masculine power, not just in the fact that the body can be taken, but also that the body can be blamed for the taking. Women are held accountable for their own victimisation unless they can prove themselves to be innocent or pure. The frequency and ways in which judges hold women responsible for the behaviour of the assailants who sexually abuse them ('victim precipitated' rape) is discussed at length in Chapter 6. But first we need to understand how this is possible.

Inscribing the feminine body with responsibility

There are three significant mechanisms underlying the notion of victim-precipitated rape in Japan. First, is the culturally specific idea of *jiseki no nen* (sense of personal responsibility). It is commonly assumed and frequently expected of crime victims in Japan that they acknowledge and reflect on their role in the events and circumstances surrounding the crime and thereby assume a measure of responsibility, although this does not automatically confer shared guilt in the legal sense. Nevertheless, the sense of shared responsibility due to one's involvement lends itself to self-blame and accusations by others.

Second, male sexuality is constructed as natural, hydraulic and uncontrollable. Therefore, women perceived as sexually promiscuous or provocative are regarded as 'asking for it', not simply because they are 'bad' but because they are seen as partially responsible for inflaming male sexual desire beyond a man's control. There is nothing new about this insight. Feminists in both Anglo-American countries and Japan have long identified this point as myth. It is, nevertheless, worth mentioning because it so clearly governs the dominant discourses on rape and sexuality in Japan. Moreover, under the guise of 'scientific knowledge', the claim that sexuality is primarily 'natural' or biologically based suggests that this is an irrefutable fact, thereby reinforcing the discourses that constitute and produce the feminine body as responsible for its victimisation.

The third mechanism underlying the notion of victim precipitation has developed from more recent feminist work that engages with Foucault or poststructuralist theories more generally. Of particular importance here is the work of Sharon Marcus (1992) and Ann Cahill (2000). Cahill explores Foucault's ideas about the diffuse nature of power, its productive rather than repressive qualities, and the construction of the social body. She then turns to the works of feminist theorists Iris Young (1990) and Sandra Lee Bartky (1988) to examine the ways in which the female body is marked as feminine. On the basis of these works, Cahill develops the argument that the feminine body is inscribed as '*guilty* pre-victim' and that female sexuality is seen as culpable.

Marcus comes to a similar conclusion although she travels a different route. Marcus (1992: 386) approaches rape as a language or, more specifically, as a script, which situates women as 'already rapable'. She highlights the significance of fear in women's lives arguing that it constitutes a fundamental process in the formation of women's subjectivity and, like Cahill, notes the degree to which this is disempowering for women. Both Cahill and Marcus are primarily concerned with exploring the possibilities of resistance and agency in the context of rape, an area often perceived as the inevitable consequence of superior male strength reinforced by natural male aggression and patriarchal structures. Both are, therefore, quick to remind the reader that rape scripts or the power dynamics underlying these scripts do not completely determine the subject. Patriarchy is not monolithic; the nature of power is localised, scattered and never complete. Therefore, the potential for resistance and agency always exists. If the body is inscribed with dominant discourses and can, therefore, be read as a text, then it can be re-inscribed, at least to a limited extent, with alternative discourses. Christine Helliwell's (2000) aptly titled article 'It's Only a Penis' also serves as a powerful reminder that rape is not a universal phenomenon and the body can be constructed in a multitude of ways.

Foucault (1977) explored the ways in which the body, as a cultural and social entity, is produced with particular powers, abilities, desires and expectations. From the mid-1980s a number of feminists extended Foucault's arguments by exploring the ways particular bodies are produced within the structures of gendered power relations (Bell 1991; Bartky 1988). A common criticism of much of this work is that it tends to be essentialist, posing a singular female body and assuming all women are similarly situated, ignoring factors such as class, age and ethnicity in the production of the feminine. Nevertheless, many of these works provide significant insights into dominant discourses on femininity, which are framed around the white, middle-class, female body. Young (1990: 150), for example, contends that women experience their bodies as weak, vulnerable and somewhat alien objects. Because of women's perceived physical fragility, women seek protection by placing restrictions on their spatial scope and movements. Young's work made an important contribution to our understanding of feminine bodily experiences of fear.

Similarly, Bartky (1988: 66–67) is particularly concerned with the 'disciplinary practices that engender the "docile bodies" of women' and thus she scrutinises the specific gestures, postures, movements and so forth that produce the recognisable feminine body. Like Young, she notes the restriction on movements and space, facial expressions of humility, emphasis placed on graciousness (entailing a degree of eroticism restrained by modesty), deference and readiness to serve in many women's jobs. She also highlights the extent to which women diet, exercise, wear make-up and so forth, which suggests that women perceive their bodies as hostile entities in need of transformation, containment and constant surveillance. Hence, Bartky (1988: 71) argues that these disciplinary practices contribute to the production of the ideal 'feminine body-subject . . . a body on which an inferior status has been inscribed'. Young and Bartky depict a feminine body inscribed by fear (of desires and harm) and, as such, women experience their bodies as creating their own vulnerability and, therefore, responsible for making danger possible. According to Cahill the feminine body is, thus, constructed as 'pre-victim':

> If [the pre-victim body] attempts something outside its highly limited capacities, if it wanders beyond its safety zone, it can expect to get hurt. The woman who experiences her body in this way does not locate the dangers presented to her body as originating from outside of her body. Rather, they have as their source the fact and nature of her body itself. If, then, the body is hurt or violated, then the blame must rest on the woman's failure to sufficiently limit its movements.
>
> (Cahill 2000: 52–53)

The restrictions on women's movements to protect the vulnerable feminine body are generated by the perceived need to reduce the risk of harm by others. Cahill (2000: 54) contends that the risk at the source of women's fear is not death but rape: 'the danger is not to the body in general but almost always specifically sexualized'.[19] Thus, Cahill argues that the threat of sexual violence plays a privileged role in the production of the feminine body.

Furthermore, this specific feminine body is integrally linked to the production of a culpable feminine sexuality. That is, while the most pervasive and significant threat to women is rape and the feminine body is constructed as vulnerable, rapable or sexually accessible, the power dynamic operating in dominant discourses also claims that women incite the uncontrollable sexual desires of men. Women can, therefore, be held responsible for the behaviour of their assailant and this process produces culpable female sexuality:

> the socially produced feminine body is precisely that of a pre-victim [moreover] it is the body of the *guilty* pre-victim. In the specific moments and movements of this body are written the defense of the sexual offender: she was somewhere she should not have been, moving her body in ways that she should not have, carrying on in a manner so free and easy as to convey an utter abdication of her responsibility of self protection, that is, of self-surveillance.
>
> (Cahill 2000: 56)

Cahill (2000: 56) therefore concludes that: '[t]he truth inscribed on the woman's body is not that, biologically, all men are potential rapists. It is rather that, biologically, all women are potential rape victims'. Therefore, until a woman can establish her innocence or prudence, the feminine body is held responsible for the acts of aggressive masculine sexuality.

These are culturally specific arguments based on US studies. Nevertheless, the work of Takie Sugiyama Lebra (1984) and Brian McVeigh (1997) who have conducted studies on the training of Japanese femininity, and the analysis of cases presented in this book suggest a degree of congruence with the US studies in the ways in which rape scripts are embodied in Japan. Whereas Lebra's study on 'Japanese Women', like that of Bartky and Young presumes a singular female body with little consideration of age or class factors, McVeigh's study focuses more narrowly on the femininity training conducted in a women's college which is primarily oriented towards the production of clerical workers or, more colloquially, 'OLs' (Office Ladies). McVeigh also explores the embodied scripting of femininity from a perspective similar to that of Bartky. Both Lebra and McVeigh note the general social emphasis on being scrutinised by one's surrounding community (*seken*) which functions as a strong disciplinary technique to secure conformity to socially appropriate standards. Lebra (1984: 154) notes that the training or discipline (*shitsuke*) in social propriety is overwhelmingly addressed to women and, therefore, propriety is essentially a gendered notion, encapsulated in the construction of femininity. Similarly, McVeigh (1997: 83) notes, 'Japaneseness and ladylike behaviour mutually construct and reinforce one another'.

The two fundamental aspects of femininity training are 'modesty' and 'moral training'. The first involves 'exposure avoidance' in terms of posture, movement and speech, elegance, tidiness and courtesy. Lebra (1984: 42–46) assumes that moral training is more 'sex-free' and 'culture-free' and therefore spends less time elaborating on its meanings. However, she does mention that it involves being subdued (*otonashii*), described as 'being around but appearing as if you didn't exist', and compliant, which results in many Japanese people's difficulty in saying 'no'.[20] In addition, McVeigh (1997: 147) describes the ways in which practices such as dieting, cosmetic surgery, make-up and so forth, inscribe the Japanese feminine body with the ideals of the 'good wife, wise mother' ideology which, he argues, 'appropriates codes of etiquette in order to embody, and therefore instil, socio-political mandates'.

However, while femininity training may be pervasive or heavily emphasised this does not mean that all women submit to the pressure to conform to the social ideal. Lebra (1984: 137) notes that some women take pride in resisting the feminine ideal and that femininity is often of less concern to women than it is to men. This point is poignantly illustrated by Lebra who notes the case of one man who beat his wife because she was unfeminine. At the same time, codes of femininity change over time. Laura Miller's study of young Japanese women's magazines suggests that older models of 'docility and submissiveness' are being rejected by young women looking to express intelligence and self assurance (Miller 1998: 45).

These sources indicate that specific femininity training takes place and that it inscribes the feminine body in particular ways, but all societies do this. The question is can we determine from the above descriptions whether fear of rape plays a significant role in producing the Japanese feminine body? First, it must be noted that domestic architecture and the traditional dress style of the kimono place considerable constraints on Japanese women's movements and that forms of etiquette developed from these continue to inform ideas about femininity even though the kimono has largely been replaced by 'Western' style dress. Nevertheless, the types of behaviours, attributes and values described by Bartky do resonate with the observations of Lebra and McVeigh.

Second, it might be argued that if low crime rate statistics and assertions of Japan as a safe country hold any sway in Japanese women's (and men's) lives then presumably women will not be particularly fearful of rape and, therefore, the feminine body will not be inscribed by the rape script. The 'evidence' of women's fear of rape in Japan is sparse. One recent study found that only one per cent of the female Japanese respondents claimed to be 'very fearful' of rape (compared to 11 per cent in the US sample), while the majority, 53.1 per cent, stated they were 'somewhat fearful' (compared to 49 per cent in the US) and 20.4 per cent stated they were 'not fearful' (compared to 0.0 per cent in the US) (Dussich *et al.* 2001). The study suggests that a moderate fear of rape is significant in the majority of Japanese women's lives but, unsurprisingly, fear is much higher in the US. There is also anecdotal evidence of the fear of rape in Japan[21] and girls are repeatedly warned to be careful of rape and to protect themselves, as a Ministry of Education handbook demonstrates. In the chapter on how to avoid the experience of sexual harm the handbook emphasises that girls must be informed about the strength of male sexual desire, warning that 'sometimes men's sexual urges become so violent/wild (*hageshii*) and uncontrollable that they cannot help themselves and therefore, given the opportunity, any man could become an attacker' (Monbushō 1974: 24–29).[22] A long list of behaviours and situations to be avoided is then provided. Thus, the question is not one of the 'reasonableness' of this fear of rape, of whether a sexual attack is likely or not, but rather of the effects of the discourse on rape, which produce fear and foster high degrees of self-surveillance circumscribing women's behaviour and movements. The feminine body may be constructed as 'guilty pre-victim' whether or not an actual attack is likely because the rape script is so pervasive.

Victim as witness: the construction of appropriate victim personae

While the feminine body may be inscribed and discursively produced as passive, vulnerable and culpable, this does not determine subjectivity. Women who testify as victims in court, for example, are not passive in their role as witnesses; they are actively engaged in a process of resistance. Rape in Japan is a crime prosecuted only on complaint (*shinkokuzai*), and before November 2000 the complaint had to be made within six months of the offence unless there was more than one assailant. By speaking out and filing a formal complaint, she has resisted the strong social pressure to remain silent. But, how does a woman whose body is marked as guilty negotiate the courts as a victim of sexual violation? The narrative aspects of her 'defence' are discussed in later chapters. My focus, here, is on how women tackle the question of constructing an appropriately feminine victim body and credible victim persona. To what extent is this important to the construction of her case and how does this impact on her ability to tell her story?

How women confronting the courts constitute their subjectivity and the impact this has on the outcome of the trial is an under-researched area. However, Amanda Konradi's study of the techniques US women use to prepare themselves for rape trials provides insights into the strategies available to facilitate and enhance women's ability to appear as credible witnesses (Konradi 1996: 404–432). The three areas discussed by Konradi that are relevant here are: 'appearance work' to construct through clothing and make-up an image that conveys what is perceived to be an appropriate victim look; 'emotion work' to produce the feelings and emotional displays in court considered to be persuasive and appropriate; and 'team building', which refers to gathering select people to support one through the trial. This is not an exhaustive list of all the strategies available to women as they prepare to go to court, but it represents the agency of women in negotiating and attempting to influence the trial. Konradi's study and my own courtroom observations and involvement in sexual harassment support groups clearly indicate that women are unlikely to adopt a passive position and rely totally on lawyers if they have the resources to do otherwise.

A successful outcome crucially depends on the presentation of self as a credible witness, which involves negotiating the contradictory and ambiguous social images of an appropriate feminine victim persona. This means the woman must distance herself from the sexualised prostitute body and possibly align herself with the weak and vulnerable feminine body, and she must demonstrate that all possible care was taken to protect herself. She must negotiate the tension between expectations that she fought off her aggressor and being too weak to do so successfully. However, conforming to appropriate feminine behaviour is complicated by the fact that women who have confessed to a sexual encounter are already suspect. The sexuality they come to embody as a result of confessing sexual violation is reinforced as they tell their story of what happened – an account that frequently sounds much like a familiar 'pornographic vignette' (Smart 1989: 39; Bumiller 1990: 125–142). The sexual violation of which she must speak is imagined and visualised by all around her and this frequently reflects more on her own character and behaviour than on the man accused of her rape. Constructing a particular physical appearance may, therefore, be an important means of counteracting or resisting the sexualisation process.

In one appeal case I observed during several hearings, the woman dealt with the complexities involved in confronting the court by constructing an image of a woman in mourning. At each court appearance she dressed in relatively loose fitting, plain, mid-calf length black dresses, black shoes and bag, and her hair was usually worn hanging straight down past her shoulders. Both in the courtroom and during the often-cheerful meetings with her lawyers and support group immediately following the hearings, she maintained a very solemn, passive demeanour, her eyes almost always downcast. The sombreness of the image of a woman of almost indeterminable age, devoid of even a hint of sexuality, who has had a life taken from her, evoked powerful contradictory and ambiguous emotions of strength and courage, disturbance and pity. The image certainly seemed an effective form of resistance to the pornographic narrative inherent in the case, but this was not the only symbolic message she wished to convey. By mid-1997 she had spent seven years fighting her sexual harassment case in court and it had reached the final stages of the appeal. According to a member of her court support group, the woman vowed to maintain the image of grieving until her case reached a positive outcome and thus released her from the oppression she experienced by both the sexual harassment and the court's original dismissal of her claims.

This particular construction of a victim image starkly contrasted with that of another woman in almost exactly the same situation – a protracted legal battle beginning in 1992 concerning sexual harassment, which was finally resolved in the victim's favour in 1998. At the court hearings I observed, the woman adopted a demure but business-like appearance to convey a sense of seriousness, respect, self-assurance and a degree of assertiveness. It was these particular aspects of her personality that she chose to emphasise and this was consistent with her approach to the case in general. She was the first plaintiff in a sexual harassment case who consented to have her name published in the media because she believed she had done nothing wrong and had nothing to hide. After her court hearings she always spoke clearly, confidently and sometimes confrontationally to her support group. Her efforts were also an attempt to disrupt the defence story of an attractive woman with a 'strong personality' and 'happy, outgoing nature' who was complicit in an affair involving some 'private trouble' (*shiteki turaburu*) but who was not disturbed or isolated by any form of conflict at work.

Both women negotiated the court proceedings in different ways, but presenting themselves as victims did not mean lack of agency. Resistance was a central element in their constructions of an appropriate victim image. The presentation of a particular appearance may also assist in allaying self-blame and fears that one may not be the 'perfect victim' in order to focus on presenting a credible account to the judge. This may also be enhanced by creating the 'right' emotional demeanour. However, as Konradi notes, the construction of an appropriate image of an innocent, truthful victim involves contradictory emotions and behaviours:

> The ideal witness was polite and composed, indicating honesty and an appropriate deference to the court's authority. Alternatively, the ideal victim was a woman overcome by tears brought on by recollection of the assault. Thus, while some survivors sought to repress displays of obvious anger or pain, which would result in loss of emotional control or make their truthfulness suspect, others prepared themselves to lose emotional control and to cry on the stand.
>
> (Konradi 1996: 415)

The contradictions involved in confronting the court were clearly expressed by Endō (interview 10 December 1996), who spoke at length about the difficulty she had in attempting to conform to expectations of what she regarded as the dominant image of a passive, vulnerable victim. She believed that her inability to resolve this conflict served to limit and contain the way in which she was able to tell her story:

> I couldn't talk at the courts about myself – I couldn't express myself. I couldn't judge if I should reveal myself or make myself look better. This inner struggle meant that I couldn't talk freely. The people who supported me advised me to try to create a good impression, to get the judge to like me. But I couldn't decide how to do that. They were watching me in the court and when I argued with his lawyer they told me that I shouldn't have because I looked like an aggressive woman (*ibazure onna*).

> The best thing for me was to be myself and to make people understand me but this means getting angry – but I had to seem gentle . . . Generally women are weak but I didn't want to accept that I was weak and so I couldn't say how scared I was when it happened because that was his point – he wanted to make me scared – so I didn't want to give him the satisfaction of knowing that he had succeeded in making me scared – and he was there in the courtroom.

Endō's statement reveals the difficulties some women have in managing their emotions and behaviour to convey a particular message while in the emotionally charged situation of being again in the presence of the assailant and the judge. Dealing with this tension can be facilitated by ensuring the broader audience in the courtroom is sympathetic. A woman may, therefore, attempt to select her audience in order to gain confidence from knowing that the majority of those listening to her story believe her. This may mean excluding particular family members and friends who might, on hearing the graphic details of what happened, become upset and thus emotionally demanding, themselves, or who may come to stigmatise or blame her for the incident. Endō and several other women who had been through sexual harassment cases decided to avoid such risks by requesting that their husbands did not attend the hearings. For some women, support groups consisted mainly of feminist activists, some of whom have links with rape crisis centres or women's refuges. This support is an important source of empowerment and symbolically underscores the validity of the woman's claim of rape. Support groups may also be enlisted in an attempt to influence the judge by demonstrating both public interest in the case and a high degree of trust in the woman.

Gaining the empathy of judges and other legal personnel by constructing a socially recognisable image of 'appropriate feminine victim' is likely to influence the outcome of the case, if only by building up the confidence of the woman so that she can present her story in a credible manner. However, the courtroom situation is fraught with emotion and, as Endō's account illustrates, the difficulties may be overwhelming. Success may well depend on how well the woman understands both the legal process and the way judges are likely to think.

Framing the judicial imagination: a summary

Three inter-linking features of the socio-cultural environment against which judges make decisions in cases involving sexual violence help to explain the patterning of those decisions. First, the discursive construction of *sukebei*, founded on and reinforcing biological understandings of male sexuality, has been normalised through the regulation of prostitution and then through its incorporation into mainstream commercial markets. This process has produced a culture of eroticised violence, which through its high levels of visibility and accessibility, is constructed in dominant discourses as non-threatening and essentially harmless. This discourse is reinforced by notions of low crime rates and safe cities. Moreover, the culturally specific configuration of private and public further renders the sphere of male sexual activity as generally a zone of non-intervention. Against this background, which tends to ignore or reinforce the silence surrounding sexual violence, it is possible, as the Ikebukuro case indicated, that in certain circumstances a 'perceptual fault line' may exist between judges and women regarding the 'harm' of a sexual assault or, indeed, whether a sexual assault took place.

The argument that the culture of eroticised violence is essentially harmless is sustained only as long as masculine sexuality is constrained by the vigilance of some women, while sexual accessibility is guaranteed through the availability of Others; sacrificed women. This leads to the second implication of the discursive construction of *sukebei* – its demand for access to female bodies. The provision of this 'need' has been facilitated by the historically situated division of women into complementary categories, ordinary women and prostitutes. Both 'types' of women are 'bound' by the inscription of a particular form of culpable sexuality onto the feminine body that marks them as 'guilty pre-victims'. Women are inscribed as potentially responsible for any sexual violation of their bodies. This explains, at least to some extent, the pervasiveness of arguments that blame the victim (i.e. arguments of victim precipitation), not only in Japan but elsewhere. While such ideas remain unchallenged they are likely to frame judges' responses to women in cases of sexual violence that cannot be easily determined. If the defendant cannot easily be recognised as a 'real rapist' the judge's attention shifts away from him and the victim then 'goes' on trial. As a result, women's stories of sexual abuse are frequently not heard, or else are distrusted or disqualified in the courtroom.

Thus, what appears to be a contradiction – the purported non-threatening culture of eroticised violence and the pervasive rape script posing a threat tantamount to death – co-exist because the feminine body is inscribed with a sexuality that is not her own but which marks her body as violable. This tension underlies the discrepancies in judgments of rape cases in which rape may be perceived as a heinous offence while others are dismissed because the woman was found to be responsible. This argument is developed in Chapters 4 to 6. However, first it is necessary to situate these judges and the women who file a complaint involving a sexual assault within the context of dominant discourses on crime and the practices of the criminal justice system in Japan. The following chapter examines ideological and structural features of the criminal justice system that contribute to the process of culling cases from further legal proceedings. The exclusion of certain types of cases from going to trial impacts on both official statistics and on the types of cases presented to judges in the courtroom. If judges are overwhelmingly presiding over cases that generally conform to the rape script then it is likely that this will reinforce their perceptions of what a 'real' rape looks like.

3 Confronting the Japanese criminal justice system

Japan has long maintained an international reputation as one of the safest countries in the industrialised world and Japanese criminal justice professionals are generally very proud of their success in maintaining low crime rates, high clearance rates and a very high conviction rate. Many non-Japanese scholars and criminal justice practitioners have looked to the Japanese example to find possible solutions to their own domestic crime problems. Reasons put forward to account for Japan's achievements in this area have included: cultural explanations emphasising perceptions of homogeneity, harmony, notions of shame and group orientation; economic considerations such as low unemployment and high standards of living; high literacy rates; political stability; strict control of drug and firearms laws; and efficient, centralised criminal justice administration (for a comprehensive literature review see Vaughn and Tomita 1990: 146–167; Finch 1999). John Owen Haley (1991) justifiably describes many of these explanations as 'shopworn', but highlights instead another familiar argument that small groups or institutions (e.g. the family, workplace, schools, local communities and friends) maintain social control by reinforcing conformity to social norms. This alleviates the necessity of relying on the coercive mechanisms of the state. Similarly, Fujieda (1989: 65) argues that Japan's low crime rate is not, as is often assumed, evidence of 'the supposed moderation of the Japanese people' but, rather, it is more likely to be due to 'the socio-cultural conditions of mutual surveillance'. Haley pushes the argument further by noting that the state's reliance on informal, social mechanisms of control represents a transfer of powers from the state to these smaller communities, thus reinforcing 'the capacity of social groups to exercise coercive controls usually reserved in the West as an exclusive prerogative of the state. The consequence is a weaker state and stronger, more autonomous and cohesive society' (Haley 1991: 138). Another consequence that tends to receive much less attention is that this transferral of state power to smaller communities consolidates patriarchal privilege.

The results of preliminary feminist research in Japan are consistent with studies elsewhere that have found significant evidence of violence against women, with the majority of those women abused by men they know.

Women are most likely to become targets of abuse from men within those same small communities that Haley argues produce a 'more autonomous, cohesive society'. The reliance on informal social mechanisms to control crime or maintain conformity to social norms means that abusive forms of patriarchal control, in all but the most extreme cases, may be exercised with relative impunity within these localised networks of gendered social relations. The point is well illustrated by a Japanese researcher on violence in the family, who stated in a 1985 interview: 'Of course Japanese husbands beat their wives. I beat my wife, too, because I am responsible for her behaviour. But I don't beat her very hard' (Scherdin 1994: 219–220). Former Prime Minister Satō Eisaku has also spoken publicly of regularly beating his wife, and the daughter of former Prime Minister Tanaka Kakuei has stated that her father encouraged her husband to beat her 'if it [made her husband] feel more like a man' (Taylor 1985, cited in Henshall 1999: 39). Similarly, at the institutional level, when schools handle complaints of sexual harassment and indecent assault, rather than follow formal channels, principals generally prefer to deal with complaints informally, usually conveying an apology to the family and suspending the offending teacher for a limited time (Tsunoda 1991: 220–223).

The patriarchal dimension of social control also complicates Daniel Foote's (1992) characterisation of the Japanese criminal justice system as 'benevolent paternalism'. Foote focuses on Japan's orientation towards prevention, in contrast to the US-orientation of deterrence, emphasising the general trust in and leniency of the Japanese system that aims to reform and reintegrate offenders back into the community. Although Foote recognises and explains that 'benevolent paternalism' encompasses both significant achievements and serious problems, he argues that, overall, the system 'works'; it is efficient and successfully maintains order (Foote 1992: 364). While the system may well be lenient and appear 'benevolent' to many offenders, the cases analysed in the following chapters suggest that many women who have been the targets of a sexual assault are unlikely to receive much benevolence at all. It seems that in many cases of sexual assault, the interests of female complainants are sacrificed in order to make the system 'work'. In David Johnson's recent work on prosecution in Japan he, similarly, concludes that the Japanese criminal justice is 'uncommonly just', but also notes that this does not extend to the treatment of sexual assault victims. 'Prosecution practice in sex crimes cases is the most conspicuous deviation' from the general orientation towards healing relations between offender, victim and community (the fundamental principle of restorative justice) (Johnson 2002: 211). He suggests that the consistent trivialisation of women's claims of sexual violation is due to sexist attitudes among criminal justice personnel and the broader social context of gender inequality. While this explanation rather oversimplifies the problem, nevertheless, Johnson's discussion sets his work apart from the mainstream literature on criminal justice in Japan, which overwhelmingly ignores or marginalises the subject of sexual assault.

Although it is widely recognised that problems such as the trivialisation of claims and under-reporting are particularly acute in the area of sexual assault in all countries, there have been few detailed studies of sexual assault in Japan. The general lack of attention reflects, perhaps, the common claim that Japan is a 'safe' country – an assertion usually based on often-problematic comparisons of international crime statistics, particularly those of the US (see Fujimoto 1994; Vaughn and Tomita 1990: 154–159; Holmberg-Okubo 1985; Kersten 1996). Japanese crime statistics for various discrete categories of sexual assault are not particularly high, certainly compared with those in the US. For example, based on the US Department of Justice and Japan National Police Agency figures, in 1995 the rate of rape per 100,000 population in the US was 37.1 compared to 1.2 in Japan while the rate of murder and homicide was 8.2 in the US and 1.0 in Japan (Dussich *et al.* 2001: 19). However, as these authors point out, great care must be taken in making these sorts of comparisons. First, many of the crime categories are classified on the basis of different data and both Dussich *et al.* (2001: 9) and Finch (1999: 504) explain the differences pertaining to homicide, considered to be the most reliable crime statistic. In terms of rape, it is also necessary to question whether statistics from other countries are limited to penile–vagina penetration, as is the case in Japan. Many jurisdictions have adopted rape reform laws that broaden the definition substantially. Japanese rape statistics also generally exclude rape figures when the crime was perpetrated in conjunction with robbery – considered the more serious crime. The one exception found is the *White Paper on Police 1995 (Excerpt)*, which included rape and robbery as a separate category from 1990–1995. It is also useful to consider whether, as in Japan, juveniles are classified as those 20 years and older. This has an impact on Japan's statistics as one third to almost half of reported rapes are committed by juveniles and 71 per cent of arrested juveniles in 2002 were 17–19 years (see Table 3.1).

Not only do legal codes impact on crime statistics, but police practices and reporting systems also have an effect. In the case of sexual assault in particular, the environment in which reports must be made have a major impact on the likelihood that victim-survivors will pursue this channel of redress. Also, until the 2000 change in law, rape statistics in Japan were limited to reports made within six months of the incident, and rape is still only indictable on complaint unless it was gang rape (*rinkan*). The rape of a minor, for example, that came to the attention of a doctor or teacher would not be included in the statistics. Moreover, Finch (1999: 502) notes that there have been cases of police tampering with statistics in Japan as a result of pressure to improve their performance and Japanese academic researchers are denied access to their raw data. Research is, thus, constrained by the criteria used by the institutions that collect and collate crime

Table 3.1 Number of reported sexual offences cleared by the police (1975–2002)

	Offences involving rape					*Indecent assault*	
Category	*Total*	*Rape (Rate)**	*Arrest rate (%)*	*Robbery and rape*	*Juvenile offenders*	*(Rate)*	*Arrest rate (%)*
1975	–	3,704 (3.3)	91.5	–	–	2,841 (2.5)	80.0
1980	–	2,610 (2.2)	89.0	–	–	2,825 (2.4)	79.2
1985	–	1,802 (1.5)	90.1	–	–	2,645 (2.2)	82.3
1990	1,629	1,548 (1.3)	82.3	81	–	2,730 (2.2)	70.7
1991	1,680	1,603 (1.3)	84.5	77	–	3,176 (2.6)	70.0
1992	1,593	1,504 (1.2)	82.6	89	–	3,505 (2.8)	74.9
1993	1,712	1,611 (1.3)	92.6	101	–	3,581 (2.9)	87.2
1994	1,703	1,616 (1.3)	91.6	87	618	3,580 (2.9)	91.7
1995	1,563	1,500 (1.2)	94.0	63	606	3,644 (2.9)	88.7
1996	–	1,483 (1.2)	88.8	–	575	4,025 (3.2)	85.4
1997	–	1,657 (1.3)	88.8	–	774	4,398 (3.5)	86.1
1998	–	1,873 (1.5)	88.2	–	839	4,251 (3.4)	82.3
1999	–	1,857 (1.5)	73.7	–	873	5,346 (4.2)	63.4
2000	–	2,260 (1.8)	68.1	–	1,006	7,412 (5.8)	48.6
2001	–	2,228 (1.8)	63.0	–	1,049	9,326 (7.3)	41.7
2002	–	2,357 (1.9)	62.3	–	1,118	9,476 (7.4)	35.5

Sources: 1 1975–1989 data: Sōmuchō Tokeikyoku (1991: 717); 2 1990 data: Keisatsuchō (1991: 1); 3 1991–1995 data: National Police Agency (1995: 46–47); 4 1996–2002 data: Keisatsuchō (2003).

Note

* Bracket indicates the rate of rape per 100,000 population (including men and women).

statistics: the National Police Agency, the Ministry of Justice and the Supreme Court. For example, to analyse the breadth of the problem of violence against women in Japan it would be useful to examine a gendered breakdown of murder and assault victims, but these are not made regularly available. The National Police Agency did, however, publish the 1995 figures.[1] Even if all these problems are taken into consideration, these statistics only relate to reported crimes.

The extent of violence against women in Japan is just beginning to emerge. Victimologist John Dussich argues that a more reliable means of ascertaining realistic levels of crime is through victimisation surveys. The first such national survey was conducted in 2000 (Dussich *et al.* 2001), but I have not yet seen any data from it. However, articles and statistics pertaining to unreported rape cases, incest and the sexual assault of women and girls, have been collected and published in the Tokyo Rape Crisis Centre (Tokyo gōkan kyūen sentā, hereafter TRCC) newsletters. In the first five years of operation (1983–1987), the TRCC provided telephone counselling in 2,899 incidents of rape. Of this number, only 1,002 of these women filed a police report (Hayashi 1990: 28). In Dussich and Shinohara's (1997: 10–11) study only 13.9 per cent of women who had experienced a sexual assault reported their victimisation and the percentage for rape victims was even lower at 9.5 per cent. Of the ten cases in which the woman was acquainted with the rapist none of the women filed a report.

There have also been various reports on domestic violence[2] since at least the 1970s. Kumagai and Donoghue's (1978: 216) survey of high-school students regarding 'conjugal power and violence in their own homes' found comparable levels of domestic violence in Japan and the US. A number of surveys in the 1980s of wives who petitioned for divorce through the family court's mediation process found violence was the most, or second most, common reason for divorce (Arichi 1987: 87; Sasaki 1989: 115).[3] In 1992 the first extensive questionnaire on domestic violence was completed by a small group of Tokyo women. Findings from the 795 respondents indicated that the level and types of domestic violence experienced by women in Japan are comparable to those found in other countries (Otto kara no bōryoku (D.V.) chōsa kenkyū kai 1993; Hada 1995; Uno 1998). In 1995 the Civil Liberties Bureau dealt with 3,648 cases of husbands abusing wives, which includes abuse (*kokushi gyakutai*), and coercion (*kyōsei appaku*) (Hōmushō 1996: 134). The Tokyo Metropolitan Government conducted its own survey on violence against women in 1997 and the first national survey was conducted in 2000. It found that almost 1 in 20 (4.6 per cent) wives were 'subjected to life-threatening violence' (Ikeuchi 2003). In 2001 the Law for the Prevention of Spousal Violence and the Protection of Victims (*Haigusha kara no bōryoku no boshi oyobi higaisha no hogo ni kansuru horitsu*) was implemented.[4] The shifting social attitudes towards domestic or spousal violence, challenging the pattern of patriarchal control in the family, and

Table 3.2 Number of reported cases by type of crime committed by husbands against wives (including de facto relationships) cleared by the police (1998–2002)

	1998	*1999*	*2000*	*2001*	*2002*
Murder	189	170	197	191	197
Bodily injury	295	403	888	1,097	1,250
Assault	35	36	127	156	219

Source: adapted from Keisatsuchō (2003).

culminating in the new law have had quite a dramatic impact on reported cases as illustrated in Table 3.2.

The sexual abuse of children is another element in the 'dark figure of victimisation' (*kakusareta higaisha*) that is of increasing concern in Japan. In 1992 there were 1,012 reported 'sexual crimes' against children under the age of 13 (*The Japan Times*, 25 December 1992: 2). A limited number of surveys have also been carried out which indicate that the problem of sexual child abuse exists in Japan as elsewhere, although discussions with Family Court judges (24 September 1996) and other Japanese citizens indicated that this is not necessarily a common assumption. Nevertheless, a 1979 Welfare Committee survey of Children's Homes found 97 cases of sexual child abuse by a parent or step-parent (cited in Miya 1984: 28). National surveys of child abuse reported to child guidance centres in 1983, 1989 and 1997 found 46 cases of sexual abuse (11.1 per cent of total child abuse cases), 48 cases (4.6 per cent) and 100 cases (4.9 per cent) respectively. Of these cases over half the offenders were fathers or step-fathers (Fujimoto 1994: 35–70; Abe 1998). In 1994, of the 2,393 'moral offences' against minors, 2,260 were cases of 'forced act of sex' and 4,337 girls were victims of 'offences forcing juveniles to perform indecent acts' under the Juvenile Protection Ordinance or the Child Welfare Law (87 per cent) (National Police Agency 1995: 58–59). In response to the increasing number of crimes involving juveniles (particularly 'child prostitution')[5] associated with Internet dating sites, in June 2003 a law was enacted to 'ban people from soliciting sex from minors and vice versa' (*The Japan Times,* 25 June 2003). Also, in 2000, the Child Abuse Prevention Law was implemented (and is scheduled for revision in 2004) in response to the increasing concern and rising number of reported cases of child abuse involving parents (23,274 reported cases January–March 2002, reported in *The Japan Times,* 25 June 2003) and this will likely raise public awareness of child sexual abuse. However, at present the primary concern appears to be identified as the problem of mothers physically (and in a few cases sexually) abusing children.

Sexual harassment has been the subject of considerable public debate since the late 1980s and surveys indicate widespread incidence. The first survey regarding sexual harassment was conducted in 1989 by the feminist group, *Hatarakukoto to seisabetsu o kangaeru santama no kai*, who then published their findings in 1991. The national newspaper, *Asahi Shinbun* published two surveys in 1996 and 1997 respectively, which indicate that around 90 per cent of women in Japan have been 'sexually victimized'. While the range of offences is very broad, from theft of underwear to rape, 63.3 per cent of respondents in the latter survey indicated signs of post-traumatic stress disorder (see Shibata 1999: 48, 79–80). The problem of stalking has also been recognised recently and the Anti-Stalker Law was implemented in 2000. Feminists have attempted to draw attention to these and similar issues (Yunomae 1990: 265–270) with many articles published in newsletters and other small, informal means of communication (*mini-komi*), but mainstream publishers are also paying increasing attention to the subject of sexual violence. In short, there are alternative sources to official statistics that document and discuss various aspects of sexual violence in Japan.

Although differentiated in legal and popular discourses, often very narrowly and in ways that make little sense to survivors of sexual assaults,[6] rape, indecent assault, domestic violence, *chikan*, incest, child sexual abuse, pornography, sexual harassment, uxoricide (the murder of women by husbands), prostitution, indecent exposure and so forth, can be usefully conceptualised in terms of a 'continuum of sexual violence' (Kelly 1987). This term highlights the inter-related nature of these forms of abuse and the link common to all these abuses of women, that is, the notion of a male 'right' of sexual access to women's bodies, which is achieved partly through the institutionalisation of marriage and, in Japan, the additional social conventions that construct male sexuality and masculinity as requiring two fronts of sexual activity. This male 'right' has been endorsed legally by the state through the practice of non-intervention and/or non-prosecution but, as indicated, there has been quite a dramatic shift in attitudes and official responses to sexual violence over the past decade. The question remains as to whether these legal changes will translate into better outcomes for victim-survivors of abuse in the courtroom.

Under-reporting

There are many reasons why women do not file a report. Some women may have been threatened by the offender or fear that making a formal complaint might lead to further violence. For example, in February 2000 the Tokyo High Court handed down the death penalty in a case where, two months after his release from a seven-year jail sentence for rape (following a 10-year sentence for homicide), the defendant murdered the woman he raped because she had ignored his warning not to file a report (*The Japan Times*, 28 February 2000). In some areas there has been no explicit name for the behaviour experienced as abusive and against which a report could be made (e.g. until recently, domestic violence and sexual harassment). In other areas, legal interpretation excludes experiences of abuse (rape in marriage, rape of sex workers and sexual harassment outside the workplace and educational institutions). For example, in theory, rape in marriage is not excluded from existing rape law, which identifies victims only as females. However, the problem lies in the interpretation of the law. A legal publication explaining each article of the criminal code states that:

> when a couple marry legally the husband has the right to demand sex from his wife and therefore there is no crime of rape existing in marriage. However, when a man has sex with his wife using assault or threats this may be the basis of the crimes, *bōkōzai* (criminal assault) and *kyōhakuzai* (criminal intimidation; threat).

This interpretation is generally accepted among legal professionals as appropriate (cited in Fukushima 1997: 37). Being able to name a behaviour as abusive is critical: '[n]ames provide social definition, make visible what is invisible, define as unacceptable what was accepted; make sayable what was unspeakable' (Kelly and Radford 1996: 20). When there is no name, behaviour experienced as abusive remains an individual concern, lacking social reality or meaning, thereby compounding women's difficulties in filing complaints and having their experiences understood.

There are also significant cultural factors and coping strategies that make it particularly difficult to define behaviour as abusive, and virtually futile to make a formal complaint of sexual violence. Values such as perseverance or endurance, will-power and self-control (*gaman*), and social proscriptions against drawing attention to oneself or problems within one's family and the shame (*haji*) that this incurs, have particular social currency for Japanese women. Demonstrating *gaman* signals maturity and strength in adversity and while Miya Yoshiko (interview 14 November 1996) suggests that for many women it is expressed as an almost 'masochistic sense of martyrdom in hardship', *gaman* is a means of negotiating cultural expectations to remain silent about one's 'private' difficulties or problems when perceived alternative solutions appear minimal. However, the value placed on demonstrating *gaman* also serves to inhibit both women and criminal justice personnel from defining and treating much of the violence directed at women as criminal behaviour. This problem is consolidated by culturally specific expectations regarding the modification of behaviour on the basis of distinctions between *uchi* (inner, inside, internal, private, us) and *soto* (outer, outside, external, public, them); *omote* (front) and *ura* (back), and between *honne* (back-stage, one's real or true feelings) and *tatemae* (on-stage, principles that one should try to act by). According to these conventions of social behaviour it is inappropriate to discuss one's feelings about what goes on in one's family, workplace or other group with an outsider. Ideally, even within their own homes women are expected to suppress their real feelings for the sake of smooth personal relations, although such feelings may be expressed when alone with female family members and friends (Lock 1987, 1993: 43–78). However, social worker Rose Aguilar Kawashima (interview 21 November 1996) argues that, 'Japanese women do not tend to confide in others, even close friends, because this is seen as rather selfish in that it places a burden on the other person (*meiwaku*), of being troublesome or causing an inconvenience'.

In line with Haley's argument, Miya (1984: 29–37, 80–81) also describes the reluctance to speak out about 'private' problems in the familiar terms of a 'village society mentality' that emphasises ideals of group harmony at the expense of individual complaints. In this context, maintaining the very ideal of group harmony may take coercive forms and it is not uncommon for local authority figures to apply pressure on both victims and their families to withdraw complaints. When the abuse takes place within the family the difficulties women face in speaking out are compounded even further. Dominant discourses construct 'the family' as the fundamental social unit, central to Japanese identity, and so to speak of rape in marriage, domestic violence or incest, potentially disrupts the ideological fabric of Japanese society.[7] The judicial expectation that women speak out about their experiences of abuse is, therefore, rather ironic given that society's means of dealing with this violence is primarily through silence.[8]

Rape myths constitute another disincentive to speak out about sexual violence in Japan and elsewhere. Lawyer Danbayashi Kazue (1990: 46) argues that ideas such as 'she asked for it', 'if a woman tries hard enough she can escape', 'all rapists are strangers' and 'rape only occurs outside and at night' are entrenched in the social fabric of Japan. Girls are introduced to these myths and taught how to behave accordingly during their adolescence if not before. For example, the Ministry of Education Handbook mentioned in the previous chapter lists a vast array of behaviours and situations to be avoided by girls and explains that if, however, a girl is violated she should be guided to consider her role in the incident, (e.g. wearing inappropriate clothing and improper behaviour) and how she could prevent the same thing from happening again (Monbushō 1974: 24–29).

The pervasiveness and salience of 'blame the victim' narratives in Japan are reinforced by the assumption that 'good' women are to some extent 'protected' by the sex industry's huge number and variety of 'accepted' outlets; therefore, those who have been targeted must have provoked their attacker or 'asked for it' in some way. These narratives thus inhibit women from reporting sexual attacks, and for those who do report, they make it difficult to convince police, prosecutors and judges that they did not willingly consent to sex (see Kinjō 1990: 34; Adler 1987; Estrich 1987).

Focusing on under-reporting and responses to violence against women makes it possible to disrupt the overwhelmingly dominant assertion that Japan does not have a crime problem and that the Japanese criminal justice system is effective and 'uncommonly just'. Challenging this claim is important because it has effectively perpetuated the silence surrounding violence against women in Japan. Ironically, Hada Aiko (1995: 266) notes that a number of recent sexual harassment court cases, in particular, have been the most effective means of raising public awareness and generating discussions about sexual violence.

Challenging boundaries: public and private

The state's reluctance to intervene in small communities, effectively privatises social relations within such communities.[9] The non-regulation or non-intervention into these areas by the state is based on a conception of the centrality of personal relations, which in legal discourse are regarded as private in contrast to public relations between the state and citizens. Social recognition of areas where state intervention is deemed inappropriate is most clearly located around the family as illustrated by the expression, '*hō wa uchi no naka ni wa iranai*' (there is no need for law in the family) (Fukushima 1997: 50). Sex, sexuality and corporeality are also regarded as private, areas ostensibly free from state intervention (providing sexual relations are between consenting adults) and, therefore, the shifting of these areas into public zones is uncomfortable and problematic.

However, it is misleading to simply characterise the private, in Japan or elsewhere, in liberal terms of non-regulation. Ngaire Naffine states that the legal notion of the unregulated family has always been a 'liberal fiction':

> The very structure and form of the private life was (and is still) determined by law. Law ordained that a family must be constituted by a husband and wife and their children . . . and it established the relations between them with the husband, not the wife, at the head, exercising legal authority over the rest of the legally constituted family. Homosexual men and lesbians had no place in the family. . . . The private was therefore utterly within (not without) the law.
>
> (Naffine 1995: 27)

The institutionalisation of marriage and law's role in defining the boundaries of what constitutes 'the family', purportedly free from state regulation, facilitates male privilege, particularly a husband's sexual subjectivity, by granting him sexual access to his wife. Naffine explains that:

> To make it possible for the man to realise his personal and sexual freedom in the private, it was essential that she (his wife) did not (for how could he be free to do as he pleased if she had the right to say no?).
>
> (Naffine 1995: 27; see also Pateman 1988: 180–188).

Law also privileges masculine sexual subjectivity outside marriage through the practice of non-intervention. The frequent rationale behind decisions to dismiss cases of rape or sexual harassment is that the issue concerned 'private relations'. Margaret Thornton's general theoretical discussion of public/private divisions is also applicable to the Japanese case. She notes that, '[t]he temporally permeable nature of the [public/private] "dichotomy" enables it to operate as an ideological device: "private" being effectively invoked if the state espouses non-intervention; "public" to the contrary' (Thornton 1995: 11). This observation has particular resonance in Japan where configurations of public and private differ to some extent from dominant Western models due both to the allocation of responsibility for social control to small communities and also to particular constructions of masculinity and male sexuality.

While dominant Anglo-European understandings of the public/private dichotomy construct the site of the family, foregrounding sex within marriage as private, notions of what is private in Japan are broadened by constructions of male sexuality as 'naturally' and therefore inevitably requiring two sites of performance. This serves to orient male sexual practices in general as private and, therefore, beyond regulation. Consequently, authorities, either the state or those responsible for maintaining social order within small communities, have been reluctant to intervene in, or regulate, activities such as sexual harassment, *chikan* and consumer practices within the realm of the various sex industries. Since the passing of the 1947 Constitution this reluctance has been phrased in terms of rights discourse. For example, leading up to the 1956 Prostitution Prevention Law, the parliamentary Vice Minister of Justice explained that the arrest of prostitutes and their clients was impossible because, 'in today's times when human rights are respected' gathering evidence of sexual acts would invariably 'infringe on human rights' (quoted in Garon 1997: 203). Moreover, non-consensual sexual relations, those clearly within the domain of state intervention such as 'acquaintance rape', are also likely to be treated as private when heterosexist and masculinist norms are applied. The expression '*fūfugenka wa inu mo kuwanai*' (even dogs are disinterested in domestic disputes) – an expression sometimes used by police called out to reports of domestic violence – suggests that arrests in these cases will be unlikely (Fujieda 1989: 61; Fukushima 1997: 50).

Distinctions between what are regarded as private or public, and therefore to be regulated, change over time as so-called 'private' issues are brought to public attention. The debate leading to the resignation of Prime Minister Uno in 1989 over his allegedly 'private' involvement with a *geisha*, debates regarding sexual harassment from the mid-1980s, recent initiatives to actively police *chikan* and the new laws concerning stalking and spousal violence are cases in point. However, two recent cases of *chikan* in December 1999 and February 2000 in which the accused were police officers (one taught a course in ethics at the Kinki Regional Police Bureau) serve as a reminder that social change is a slow and uneven process (see *The Japan Times*, 14 December 1999). Nevertheless, women's attempts to make public their 'private' violation do subvert distinctions between public and private and criminal statistics are likely to reflect this, at least to a limited extent, as more women assume support for the reinterpretation of certain abusive '*sukebei*' practices as legitimate sites for state intervention.

Diversionary tactics: prosecutorial discretion

There are also a number of uniquely Japanese characteristics of criminal justice processes that impact on official statistics. These tend to mask or deflect cases of violence against women from proceeding through to judgment in the court and they may also have a negative impact on the final outcome of the case. Of particular significance is the prosecutors' broad discretionary power in decision-making, summed up by the term 'prosecutor justice' (*kensatsukan shihō*) (Hirano 1989: 131). Prior to the recent authoritative work by Johnson (2002) there had been little research in the area of prosecutors' discretionary powers, partly because investigation takes place behind closed doors and access to relevant information is particularly difficult to obtain. Nevertheless, there is evidence of a general principle of non-intervention in the private arena, which means that it is likely many cases of sexual violence are diverted from further legal proceedings at this stage.

A criminal investigation is an 'inquisitorial' process that takes place behind closed doors (Hirano 1989: 132–133). The primary aim at this stage is to obtain a confession and detailed statement corresponding to the investigators' hunches and opinions. Retired judge Ishimatsu Takeo argues that, as a result of this priority, original or physical evidence viewed as 'unreliable' (or, perhaps, contradictory) is sometimes discarded rather than left to a judge's evaluation. Ishimatsu is critical of the Japanese criminal justice system, arguing that investigative powers are over-expanded, the investigation of material evidence is completed before the trial, and the consequent nature of the trial is little more than ceremonial (Ishimatsu 1989: 150–151).[10]

Prosecutors in Japan, as in other countries, decide not to prosecute for a variety of reasons, including insufficient evidence. Japanese prosecutors also have the legislative power to suspend prosecution (*kiso yūyo*),[11] which they do in about 37 per cent of cases in which they believe there is sufficient evidence to convict (Johnson 2002: 37). A suspension of prosecution is granted when, after extensive investigation, usually having obtained a confession, the prosecutor concludes that the suspect is guilty but nonetheless foregoes prosecution. Like sentencing decisions, prosecutorial decisions take into account factors such as: criminal character, age, sex, work history, schooling, place of residence, occupation, gravity of the offence, the extent of damage or injury, remorse and payment of compensation following the crime, prior relationship with the victim, and aggravating or mitigating circumstances (Goodman 1986: 26). In 1995, the lowest suspension rate for penal code offences was homicide at 4.3 per cent followed by robbery at 6.4 per cent, rape at 13.7 per cent and indecent assault at 14.3 per cent. This pattern is in keeping with the general ranking of seriousness of offences. In 1995, of the public prosecutor's 1,425 settled rape cases, 766 (53.8 per cent) were prosecuted and 372 (26.1 per cent) were not prosecuted, of which 122 cases (32.8 per cent of non-prosecuted rape cases) resulted in suspended prosecution (see Table 3.3).

There are grounds to suggest that prosecutors are likely to drop or suspend cases that do not conform to dominant or 'common-sense' understandings of violence or stereotypical images of rape, that is, those cases that are least likely to result in a conviction. For example, the high number of 'stranger' cases that go to trial and end in convictions suggests that conviction is more difficult in cases involving a relationship between the victim and the offender. In 1995, 1,115 cases of rape (79.5 per cent) were committed by a stranger (see Table 3.4).

Questioning the consistently high figure for 'stranger rape', the Tokyo Rape Crisis Centre compared its own statistics with those of the Ministry of Justice. The Ministry's 1989 statistics revealed that, of prosecuted cases, 0.7 per cent of rapists were family relations, 26.7 per cent were known to the victim, and 72.6 per cent were strangers. In stark contrast, Tokyo Rape Crisis Centre statistics revealed that of victims who contacted the Centre, 15 per cent of rapists were family relations, 55 per cent were known to the victim, and 30 per cent were strangers (*Tokyo Gōkan Kyūen Sentā Nyūsu*, 24 May 1993).[12] The Tokyo Rape Crisis Centre statistics support feminist findings in other countries, which have found that women are most at risk in their own homes and from men they know, particularly those with whom they have had sexual relations. Contrary to claims by legal scholars such as Aiba Hiroshi (cited in Vaughn and Tomita 1990: 159) that women are more likely to report rapes in cases where the offender is known because he can be readily identified, one study in Japan (Dussich and Shinohara 1997: 10–11) and feminist research in other countries have found that when a prior relationship exists between victim and offender, women are less likely to file a formal complaint of rape. This decision is often based on the women's perception that they will not be believed given the circumstances and/or that legal personnel will perceive the harm they have suffered as trivial.

Ministry of Justice statistics are consistent with the unofficial practice of non-intervention in cases regarded as 'private matters'. The official figures also indicate that winnable rape cases conform to the stereotype of an attack on a respectable woman in a public place by a stranger. That is, prosecutorial decisions are likely to be informed by the same dominant narratives of gender and sexuality underpinning rape myths, which are thus reconstructed in the courtroom generating further authority and legitimacy. In a sense, it is a 'catch-22' situation: judges most often confront stereotypic

Table 3.3 Number of suspects whose cases were disposed of by Public Prosecutor's Office, by category of offence and disposition (1995)

			Non-prosecution								
Offence	*Total*	*Prosecuted*	*Total*	*Suspended prosecution*	*Insufficient evidence*	*No facts which fit the crime*	*Lack of mental capacity*	*Complaint: invalid or withdrawal*	*Expiry of statute of limitations*	*Others*	*Referral to Family Court*
Homicide	1,822	781	1,001	35	84	556	147	–	42	137	40
Robbery	2,072	1,035	252	74	84	3	16	50	25	785	
Robbery and rape	83	51	11	2	4	–	–	–	5	–	21
Rape	1,425	766	372	122	90	5	3	129	19	4	287
Indecent assault	1,555	587	649	98	34	–	11	498	5	3	319

Source: adapted from Hōmushō (1996: 74–79).

Table 3.4 Suspect–victim relationship in rape cases

	Total	*Wife; step-mother*	*Child; step-child*	*Sibling*	*Other family relative*	*Lover*	*Employer/ senior*	*Colleague*	*Employee/ junior*	*Friend/ acquain-tance*	*Other*	*Stranger*
1990	1257	–	4	–	2	1	4	12	7	118	174	935
1991	1225	–	5	1	6	1	2	14	10	107	161	918
1992	1225	–	5	1	6	1	2	14	10	107	161	918
1993	1464	–	4	–	2	2	4	16	5	135	176	1120
1994	1465	1	1	–	6	3	4	14	10	123	169	1134
1995	1402	1	4	–	2	2	6	10	10	94	158	1115

Source: adapted from Keisatsuchō (1991–1995)

rape scenarios (perpetrated by a stranger, visible physical injuries, etc.) and these women then come to be seen as the only legitimate 'normal' (*tsūjō*) rape victims and so prosecutors only commit these sorts of cases to trial. Would judges' perceptions change if they saw a greater variety of cases – would this foster a deeper level of understanding of the harm of sexual violence? Perhaps, but the possibility is limited by the social context in which judgments are made. Legal knowledge is framed and informed by the general culture of eroticised violence, which does not acknowledge the harm of sexual violence.

Prosecutors do not operate in a social vacuum; they are influenced by ideas circulating in society and this, in fact, is cited by the Prosecutor's Office as one measure for making sure that decisions are 'socially acceptable' or seen to be appropriate. The Prosecutor's Office assumes that prosecutors' individual value judgments are avoided and discretionary decision-making is held in check partly by the prosecutor's ability to tap into and employ ideas that are *shakai tsūnen*, that is, ideas held in common throughout society, or a community standard (Goodman 1986: 48; Yasaki 1982: 1–10). Even if one were to accept the notion that a single, uncontested moral or ethical standard could ever exist in Japanese society, or anywhere else, shifting debates reflected in recent government policies and policing practices suggest that consensus around issues involving violence against women and measures to deal with this problem are far from being achieved.[13] The principle of relying on *shakai tsūnen* for regulation in prosecutorial decision-making is a very conservative approach to the role of law in society and it also means that prosecutors are likely to be influenced by, and draw on, the same rape myths and familiar narratives that have normalised the eroticisation of violence against women. In the December 1996 interview, Endō questioned the depth of the prosecutor's understanding of *shakai tsūnen* in the area of sexual relations:

> It was the prosecutor's opinion that women are passive and so in relationships between men and women it's quite normal for men to be active and always trying to have sex with women – so it was normal for him [the manager] to try to have sex with me . . . this sort of thing is common, not a crime . . . because he [the manager] said that he liked me, it was a love affair. I said that this wasn't true but they didn't listen.
>
> The prosecutor said . . . that my husband was angry and that's why I went to the police, meaning that I made the report because my husband found out about the love affair and threatened divorce. Their ideas were like those in trashy romance novels.

Legal scholar Marcia Goodman asked Japanese prosecutors about cases they had trouble deciding and found a general reluctance to prosecute cases involving 'private relationships'. In one of these cases, a woman filed a complaint accusing her former lover of attacking her on the street, resulting in injuries that took three months to heal. The prosecutor did not prosecute, primarily because 'the incident involved a love affair and was to some extent a private matter'. The prosecutor forced a negotiation, which included the withdrawal of charges, a financial settlement, and an agreement to terminate the relationship. Goodman concludes that prosecutors seem to believe that when factors peculiar to a familial or personal relationship have a strong bearing on a particular crime, the matter should be resolved by the parties involved rather than in the public arena and, hence, the decision not to prosecute, or to suspend prosecution, is regarded as preferable (Goodman 1986: 40–41, 47). Such decisions amount to the state's transferral of its power to maintain social control to patriarchal systems operating within the family, workplaces or small communities. These types of decisions do not take into account the gendered distribution of power within those situations.

Women's alternative accounts of abuse are also excluded through the police and prosecutors' practice of summarising and writing up all statements of both suspects and witnesses (Goodman 1986: 47). Endō (interview 10 December 1996) described a mixture of anger, embarrassment and powerlessness to do anything about the fact that she barely understood 'her' statement drawn up by the police officer:

> I felt weird about their questions regarding how many sexual partners I'd had, was I a virgin when I married, what about my husband's sexual experiences and so on – all these questions were not related to what happened and were none of their business and I didn't want to talk about them, but I answered them honestly. But, thinking back, these questions may have had an impact on the decision of the case and perhaps I shouldn't have answered them so honestly. It wasn't necessary to take them so seriously.
>
> At the police station when they wrote the report, they used words that I either didn't know or use . . . like words you don't hear on TV. I always thought these words shouldn't be used openly, and at the police station they also used medical terminology which I wasn't very familiar with. The police officers said, was it this or was it that, but I never use these words and so I didn't feel comfortable talking about these things. There were no words for me to explain exactly what happened. In the statement there was something I wanted to say . . . he grabbed my legs and spat on my vagina. It was really too disgusting . . . I wanted to say this in the statement but it was too hard to say and I couldn't judge whether I should have or not.

The process of producing statements in Japan excludes alternative accounts of sexual violence, by silencing women's explanations of their experiences, particularly those that do not conform to the stereotypic 'ideal' rape narrative. At best, women's experiences are reinterpreted through police and prosecutors' perceptions of their accounts – shaped by dominant notions of gender and power relations, and paraphrased in legal and medical jargon. What is regarded as relevant by the complainant may not be deemed so by the investigators, and vice versa.

Goodman also questions the merit of the prosecutor's power to draft statements, and demonstrates the way in which this may significantly impact on the outcome of a case. She describes the case of a 20-year-old man arrested on suspicion of robbery and attempted rape. While the suspect was held in detention, his parents apologised to, and financially compensated, the victim. The prosecutor found the parents to be worried, apologetic and shocked, which convinced the prosecutor that rather than attempted rape, the lesser charge of 'bodily injury' was more appropriate. The prosecutor's production of the suspect's final statement minimised any facts supporting a charge of rape and emphasised the chance nature of the stolen money so that, in the end, the statement was consistent with the charge of 'bodily injury' and the requested penalty of a ¥75,000 fine. Goodman notes that, 'even though the prosecutor seemed to have some doubt about the suspect's innocence, he felt there were enough outside pressures to guarantee good behaviour in the future' (Goodman 1986: 42).

There is a strong argument that reliance on the informal social control mechanisms of small communities and the family is preferable to jail sentences in terms of the offender's reintegration into society (see Haley 1996), but questions need to be asked about how this process impacts on the needs of the victim-survivor seeking social justice through the criminal justice system. Do decisions not to intervene serve to further victimise women who have been targets of sexual assaults? Does this system leave these women with feelings of not being believed or even heard and, if so, are the democratic rights of these citizens being addressed by the state? Although Haley discusses the very positive benefits of incorporating victims of crime into the criminal justice process in Japan through the emphasis on apologies and payment of compensation by the offender to the victim (Haley 1996: 359–366; Haley 1991: 130–131), it is also the case that, for many victims of sexual assault, the process of weeding out 'flimsy' cases constitutes, or is experienced as, a second assault. For many women who choose to seek legal redress and vindication, the formal acknowledgment that the abuse inflicted upon them was serious is instrumental in their healing process (Townsend 1996). It is also possible that prosecutors' discretionary decision-making privileges or protects the interests of, particularly, middle-class, middle-aged, ethnically Japanese men whose employment and family backgrounds are most similar to those making the judgments. Such backgrounds are seen as constituting enough outside pressure to guarantee good behaviour in the future.

Of the 25 rape and indecent assault trials I observed at the Tokyo District Court in June–July 1997 only one first-time offender could be classified as middle-class: a teacher. It is also noteworthy that the only two non-Japanese defendants, of seemingly African and Middle-Eastern descent, received very heavy sentences compared to Japanese defendants on similar charges. The defendant of Middle-Eastern descent (who had no criminal convictions) received five years' imprisonment for indecent assault and robbery.[14] Although it is difficult to compare cases given the quantity of detail taken into consideration, in another indecent assault and robbery case the Japanese defendant received the lesser sentence of four years' imprisonment despite a more serious degree of sexual assault, a significantly higher sum of stolen money and two previous criminal convictions for robbery and bodily injury.[15] Unlike the Middle-Eastern man, the defendant in this case apologised, returned the stolen money, paid additional compensation and the woman requested a degree of leniency. The defendant of African descent (who had no criminal convictions), like the Middle-Eastern defendant, was found to have lied, failed to apologise or pay compensation. He received a sentence of 14 months' imprisonment for indecent assault. In the majority of similar indecent assault cases observed, the Japanese defendants received suspended sentences. As a point of comparison, similar sentences of 18 months were handed down in two other cases I observed of indecent assault. In one of these cases the victim was a 13-year-old boy, and in the other the defendant, a teacher, committed multiple offences against a number of his male students.[16]

The construction of a homogeneous judiciary

Ishimatsu Takeo and legal scholar Hirano Ryūichi claim that in Japan courts have little to do with fact-finding and that this power lies with prosecutors and police. Moreover, both emphasise the significance of the fact that the Japanese judicial process, in which decisions are based not on evidence presented in court but on later reading the written dossier, is characterised as 'trial by dossier' (*chōsho saiban*). They argue that courts in Japan are not places that determine whether the defendant is guilty or innocent, but merely ceremonial places that confirm the defendant's guilt, or at most, a place to inspect the results of the investigation (Ishimatsu 1989: 143–153; Hirano 1989: 129–142). A strong indication of the importance of the investigative stage is the very high level of suspicion required to file an indictment and the extremely low acquittal rate at trial, consistently well under 1 per cent.[17] Hirano argues that, 'if one requires great suspicion for indictment, then the substance of the criminal proceeding inevitably must shift to the investigation level and the investigative bodies must be provided with considerable coercive authority' (Hirano 1989: 131).

Although much of the research on policing in Japan portrays a very positive or benign picture (Ames 1981; Bayley 1976, 1984) there are also convincing alternative accounts of disturbing police powers and practices at the investigative stage (see Saitō 1992: 182–192; Igarashi 1986;

Miyazawa 1992: 21–23, 159–166). Ishimatsu and Hirano convincingly argue that police and prosecutors are endowed with significant power and coercive authority, however, the extent to which they infer this transferral of power diminishes judicial control of the trial is questionable. The authoritative voice of the judiciary in interpreting meaning is essentially beyond dispute[18] and presumably this influences police and prosecutors' practices in ways that mutually reinforce common assumptions and values. The very general wording of the penal code (the article on rape is a clear example) necessitates the broad discretionary authority of judges in interpreting the law (Terrill 1992: 241–242). Judicial authority is also reinforced by the high level of conformity that generally characterises judicial decisions. Evidence of this conformity is found in the low success rate of appeals. Seventy-five per cent of high court appeals uphold the lower court's decision and 97 per cent of Supreme Court appeals uphold the decisions of the lower appellate courts.[19] Judicial conformity is achieved by the organisational mechanisms and processes described below, which aim to create a homogeneous judicial community.

It is generally accepted that judges in Japan and elsewhere in the world are overwhelmingly conservative, preferring to uphold rather than challenge the status quo. This situation is compounded by a number of factors in Japan. First, without juries,[20] in all cases judges bear the burden of ultimate responsibility for determination of fact and law. Second, under the civil law tradition, emphasis in the application of the law is placed on legal certainty and uniformity. Haley (1995: 3) argues that the result is 'greater caution and passivity in the exercise of judicial authority than their counterparts in the common law tradition'. Legal change in Japan is an extremely slow process, carefully managed to keep it in line with the 'judges' sense of community values' (Haley 1995: 17). These observations make a number of recent judgments in favour of the plaintiff in sexual harassment cases particularly interesting. Leon Wolff interprets the new sexual harassment findings as an indication that judges are not as passive as is commonly believed, arguing that Japanese 'judges *develop* law – by exploring the whole context of the legal system to derive principles which would justify new concrete rights and duties' (Wolff 1996: 511). Certainly, this seems to be the case, but it is also important to recognise the role of feminist lawyers and others who have been active in providing the groundwork for the innovative legal decisions. It is on the basis of the cases brought to the courts by feminist lawyers and these lawyers' legal arguments that the judges are being required to respond. As a result, new sexual harassment findings suggest that a space is opening up for feminist resistance to dominant legal discourses.

Nevertheless, there are a number of institutional practices that inhibit judges from making 'land-mark' decisions. Due to the enormous caseload of Japanese judges there is strong pressure to settle cases prior to judgment, which reinforces the conservative nature of the judiciary and their reluctance to make new law. The number of judges in Japan is very small: in 1994 there were 2,200 judges in the courts of first instance (compared to 28,500 in the US, 25,000 in the UK and approximately 18,000 in Germany). Each of these judges in Japan hears an average of 1,100 cases per year (compared to 700 in the US) (Davis 1996: 80). Judges generally work on about 50 cases at a time, hearing two or three trials per day. Hearings are not held consecutively and each one is generally quite short (10 minutes to 3 hours).[21] While this system was adopted from European traditions during the Meiji period, it is currently justified in terms of allowing time for emotions to diffuse and, therefore, being conducive to settlement. At the same time, given the high caseloads of judges and their obligation to produce a text detailing the findings of fact and application of law if the case proceeds to judgment, settlement prior to judgment is an efficient means of disposing of cases. In-court settlement also avoids the possibility of a future appeal (Obuchi 1987: 86–87). According to Haley, efficiency and case management take priority over the social consequences of particular decisions and even uniformity in decision-making within the judiciary (Haley 1995: 15).

However, there are numerous measures and internal controls that ensure a high degree of uniformity. The justice administration in Japan effectively ensures that one 'socially appropriate' standard is maintained by centralising administration. Legal scholars Abe Masaki (1995: 304) and Mikazuki Akira (1976: 450) emphasise the highly centralised hierarchical control of the judiciary in Japan and note that the internal control mechanisms foster tacit norms and a high degree of homogeneity within the judiciary.[22] The internal control is directed by the judges, who form the top management staff of the General Secretariat (*Jimu-Sōkyoku*) of the Supreme Court. Although judicial appointments are ostensibly made by the Cabinet, the real decision-making power rests with the judges within the General Secretariat, who are in a position to reward and punish judges and prosecutors through promotions, pay rises and transfers. Thus, Abe asserts that 'the control over judges by the General Secretariat is, after all, control over judges by judges. It is internal control within the judiciary' (Abe 1995: 312).

Assistant judges and judges are transferred on average every three years to a variety of courts around the country and there is a general understanding of the places regarded as favourable and those that are not. This practice serves as an important means of control over judges. For example, Davis (1996: 78) notes that the reversal of judges' decisions on appeal tends to reflect badly on their performance record and, although the dismissal of a judge is extremely rare, judges may be 'punished' by assigning them to positions in remote locations. In addition, assistant judges attend special training programmes conducted by the General Secretariat. Haley argues that these programmes and the practice of rotation among the courts:

> represent a process of socialization through which the values, expectations, and underlying assumptions of senior judges are passed down. Younger judges learn – and are intended to absorb – the standards and expectations that will be applied to them for promotion and assignment. Judicial uniformity and cohesion are the result.
>
> (Haley 1995: 15)

In addition, Miyazawa (1991: 55–59) argues that the General Secretariat's periodic judicial conferences are a means to educate judges on the General Secretariat's interpretation of particular issues, rather than opportunities for judges to engage in constructive dialogue. Miyazawa also describes a number of incidents where judges have been punished for establishing forums in which they could freely discuss topics of their own selection and he details the General Secretariat's shift from 1968 to constrain 'more independent-minded, liberal judges'. The result has been a more cautious and conservative judiciary and, according to Haley (1995: 17), 'a lost opportunity to transform the judiciary into a more politically responsive and reforming institution'. However, Haley also argues that this cautious approach by the judiciary may well be responsible for the institution's continuing autonomy and influence, free from political intervention. Haley's main argument is that judicial independence rests on 'parliamentary trust and public confidence' (Haley 1995: 17).

Judicial homogeneity and the maintenance of uniform standards are also reinforced by the limited range of social backgrounds and experiences of legal personnel. As lawyer Yanagawa Tsuneko noted, judges lead very cloistered lives not so different from priests. The majority began their careers as judges in their mid-twenties and, therefore, have not even experienced life in a legal firm (interview 5 November 1996). Similarly, Davis notes that judges are a tight knit group working and socialising together. He explains that because of frequent transfers and heavily subsidised housing provided by the government, judges also tend to live in 'conclaves of apartments and houses' and thus, due to their 'sheltered lifestyle and long hours of work, judges seldom have contact with and insight into the reality of everyday life' (Davis 1996: 79).

Moreover, a very high percentage of judges, public prosecutors and practising attorneys graduate from a very small number of select universities[23] and all must then pass the highly competitive National Legal Examination (*Shihō shiken*) which, Abe argues, rewards students willing to accept the status quo.[24] Those who pass may then proceed to the Legal Training and Research Institute (LTRI), which is managed by the Supreme Court. Educators at the Institute are predominantly career judges, 'carefully selected by the General Secretariat to teach mainstream doctrines and forms of practice' (Miyazawa 2000: 27). While the percentage of female students enrolled in the LTRI has been steadily increasing over the past decade, they remain a very small minority – 7.6 per cent in 1997 (Levin 1998).

Given the small numbers of women entering the Institute it is no surprise that the Supreme Court remains a male bastion: the first woman, Takahashi Hisako, was appointed to the Supreme Court in 1994; she is now retired.

Ministry of Justice professionals are, thus, dominated by an elite, urban, ethnically Japanese, predominantly male identity. In April 1997 there were 282 female judges (9.7 per cent), 113 female prosecutors (5.2 per cent) and 1,176 female lawyers (7.4 per cent) (Office for Gender Equality 1999). In 1986, of the 256,546 police personnel (including those in charge of clerical duties) 16,600 were women (United Nations Asia and Far East Institute for the Prevention of Crime and Treatment of Offenders 1990: 112). Age is also a common factor at the Supreme Court level. Haley (1995: 13–14) notes that at the time of writing (1989) only two Supreme Court Justices had been under the age of 60 (both were 58 years) since 1952, and up until 1990 none had received their legal education in the post-war period. This presents a number of problems for 'outsiders' attempting to gain entry or fit in. For example, it is generally asserted that graduating students from the LTRI can choose one of the three professions (Davis 1996: 77). However, the element of choice is moderated by the Institute staff who, according to one female graduate, often 'strongly recommend', if not coerce, the 'choice' of one path over another, and women are usually advised to pursue private practice. Yet, as noted in a 1997 report by the Japanese Federation of Bar Associations, finding a placement on graduation is not always easy for women (cited in Mossman 1998: 42). Similarly, freelance writer Miya Yōko (1995), who interviewed a number of female lawyers, notes that these women expressed mixed reactions regarding their acceptance and difficulties in working in this 'male world'. There is nothing unique here. In a recent Australian study of female barristers in Victoria (constituting only 15.8 per cent of the total number), Rosemary Hunter (2003) describes patterns and sources of homosociability – an important marker of hegemonic masculinity – similar to those mentioned above. Hunter argues that there is a distinctive culture of the Bar, consisting of a range of exclusionary practices that involve the production and performance of hegemonic masculinity, that adversely impacts on female barristers' opportunities for advancement. Compulsory heterosexuality is also a central component of hegemonic masculinity produced in both the Australian Bar culture and the Japanese (hostess/*geisha*) bar culture. Two Japanese female lawyers interviewed by Miya commented on the necessity and discomfort they experienced in having to participate in regular work outings to hostess bars and at Bar association functions attended by *geisha*. Another common obstacle was the general perception that married women are less committed and therefore unable to carry out the degree of work required of a competent lawyer (Miya 1995). Presumably, female judges face similar difficulties.[25]

The high degree of homogeneity, cohesiveness and uniformity within the legal community, and judiciary in particular, makes it difficult for women not only to enter and to work within the legal community but also to make independent decisions that might not conform to precedents. It is possible that such decisions would be met with accusations of being 'biased', opinion based on personal, gendered experiences rather than 'neutral' standards. The structure and nature of the judicial community also has serious implications for other sorts of 'outsiders' who come before the courts. Witnesses entering the court must reconstruct aspects of social life that are usually taken for granted and they must make these visible to judges who may have very different life experiences. Making one's story comprehensible to judges is much easier for those whose life experiences approximate those of the judge because what is accepted as 'common sense' is drawn from a shared pool of knowledge. The most effective arguments or the most credible stories among multiple and contesting accounts are those that rely on 'common knowledge' – assumptions that go without saying. The result is the likely exclusion of alternative accounts of sexual violence that do not conform to either dominant (common-sense) understandings of violence or stereotypical images of rape.

The discussion of both socio-cultural elements, discussed in the previous chapter, and particular structural features of the Japanese criminal justice system outlined in this chapter, provides a context or background that, together, create a framework that is likely to shape judges' decisions in specific ways. The following chapters examine the pattern in judicial decision-making that emerges from my sample of cases. Chapter 4 analyses the cases that required little deliberation in determining that rape took place. These are the cases that conform to perceptions of 'normal' or *tsūjō* rape, rapists and rape victims.

4 Credibility in the court

Scripting rape

How is rape law understood by the judiciary in Japan? What kinds of knowledge count? The definition of rape in the Japanese Penal Code (translated in Appendix 1) is broad and, therefore, provides considerable room for interpretation in the determination of cases. However, within Japanese legal circles there has been little discussion regarding the nature of the crime and its central elements. Legal scholar George Koshi (1970: 140–141) outlines the key aspects of rape law as follows: (1) penetration of the vagina by the penis, (2) without the consent of the victim, (3) achieved by the perpetrator's use of force or intimidation. To these elements should be added *mens rea*, that is, where the perpetrator intended to have intercourse against the victim's *will* (as opposed to consent).

Although *mens rea* is not mentioned by Koshi, it is an accepted legal principle in Japanese law, and the legal discussions in a number of cases analysed in this study state that it is a necessary element of the crime of rape (see Case 9; Case 10 Watanabe; Case 11 Takeda; Taniguchi 1970: 5–9). Article 177 is based on the assumption that consent and *mens rea* can be determined on the basis of the perpetrator's violence and coercion. When questions concerning consent and *mens rea* were raised in the sample of cases, the legal points of argument focused on the defendant's degree of force and intimidation, which was defined primarily in the context of the victim's resistance. In other words, the woman's resistance to the defendant's violence acts as a proxy for determining consent and *mens rea* in the majority of ambiguous cases – cases which Japanese judges regularly described as containing evidence that was *fushizen* (unnatural).

Thc legal commentary preceding a rape case detailed in *Hanrei Jihō* (Case 13 Matsumoto: 111) states that a minority of legal scholars argue that consent rather than the degree of violence and threat should be the central question in determining the crime of rape. However, the dominant legal opinion is that consent and the victim's will are unreliable standards on which to determine whether rape took place because they rely on the subjective opinion of the victim and are thus likely to lead to appeal challenges (Tsunoda 1991: 27). The majority of scholars, therefore, concur that it is necessary to focus on the 'objective' standard of the behaviour involved, that is, the degree of force used to commit the crime. Therefore, rather than Koshi's explanation of rape law in terms of 'without the consent of the victim', more appropriate is 'against the will of the victim'. This is in view of the fact that current interpretations of rape law in Japan, discussed in Chapters 5 and 6, are generally more consistent with the early English common law definition of rape as 'carnal knowledge of a woman forcibly and against her will'. Like interpretations of rape law in Japan, this definition required the perpetrator's use of force and the victim's resistance. The nineteenth-century change from 'will' to 'consent' was an attempt to broaden the scope of rape law to include cases in which neither violence nor fraud were used and the change meant that it was no longer necessary for the prosecutor to establish an outward manifestation of lack of consent in the form of resistance.[1] However, the simplified understanding of rape as penetration 'without consent' retains the emphasis on consent and thus the focus of attention on the victim-survivor and her state of mind. Consequently, in many cases the central focus of the trial remains on the woman rather than the man, and violence and resistance are still frequently considered relevant to determine lack of consent (Bronitt 1992: 290).

Law protects especially valued interests and although the law is concerned more with wrongs than rights it is difficult to understand these wrongs without an understanding of what these particular values and interests are. The particular values and interests to be protected by rape law and different ideas about the harm of rape are open to interpretation and it is on this basis that several theories on rape have developed. Rape law in Japan closely corresponds with Keith Burgess-Jackson's conceptualisation of a 'conservative' theory of rape. He argues that general debates concerning rape and variations in rape laws can be categorised in terms of three theories of rape: conservative, liberal and radical. While elements of all three approaches may be incorporated into existing rape laws, the conservative theory, which accords with the historical or traditional approach, still remains at the foundations of 'modern rape law' in Anglophone and other countries. The familiar conservative theory of rape can be likened to the law of trespass. A woman's reproductive capacity, sexuality and virginity are conceptualised as valuable commodities that belong to her father, husband or sovereign. Women merely hold (or hoard) their sexuality, in trust, for the lawful, male owner. Rape is, thus, regarded primarily as the appropriation and violation of the male's property right to these commodities. The question of consent is redundant as the woman's interests are presumed to coalesce with those of her male protector (Burgess-Jackson 1996: 44–45).

Under the conservative approach, rape in marriage is inconceivable because the husband already owns the property rights to his wife's body. The conservative approach also has difficulty in dealing with the rape of prostitutes who, by making their sexuality available to numerous men, forego the right to protection by one man and, thus, by the legal system, which exists to uphold his interests. In addition, Burgess-Jackson explains that:

> the theory of rape as trespass explains why women become, in effect, 'co-defendants' in a rape trial. . . . female victims of rape are accused by defense attorneys of acting irresponsibly with what has been 'entrusted' to them by men, namely, their sexuality. If a woman has been raped she hasn't done her job properly. She must have provoked a man, been in the wrong place, or been out without a male chaperone. She has been reckless. The fact that many women blame themselves for their own rape testifies to the continuing strength of this theory.
>
> (Burgess-Jackson 1996: 47)

In contrast, the liberal theory views rape as a form of gender-blind assault, 'the unlawful touching of another person (understood discretely rather than relationally) without his or her consent' (Burgess-Jackson 1996: 49). Consent is central to this approach because sexuality is regarded as an object or a form of commodity, which the individual owns and has the right to control. Thus, rape is conceptualised as a violation of a will and an individual's right to bodily integrity or autonomy – male or female. Both the conservative and the liberal theories, therefore, regard sexuality as property that can be violated.[2]

The radical theory of rape, conceptualising rape as a form of degradation, rejects the gender-blindness of the liberal view and emphasises the fact that rape is overwhelmingly perpetrated by men against women. Rape is 'about power, fear, status, and control, not individual transgression of social norms' (Burgess-Jackson 1996: 53). According to the radical approach, rape is seen as a means of subordinating women and, therefore, the political context of gendered power relations in which rape takes place is emphasised. Sexuality is not biologically given but socially constructed, reflecting the prevailing power structures that privilege male interests and desires. Both the conservative and liberal approaches fail to recognise the way in which sexual relations are shaped by gendered power hierarchies.

The conservative approach to rape is contested by Japanese feminist lawyers currently attempting to introduce 'radical' interpretations to rape law in Japan. They argue that the current interpretation of rape law in Japan continues to reflect the patriarchal interest in women's sexuality and reproduction by regarding rape as an injury against the property rights of husbands or fathers and, thus, the patriarchal order. In their view, the *honne* (real intention or true substance) of the Japanese rape law is the protection of chastity (*teiso*) (Tsunoda 1991: 17–20; Fukushima 1997: 257–268). Judges have little difficulty convicting and severely punishing defendants in cases where the victim's virtue was clear and unambiguous and she defended it to the utmost of her ability. Moreover, the injury of the crime, 'rape resulting in bodily injury' (*gōkan chisho*) is frequently interpreted as damage to the hymen (Taniguchi 1970: 7) – reflecting the common view among judges and others that the harm of rape is most significant when the victim was a virgin (Tsunoda, interview 8 April 1997). Once a woman has experienced sexual intercourse, additional acts of penetration are not regarded as damaging. Little attention has been paid to the psychological harm of rape.

Under the 1907 criminal code, crimes are defined in terms of three types of interest or rights protected by law (*hogohōeki*): national, social and personal rights (*kokka-teki hōeki, shakai-teki hōeki* and *kojin-teki hōeki*). The section of the criminal code explaining social rights mentions rape and indecent assault in terms of protecting the social order and the maintenance of a healthy sexual environment.[3] The right to be protected by rape law is, thus, not conceptualised as an individual or personal right. Tsunoda points out the contradiction between this conceptualisation and the 1947 Constitution's guarantee of equality based on the notion of liberal individualism, under which rape and indecent assault are clearly violations of sexual or personal freedoms and thus belong to the personal category (Tsunoda 1991: 13–16; see also Fukushima 1997: 250). This idea has gained acceptance to some degree within legal circles and is certainly expressed at the level of rhetoric in legal rape discourse. Although there has been no significant rape law reform in Japan since 1907,[4] there is evidence of shifts in interpretation of the existing law. The post-war legal discourse of rape began to include the notion of 'women's right to sexual freedom', and discussions concerning the nature of woman and the nature of rape were thrown into question. Taniguchi Masataka, Supreme Court Justice 1980–1987, writes that 'the essential element of rape is that it violates women's sexual freedom'. However, this statement is moderated by his following question and discussion regarding the nature of woman, rationality and rape:

> Is it possible to have sex with a woman who is seriously resisting? This became an obvious question to ask immediately after the end of our class society when women gained the legal freedom to be independent individuals. . . . We faced the fundamental problem of deciding whether women were rational people (*riseijin*) . . . at the same time we must not forget the fact that as the central characters of the crime of rape, women are not ideally positioned rational beings, but humans with sexual and emotional instincts. Therefore, considering the essential element of rape, it is not enough to define it as a crime which invades women's sexual freedom, but it also involves the immorality of the behaviour itself, that is, the intentions of the offender.
>
> When we think about the degree of assault and threat used to commit rape, we come to different conclusions depending on how the woman is positioned in relation to the crime and how we understand the true nature (*honshitsu*) of woman. That is, when we understand rape as a violation of women's sexual freedom and position women at the centre of the crime of rape as rational human beings, the degree of threat and

> violence must be sufficient to overcome the resistance stemming from her natural rationality. . . . if rape is a means to satisfy sexual desire and we accept women as rational humans but still with sexual feelings, the degree of threat and violence necessary to accomplish the crime is sufficient to symbolise the immorality of the behaviour.
>
> (Taniguchi 1970: 6)

Despite post-war rhetoric concerning the harm of rape in terms of women's sexual freedom, humiliation and psychological injury,[5] dominant legal opinion, illustrated by Taniguchi's argument above, offers women very limited sexual freedom at best and only if they prove to be deserving of protection by conforming to norms of rationality that accord with a presumed male response to aggression.

In the written law of rape, as well as case examples, the issues of force and intimidation are clearly central. It is the degree of force and intimidation deemed necessary to commit rape that is contested. Nevertheless, as Taniguchi notes, this debate has probably been constrained due to the lack of cases coming before the courts that focus on determining the degree of force and intimidation as proof of rape. He notes that cases in which lack of consent is unclear rarely come before the courts because, in the majority of cases where no physical injuries are incurred or the degree of violence and threat is light, victims tend either not to file a complaint or to drop their case before it comes to trial (Taniguchi 1970: 7), often at the recommendation of the prosecutor (Tsunoda 1991: 32).

Presumably on the basis of Article 178 of the Penal Code (see Appendix 1), which relates to constructive compulsory indecency (*junkyōsei waisetsu*) and quasi-rape (*jungōkan*), the conventional wisdom is that:

> it is not necessary that the perpetrator overcome all power to resist, nor does the law require that the victim offer resistance to the limit of her capability. In actual practice, if the force or intimidation used is such that it would create an apprehension on the part of the victim that any further resistance is useless and dangerous, the requirement that force or intimidation be present is satisfied.
>
> (Koshi 1970: 140)

However, an examination of the cases in this study shows that in certain situations women are required to demonstrate much more than 'apprehension' that resistance is useless or that it will place them in further danger. It is only when the circumstances fit the stereotypical or *tsūjō* rape scenario that a victim's failure to resist is perceived as evidence of the existence of significant force and intimidation. It is in these types of cases that the threat is considered unambiguous and non-consent can be easily assumed. However, as the Ikebukuro case in the Prelude demonstrates, even in such situations a woman's non-consent is not automatically or necessarily assumed if the scenario simulates familiar pornographic narratives and/or if the woman is deemed to have provoked her sexual assault.

Taniguchi (1970: 5–9) attempts to clarify the debates concerning the degree of necessary force to commit rape by analysing four main approaches to rape in Japan. These approaches provide an important insight into the links and tensions between constructions of sex and gender within dominant legal discourse. The first approach, to which Taniguchi adheres, recommends that the necessary level of force in rape must be the same as that pertaining to robbery, that is, the force must *overcome* (*yokuatsu*) the victim's resistance. Taniguchi explains that this position is based on the premise that rape is the use of a woman's body as a tool to achieve a man's sexual gratification. Therefore, the essential element of rape includes not just the violation of a woman's sexual freedom and will, but also the intentions of the rapist. As the intention is to achieve sexual satisfaction and the means to do so is the use of violence and intimidation, it is therefore not enough to determine rape on the basis that the sex was against the woman's will alone. It is necessary to prove the man's intention to rape with evidence of the means to commit the crime, that is, that the force and intimidation was sufficient to overcome the woman's resistance. A real rapist is, thus, conceptualised as a man who will resort to any means necessary to achieve sexual gratification.

This shift of focus from the woman's consent to the man's intention is due in part to the difficulty the law has in dealing with women who do not act like men. Taniguchi explains that because women have been granted citizenship and accepted as independent and free individuals, they must, therefore, be accorded with the appropriate status of rational beings (*riseijin*). Yet, for Taniguchi, this is complicated by the fact that women also have sexual and emotional instincts. Thus, in potential rape situations women do not always behave as rational actors by resisting earnestly to the end; they do not always run away, and some eventually submit, their 'instincts' taking over from rationality. Taniguchi argues that although we cannot call sexual intercourse under these circumstances consensual sex, neither can it be called rape. Rather, the offence falls more appropriately under the crime of compulsion (*kyōseizai* Article 223, see Appendix 1), which pertains to violations of free will or human freedom rather than sexual freedom.

The second approach argues that the degree of force should be such that it *makes resistance significantly difficult* (*ichijirushiku konnan*). This argument emphasises the point that it is often difficult to distinguish between consensual sex and rape because of *yūkeiryoku*, that is, the degree of force that may be used in 'normal' heterosexual sex that is not against the woman's will. Therefore, it is necessary to demonstrate that the resistance was very strong, as evidence that the level of force and intimidation was above and beyond that accepted as part of 'normal' sexual relations. Taniguchi states that while the required degree of force and intimidation is similar to that of the first approach, it fails to adequately address one of the fundamental elements of rape, that is, the violation of women's sexual freedom.

To illustrate the second approach, Taniguchi cites two cases. The first is a 1949 case in which the court did not accept the claim that it is necessary that the force and intimidation 'be as strong as to disable the victim's resistance and free will', but decided that it was sufficient when it 'makes the resistance of the other party significantly difficult' (Taniguchi 1970: 8). Taniguchi notes that although the expression of the judgment conforms to the second approach, the actual details of the case were also sufficient to convict under the first approach: the defendant pushed a 15-year-old girl down on the ground and when she screamed for help he threatened to kill her, and hit her in the face. The injury to her head and vagina required two weeks' hospitalisation. This case is frequently cited in Japanese legal textbooks as an example of the *minimum* standard of force required to establish rape and, thus, as Tsunoda (1991: 15) points out, the problem is that cases not involving this degree of violence are dismissed.

The second example is a 1958 case in which the judge stated that the force and intimidation is sufficient when it 'immobilises the other party's resistance or makes it significantly difficult considering the person's age, sex, lifestyle, history, the time and place of the act, the general environment and other details'. Taniguchi (1970: 8) adds that judgments in cases of robbery, similarly, make it clear that the degree of force and intimidation should not be decided on the basis of the victim's perspective but should be decided on the basis of 'objective' facts concerning the act. Thus, in principle, the two approaches are fundamentally similar in terms of judgment considerations.

The third and fourth approaches to rape differ significantly from the first two approaches in that they are premised on the assumption that the central principle of the law of rape is the protection of chastity, arguments that Taniguchi asserts are reminiscent of ideas that sex outside marriage should be punished. While Taniguchi is critical of these theories because he argues that morality should not be the basis of the *hogohōeki* of rape law, he explains the third and fourth theories less clearly than the first two theories. However, he states that the third position argues that a narrow definition of force (demanding a high degree of resistance from the victim, as in the first theory) fails to include some immoral behaviours and, therefore, the degree of force and coercion is sufficient when it *makes resistance difficult*.[6] As an example of this level of force Taniguchi (1970: 8) cites a 1969 High Court judgment concerning a case in which the defendant took a woman he was secretly meeting at night to a bush, ordered her to lie down, lay on top of her and had sex while she was resisting. The judge stated that the law pertaining to rape, Article 177, does not require that the degree of force and intimidation be as strong as to overcome completely the resistance of the victim. Rather, it is sufficient when it deprives a woman of her free will.

The fourth approach maintains that the force is sufficient when it *restrains resistance*. The rationale behind this argument is that it is unacceptable that cases not meeting the high level of force required in the first two approaches be prosecuted under the law of coercion (or 'compulsion'), which does not pertain to the essential element of rape, that is, the protection of women's chastity. According to Taniguchi (1970: 8), an example of this level of force was described in a 1949 High Court judgment of a case in which the defendant held a woman down with both hands and raped her. The court stated that according to Article 177 the necessary force is physical violence against the victim's will regardless of the degree.

The main problem with the third and fourth approaches is that although they require a lesser degree of force and intimidation and, therefore, appear to be more conducive to understanding women's fear and experiences of rape, the emphasis on chastity is likely to mean that women who do not meet the conventional standards of virtue or whose character or behaviour could be construed as blameworthy, are unlikely to receive much sympathy. The woman of virtue may be protected, but at the expense of those who transgress conventional constructions of appropriate femininity and female sexuality.

The main problem with the first two approaches outlined by Taniguchi, which demand a high level of resistance, is that they are formulated on the basis of a 'rational' response to an assault which, as Estrich (1987: 60) puts it, conforms to behaviour expected of men in a bar-room fight. That is, a reasonable man fears the threat of attack by a male stranger, particularly if he is outnumbered, and he reasonably fears the threat of a weapon, which clearly disturbs the otherwise relatively equal balance of power between two men in a fight in terms of size and weight. The expected response to such threats is either 'fight or flight'. No doubt the interpretation partially reflects the fact that when the criminal law was written, there were no female legal professionals or members of the imperial parliament, and consequently the degree of violence and coercion was defined by men. Similarly, the extent of injury is defined in masculinist terms. In Tsunoda's words, 'the amount of pain felt when punched in the face is decided by the man who throws the punch' (Tsunoda 1991: 17).

Numerous studies in Anglophone countries have demonstrated that women respond to perceived threats often much earlier and in different ways to men, at least partially due to different socialisation processes, and partially due to the socio-cultural rape scripts, which assert women's vulnerability and weakness (see Box 1983: 148–150; Estrich 1987: 60). While masculine fear typically triggers a 'fight or flight' response, women frequently respond by 'freezing', that is, involuntary immobility and silence. Sharon Marcus argues that women's learned responses to fear are part of what she terms the 'gendered grammar of violence', which precedes and structures rape. She explains that:

> the grammar of violence dictates that feminine fear concentrates the self on the anticipation of pain, the inefficacy of action, and the conviction that the self will be destroyed. Feminine fear precipitates all violence and agency outside of its subject; it thus disables its subject from risking possible pain or death in order to defend herself, since that risk can seem viable only if the subject perceives herself as possessing some violent capacity on which she can draw to try to survive pain or elude injury. Feminine fear also seems to entail a complete identification of a vulnerable, sexualized body with the self.
>
> (Marcus 1992: 394)

The relevance of these theories to Japanese women's responses to fear is open to conjecture as studies in this area have not to my knowledge been carried out in Japan. However, my analysis of sexual assault cases suggests that these observations are also salient in the Japanese context. Endō explained that the sound of her attacker's raised and threatening voice (a tone that she had never heard before) reduced her to a state of fear, compelling her to compliance and passivity. However, the judges in all three trials relating to her case failed to understand her response, interpreting her submission not as consent but as inconsistent with rape. Women's alternative experiences of fear and violence are, thus, denied credibility and silenced by the masculine legal standards on which force, intimidation and resistance are evaluated.

Taniguchi's discussion of the four approaches to rape law highlights the lack of consensus concerning the nature of rape and, to some extent, explains the variations in interpreting rape law. Identifying such differences is important to the project of feminist law reform because such fissures indicate possible space for the intervention of alternative feminist-inspired interpretations of rape. However, Taniguchi's conceptualisation of approaches to rape does not account for the patterning of judgments that emerge on closer analysis of specific cases. Despite the differing assumptions of the four approaches, the force and coercion requirement tends to be interpreted in much the same way when particular variables or conditions exist, as demonstrated by the cases in this study.

To highlight the judicial pattern in decision-making the 20 cases have been divided into two sets on the basis of whether or not they conformed to stock stories of rape and could, therefore, be decided with apparent ease, and those which demanded further consideration of the 'facts' (see Appendix 2). The first set outlined below (cases 1–9)[7] conformed to the stock stories of rape and/or on some other basis were quickly and easily classified as *tsūjō* rape cases – those the judges deemed normal or natural rape situations. The second set, outlined in Chapter 5 (cases 10 to 20, which are referred to by pseudonyms) required more careful deliberation because some aspect of the story or circumstances was regarded as *fushizen*, not normal or unnatural for a case of rape. In these cases, additional evidence of rape is required and this most frequently takes the form of proving the defendant used a degree of force and/or coercion and that the woman resisted. The focus of the trial, thus, shifts at this point from the defendant to the woman. In order to understand the judgments in these cases it is necessary to first consider the sorts of cases that judges have little difficulty in deciding – the *tsūjō* or benchmark cases.

Tsūjō rape cases

Case 1

Over a three-month period the defendant received substantial amounts of money through blackmail from five women. He raped two of the women and attempted to rape the other three (two of these women were forced to perform oral sex, which constituted 'attempted rape'). The primary legal argument focused on whether he was guilty of one crime or two. The case was novel because it was the first involving rape and blackmail.

The defendant was found guilty of two crimes because (a) the nature of the crimes are different: the aim of the blackmail was to obtain money, the aim of the rape was *seiteki yōkyu* (to satisfy his sexual desires), and (b) the crimes did not take place at the same time. The defendant was sentenced to five years and six months' imprisonment including the 180 days detention. The sentence took into account the seriousness of the crimes, that the defendant had no prior relationship with the women, that the total ¥700,000 obtained through the blackmail was a substantial amount, that the women refused a private settlement, and that he had been questioned by the police in connection with similar cases. In his favour he had attempted to make a private settlement, he had paid back the money, he had no previous convictions and his family was supportive.

Case 2

This case was primarily concerned with the question of warrants. The defendant, a fisherman, was arrested in a pachinko parlour[8] without a warrant because the following day he was due to go to sea and there was insufficient time to follow the correct procedures. One of the six women sexually assaulted by the defendant recognised him from a photograph and he was arrested.

The case involved six separate incidents beginning 18 months after his early release from prison. The judge found that the seriousness of the crimes outweighed the question of the warrant. The judge noted that in the first incident the woman was subjected to extreme fear because the attack took place in a dark deserted street, and in all cases the women were unmarried and none of them had 'made a mistake' (presumably acts such as drinking alcohol or engaging in provocative behaviour). The judge also took into account the defendant's criminal record (rape resulting in bodily injury, for which he was released 15 months early for good behaviour), the fear he caused in the small community, that he did not apologise in any form to the victims and his escape from police custody. The defendant was sentenced to six years including the 250 days detention.

Case 3

This High Court appeal focused on the argument that the original judge did not explain the evidence in the judgment. The High Court found that the facts were written in the judgment and so there was no need to verbally explain the details and, furthermore, this did not affect the fact that the defendant was found guilty.

The defendant was one of eight men convicted of raping a 14-year-old girl. The defendant admitted that he was in the room but denied taking part in the rape. However, the judge argued that the element of *mens rea* existed. The defendant's father paid the girl's mother two lots of ¥1,000,000 and on this basis requested a reduction in the sentence. The judgment, including the sentence, remained the same: 20 months' imprisonment.

Case 4

This case, which sparked a major controversy over the US bases in Okinawa, involved three Afro-American military servicemen (A, B and C) who were convicted of the rape of a 12-year-old Japanese girl. The judgment focused on the evidence concerning B because he withdrew his initial confession, arguing that he neither hit nor raped her.

The judge found that A planned and orchestrated the crime and was the first to rape the girl. According to the judge, after the first rape the girl was understandably confused and hurt and so she could not clearly remember if B raped and hit her. However, the judge said that this was not evidence that he did not commit rape. B was found to have lied and was therefore sentenced as heavily as A. In sentencing the men, the judge considered the facts that A told the truth, apologised, has a family and A, B and C combined paid the girl's family ¥900,000. The judge also noted the wives of A and B and one of C's superior officers pleaded for leniency. A and B were sentenced to seven years' imprisonment and C was sentenced to six years and six months' imprisonment.

Case 5

In this case the victim was a 20-year-old virgin. The defendant posed as a doctor convincing her that to clear police suspicions that she was a prostitute and that she might have a sexually transmitted disease she would need to have sexual intercourse with him.

The judgment focused on the question of whether the victim was unable to refuse due to the defendant's actions, in which case the crime constituted quasi-rape and constructive compulsory indecency (Article 178). The judge found that Article 178 does not only pertain to physical inability to refuse: the defendant created a situation where the victim was unable to refuse psychologically and mentally (*shinriteki* and *seishinteki*) and, therefore, the sexual act constituted a violation of her sexual freedom. In sentencing the defendant the judge noted: the 'shameful and vicious' nature of the crime; the woman's loss of virginity and the defendant's disrespect for her chastity, the enormous physical and mental pain inflicted on the victim; that the victim and the parents' refusal to accept an apology and their wish that the defendant be punished for the protection of society was understandable; the defendant's repeated illogical self-defence with no shame or sense of remorse; the intention of the defendant to commit the crime (i.e. *mens rea*); the defendant's long criminal record including four similar offences and previous imprisonment (in 1964 sentenced to two years for attempted rape; 1966 sentenced to two years and six months for attempted quasi-rape and quasi-rape; in 1975 sentenced to five years for indecent assault and quasi-rape; in 1981 sentenced to two years and six months for illegal restraint (*kankin*); and in 1985 sentenced to nine months for intimidation (*kyōhaku*)). The defendant was sentenced to 10 years' imprisonment, including the 100 days' detention.[9]

Case 6

This High Court appeal focused mainly on the question of whether the defendant's confession was admissible evidence or not. The case involved the rape of a 19-year-old woman at night in her apartment where she lived alone. After being raped she immediately sought help and called the police. During the investigation, the defendant denied the rape, confessed, retracted his confession and then later confessed again. This 'confession' and the woman's identification of the defendant were the only pieces of evidence, both of which were found to be trustworthy in the District Court. Therefore, although the defendant totally denied the charge in the courtroom he was found guilty and sentenced to three years' imprisonment.

However, while the High Court judge accepted that the woman was raped, threatened with a weapon and tied up, the evidence establishing that the defendant was the perpetrator was found to be questionable and, thus, the original decision was overturned. The High Court judge decided that she could not have accurately identified the defendant because (a) he was a stranger, (b) he was not identified in a line-up, (c) she had weak eyesight and was not wearing contact lenses at the time of the rape, (d) the early morning light was bad, and (e) she had little opportunity to see his face. The judge also found that the defendant (a) had a low IQ and did not have sufficient ability to explain what happened including how he committed the rape, (b) the defendant was led by the police in his explanation and (c) there were significant changes in his story and contrasts with the woman's account. The High Court judge, therefore, decided that his confession was not entirely trustworthy and the defendant was acquitted.

Case 7

This case is unusual in that it concerns the re-examination of a case in which the man had served his full three year jail sentence for the rape and assault of a woman in 1954 and then he died shortly after his request for the re-examination was accepted. Moreover, all the original court records had been destroyed.

The judge assumed that the impression (*shinsho*) of the first judgment was based on the statement of the witness who accompanied the victim, the confession, and the investigation that found the presence of semen. However, the 1989 judgment overturned the verdict. The most compelling evidence came from new DNA testing techniques which indicated that the semen and blood type found on the woman's dress and underwear did not match that of the accused. The judge argued that there was no doubt that the woman had been raped in the dark, deserted field late at night. The statements of both the woman and her female friend who witnessed the attack were regarded as trustworthy because of their continuity, detail and clarity. However, the credibility of the confession, the positive identification of the defendant, and his actions following the rape were questionable. The man argued that he initially denied the accusation but as a result of police intimidation and coercion he concocted a confession, but this was later withdrawn and he maintained his innocence throughout the trial and requested an appeal on several occasions. Concerning the identification of the man as the offender, the judge argued that it was dark and the man had no distinctive features in terms of dress or physical structure. Furthermore, not running away after the rape is not the natural behaviour of a rapist.

Case 8

The defendant was riding home on his bicycle in the middle of the night and started to follow a 17-year-old girl with whom he had no prior relationship, who was walking along the road. The girl became frightened, went to a house to ask for help and then when she thought she was safe she began walking again. The defendant continued to follow her so she went into a primary school to find a phone to call the police. He then attempted to rape her but gave up when she resisted and pleaded with him to stop.

The judgment focused on the question of why the defendant stopped – compassion or fear of being caught. The judge decided it was a combination of compassion and guilt because he gave up even though the girl had stopped struggling. The judge emphasised the girl's youth and the grave fear and psychological injury caused to her. However, in the defendant's favour the judge took into account the facts that the defendant had a family to maintain, that the defendant's wife apologised to the girl's family and paid them ¥1,000,000, and that the girl's family then also requested leniency for the defendant. The defendant received an 18-month jail sentence suspended for three years.

Case 9

In this case the defendant took amphetamines and then at 3 a.m. entered the unlocked home of a de facto couple who were sleeping together at the time. The defendant touched the 17-year-old girl who thought it was her partner so she did not resist. The defendant then undressed and lay beside her. She then woke up, called the police and the defendant was arrested.

The judgment focused on the reasons the crime was consistent with constructive compulsory indecency, not attempted quasi-rape, and the main legal argument concerned the issue of *mens rea*, whether his initial intention was to rape her. The judge accepted the defendant's statement that initially he just wanted to touch her but then gradually came to want sex because she did not resist. The defendant's statement was supported by the judge's assumption that it would be unnatural for the defendant to immediately think of raping the woman given that there was another man asleep beside her who might wake up at any time. The judge noted that the case was complicated by the fact that there was no evidence of the usual objective means of determining rape, that is, violence and coercion. According to the judge:

> for the crime of attempted quasi-rape to apply the defendant not only had to have an intention to commit quasi-rape but also it is necessary for him to carry out quasi-rape behaviour based on that intention . . . he took off his trousers and underpants and lay next to the victim, but objectively speaking (*kyakkanteki*) he did not do anything further to rape her. Therefore the defendant formed the criminal intention of quasi-rape but he did not reach the point where he carried it out.

The defendant was, therefore, sentenced to 20 months' imprisonment suspended for four years.

Content analysis of Cases 1–9

In contrast to the cases discussed in the following chapters, the above nine cases did not raise the question of force, coercion or the woman's resistance. Each of these cases included several elements of the stock rape story, which to some extent served to vitiate the requirement to prove non-consent by establishing the degree of force and resistance. The judge appeared to have little difficulty determining rape or sexual assault and did not require the victim to demonstrate strong resistance when at least one of the following factors was present:

1. *Offender is a stranger (all cases with the exception of Case 3 – involving eight offenders – in which this detail is unknown).* The existence or lack of a prior relationship between the victim and the offender is the most outstanding difference between the two sets of cases. In the set of cases involving a discussion of the degree of force and resistance (outlined in the following chapter below), only Watanabe (Case 10) in the second set had unambiguously no prior relationship with the defendant. This finding suggests very clearly that unless the defendant is a stranger, a woman must expect to prove lack of consent by demonstrating a physical struggle.
2. *Multiple victims (Cases 1 and 2).* In Case 1 there were five victim-survivors of rape or attempted rape in addition to blackmail. Regarding the first and most serious incident involving rape, the judge barely mentioned the degree of force or resistance, merely stating that, 'in his attempt to have sexual intercourse he assaulted her by undressing her and so forth and she resisted' (Case 1). Case 2 involved six victim-survivors.
3. *Multiple offenders (Cases 3 and 4; also Case 15 Sasaki and Case 11 Takeda).* In Case 3 a 14-year-old girl was raped by eight men and in Case 4 a 12-year-old girl was raped by three US marines.
4. *Offender has a previous sexual assault conviction (two known cases, Cases 2 and 5).* In these cases the defendants had served previous prison terms for at least one similar sexual offence. In the second set, Case 15 Sasaki and Case 12 Nakajima involved defendants who also had previous convictions but these did not include a sexual offence.
5. *Offender is black (Case 4).* While there are insufficient cases to provide a lot of support for this hypothesis, it is worth noting that in one indecent assault case observed at the Tokyo District Court, the African defendant's presence alone was deemed sufficient threat to overcome the victim-survivor's resistance. A conventional post-war pornographic theme distinguishes rape from seduction by depicting the rapist as a black G.I. and the victim as a young Japanese girl. Black men are associated with 'sexual and athletic prowess, disease, and violence' (Russell 1998: 114). Drawing on this theme, film director Takechi Tetsuji in his 1965 film *Black Snow* (*Kuroi Yuki*) tells the story of a black G.I., ostensibly symbolising American imperialism (and virility), who is murdered by an impotent Japanese man (Buruma 1984: 57). John Russell (1998: 124), similarly, notes that a number of Japanese male writers in the post-war period have equated black male sexuality with 'rape, primitivism, and hypersexuality'.[10]

I also expected to find a correlation between (a) the use of a weapon, (b) physical evidence of injuries and (c) the youth or virgin status of the victim, and the mitigation of the requirement to demonstrate force and resistance. However, a weapon was mentioned only in Case 6 and regarding the latter categories there is significant variation in the ways the judge responded to this information. For example, in both Cases 3 and 4 the judges mentioned that the harm was significant due to the girls' young age – 14 and 12 years respectively. Similar comments were also made of 17- and 20-year-old virgins (Cases 2, 5, 8) but not of 16- or 17-year-olds with (assumed or established) sexual experience. Claims of virginity and physical injury were not always accepted and, therefore, these issues are discussed in detail in the following chapters.

The integrity of the claimants was not questioned in any of the nine cases that did not deliberate on the degree of force and resistance. Their accounts of sexual assault were believed and validated. However, this does not mean that all *tsūjō* cases necessarily result in convictions (see Table 4.1). Of the nine cases discussed above, seven resulted in convictions. The two acquittals accepted the fact that the woman was raped but not by the defendant.

Questions regarding the degree of force and intimidation, emphasising the woman's requirement to resist, were raised in 11 of the total 20 rape and attempted rape cases (the second set) in this study. Of these 11 cases (analysed in detail in Chapters 5 and 6), seven resulted in an acquittal and four resulted in a conviction. My analysis of the 20 cases suggests that a woman is required to resist to the utmost of her ability only in particular circumstances, that is, certain factors or combinations of factors may mitigate the necessity of 'proving' the extent of force and coercion.

The variation in the way different cases were interpreted in the total sample of cases clearly suggests that an understanding of rape law requires a qualitative analysis of specific cases. While Western legal commentators who have examined the black-letter law of rape in Japan, such as Koshi (1970) and Naftulin (1980), argue that the element of force and coercion

Table 4.1 Primary sample of 20 rape cases by type of case (*tsūjō* or *fushizen*) and case outcome

	*Tsūjō rape**	*Fushizen rape***
Conviction	7	4
Acquittal	2	7

Notes

* *Tsūjō* rape scenario: a sudden and brutal attack by a stranger whose criminality can be clearly demonstrated with evidence of multiple offences or prior convictions.

** *Fushizen* rape scenario: the man and woman were acquainted, her behaviour could be interpreted as provocative or foolish and, therefore, the use of utmost force and resistance standard is applied.

is not a necessary requirement for the prosecution of rape, a closer analysis of case law suggests that such an interpretation is misleading. Taniguchi's discussion of this issue clearly indicates that the degree of force and coercion is central to the determination of rape. Nevertheless, the cases in this sample suggest that this requirement may be mitigated under particular circumstances. The following two chapters develop this analysis of how judges interpret rape. I also attempt to move beyond this question by examining the ways in which judges construct sex, sexuality and gender to demonstrate that the legal discourse of rape extends the power of male sexuality through the negation of women's subjectivity.

5 'In truth she was probably very drunk'

Women subject to scrutiny

Where there is a prior relationship between the woman and the defendant, to the extent that it might be possible to imagine that the woman enjoyed the defendant's company even though that moment might be fleetingly brief, Japanese legal discourse on rape demands proof of force and resistance. In so doing, the law constructs the male subject as having the power to disregard a woman's lack of consent if she does not physically fight back. Women are not constructed as freely consenting subjects. The legal notion of consent in Japanese rape law accommodates not only submission or acquiescence under circumstances of gross power inequalities, but also in situations in which a woman clearly signals unwillingness but does not physically resist her attacker to the extent that she is overcome.[1] A woman's consent is, therefore, essentially meaningless. She has no voice to express non-consent because she is reduced to a sexualised body, always already presumed to be consenting. Sheila Duncan (1995: 340) states this idea succinctly:

> The law has constructed a fiction to provide space for the satiation of the sexual desires of the male subject. Such violence constructs a further space for the identity and subjectivity of the male subject, enabling him to treat this other, across a range of areas, as body without subjectivity for the male subject's sexual gratification.

The 11 rape and attempted rape cases (Cases 10–20), discussed at length in this and the following chapter, provide the basis for investigating how judges approach complaints of rape that do not conform to *tsūjō* rape stock stories. A summary of each of these cases will be followed by a thematic analysis of the cases, supplemented with material from additional indecent assault and sexual harassment cases in particular, where the judicial comments are relevant to the discussion. While the primary focus of the chapter is on rape, my aim is to identify the dominant constructions of sex, gender and sexuality that are used to make sense of competing accounts of sexual assaults and to claim 'truth' in Japanese legal discourse. In each of the 11 cases, the defendant and the woman had spent at least a few hours together in a social context before the alleged offence, there was no definitive evidence of rape and, thus, the trial focused on his word against hers. In only one case (Case 17 Atsumi) did the offender deny that sexual intercourse had occurred, withdrawing his earlier confession. All other cases focused on the question of whether the woman consented or not – interpreted on the basis of the degree of demonstrated force and resistance.

Fushizen rape cases

Case 10: Watanabe[2]

In this 1969 case, the defendant and Watanabe, both aged 26, and Watanabe's husband were staying in the same hotel. The defendant and Watanabe were strangers but greeted each other in the lobby as is customary between guests. The defendant entered Watanabe's room while her husband was out. He asked if she was free, if she was lonely, and suggested they sleep together. Watanabe asked him to leave but he held and kissed her, pushed her down and raped her.

The defence constructed a story of two lonely people needing company and argued that he entered the room because he wanted to talk to her. It was only later that he gradually began to want to have sex with her and, therefore, there was no intention to rape. The trial focused on the degree of violence and threat necessary to commit rape as distinguished from the force involved in consensual sex. The defendant was acquitted because Watanabe did not sufficiently resist or attempt to escape and, thus, it could not be said that 'the degree of violence and intimidation was sufficient to make her resistance significantly possible'.

Case 11: Takeda

In 1969 the 16-year-old complainant Takeda was in a café-bar at night with a group of friends, where she met the three defendants. The defendants talked about taking her to a hotel to have sex with her. At one point in the evening Takeda became nervous of the three men and thought of leaving but stayed because she and her friends had no money to pay the café bill. In the early hours of the morning they were asked to leave the premises by a staff member because a guidance officer would arrive soon. The defendants paid the bill and suggested they all get something to eat and so the three defendants, Takeda and one of her male friends caught a taxi. Instead of going to a restaurant they went to a hotel and, after entering the room, Takeda's friend was asked to leave, which he did. Defendant U cajoled Takeda with offers of marriage and threats that he was just out of jail, that he could kill her family, and that he would never let her go. According to the judge, Takeda refused to have sex at first but then 'agreed' to sex with U, but not with the others. She resisted by moving her legs but did not scream or try to escape. She then dressed and defendant U left the room. The second defendant, R, entered the room and tried to have sex. Takeda asked him to stop, moved her legs but did not push him or scream and sexual intercourse took place. The third defendant, K, then entered the room, but left without touching her. Afterwards, R suggested selling her to a brothel but U decided he wanted to 'keep her'. Ten days after the incident Takeda called her friend and, by chance, there was a police officer present who was looking for her. As a result she was found and Takeda's father then reported the rapes.

U's defence rested on the argument that he lived with Takeda for those ten days during which time they had a physical relationship, he looked after her, gave her money and they even discussed marriage when visiting his sister's house. However, they argued during these ten days and Takeda 'played' with the milkman. He emphasised that even though Takeda was sometimes alone in the apartment she did not try to escape or call anyone for help. Moreover, it was noted that even though Takeda was only 16, she was sexually experienced and she played around in cafés late at night with boys.

The judge determined that the defendants' threats were 'insufficient to make it impossible for her to resist', her behaviour was considered blameworthy and although Takeda did not consent to sex with R she only resisted verbally, not physically. Therefore, the judge reasoned, the three men did not intend to rape her and they were acquitted.

Case 12: Nakajima

In this 1970 case, Nakajima, aged 20, and the widowed defendant were acquainted through her work in an electrical goods shop. He was a regular customer and on this occasion he asked Nakajima's boss to allow her to leave the shop for a short time so he could talk to her. She got into his car and he told her another man liked and wanted to meet her. She agreed and the defendant drove to a love hotel (*rabu hoteru*)[3] although she argued that she did not initially recognise it as such. When she did realise the nature of the place on entering the room, the defendant persuaded her to stay, arguing that a coffee shop would be too noisy. He soon admitted his earlier story was a lie and when she then asked him to take her back to the shop he said he first wanted a kiss and that if she refused he would force her to have sex and keep her until morning. She again asked him to let her go. The defendant continued his carrot and stick game asking for one more 'favour' after another with the promise of letting her go or the threat of ripping her clothes and keeping her until morning, and warning that if she screamed no one would hear. Finally, sexual intercourse took place.

Because the defendant did not have enough money Nakajima paid for the hotel and he drove her back to the shop. During the drive they argued about the time taken from her work and the possibility of pregnancy so they arranged to meet again to discuss the issue further. Back at the shop the owner asked Nakajima what happened but at first she just cried and then she told him the defendant had raped her. The owner's wife took Nakajima to a doctor and she then filed a police report.

The judge found no evidence that he 'beat, kicked or pushed her with force', his threats did not make resistance impossible nor were they sufficient to cause her grave fear, and there was no evidence of an attempt to escape or even of her desire to escape. In addition, the judge stated that the extent of the damage to her vaginal tissue was no greater than that which might result from ordinary sexual intercourse. The defendant was, therefore, acquitted of the charge rape resulting in bodily injury.

Case 13: Matsumoto

This 1978 Appeal overturned the District Court's verdict of guilty. The defendant and Matsumoto, both in their mid-thirties were acquainted through Matsumoto's husband. The alleged rape took place in the defendant's car, parked far from the city at midnight. The defence argued that the defendant had wanted to tell Matsumoto he loved her so he asked a friend to fabricate a story regarding a business meeting and arranged that the friend would drive Matsumoto to him, which he did. The defendant confessed both his dishonesty and his 'love' for her, his passion driving him to threaten to kill her and then himself. When Matsumoto would not commit herself to seeing him the next day he realised that if he missed this opportunity he may never get another chance to have sex with her. The prosecution emphasised the fact that there was a big difference between them in terms of physical size and strength, that Matsumoto was crying, she had asked him to stop and to take her home, that given their location it was difficult for her to escape, but that for the sake of her husband and two children she did everything that was possible.

Like Watanabe's case, the judgment focused on the degree of force and coercion and found that it was no more than that of normal sex and that it was not sufficient to make Matsumoto's resistance significantly difficult. The judge dismissed her testimony regarding the violence and threats because she could not remember all the details and because the prosecutor had led Matsumoto in her answers.

Case 14: Takahashi

In May 1993, the defendant and his male friend met Takahashi, aged 28, who was with four other girls in a bar. The group played drinking games with sexual innuendoes including a strip game in which Takahashi took off her pantyhose (the defendant alleged she also took off her underpants). The group then moved on to another bar where they continued drinking until 3 a.m. They all decided to go home in two cars and, after dropping his friend home, Takahashi remained alone with the defendant in his car. The defendant told her he wanted to pick up something from his home and so they drove there. The alleged rape took place in the car outside his home. There were no witnesses and the only 'objective' evidence were inconclusive injuries, which the judge reasoned might have resulted from consensual sex in the confined space of the back of the car or, given her state of intoxication, by stumbling into an object. The case was, therefore, a classic one of his word against hers. The two main points of argument were whether Takahashi had consented to sexual intercourse, and whether her statement was trustworthy.

Takahashi argued that while waiting in the car she began to feel nervous and, therefore, decided to leave. When she started to walk off, the defendant chased her, kicked her and pushed her into the back of the car. She screamed, tried to resist and then vomited. He became angrier, slapped her across the face, punched her thighs and then raped her. He then drove her home during which time she was crying and said she would report him to the police. She mistakenly left her keys in the defendant's car and so she went to her friend's house and told her what had happened. Takahashi later went home and got a key from the landlord and took the clothes she was wearing to the cleaners. She went to a clinic but the doctor said that because two days had passed even a gynaecologist could not conduct adequate tests.

According to the defence narrative, Takahashi led him on, she was very drunk, acted provocatively and agreed to go to his room but when they got to the door he became nervous about the possibility of his girlfriend arriving so they went back to the car. She took off her clothes so he had sex with her. Afterwards, she asked to be dropped home but while driving in the car she vomited and he got angry because the car was new and belonged to his father.

The judge noted that in addition to taking one month to file a complaint, she lacked integrity, behaved provocatively, failed to admit her mistakes, and lied about the amount of alcohol to emphasise her chasteness which, contrary to her assertions, was highly questionable. The judge commented that due to her drunken state her 'chastity would have been weaker and her memory unreliable and therefore untrustworthy'. In short, Takahashi's testimony contained many 'unnatural and illogical' elements. The defendant was acquitted because although his testimony also contained untrustworthy points it was, on the whole, more believable.

Case 15: Sasaki

The judgment in this case concerned only one of two defendants, aged 25 years and unemployed. The two men picked up two 19-year-old women who, because trains were no longer running, were hitchhiking home after work around midnight. After dropping her friend home, Sasaki agreed to drive to an amusement park. However, the defendant stopped the car before reaching the park, the two men got out of the car and the defendant climbed into the back seat with Sasaki. The defendant attempted to have sex, Sasaki resisted strongly and he punched her. He took off her blouse, she asked him not to penetrate and he forced her to perform fellatio. The other man then attempted to have sexual intercourse with her but she resisted and he gave up. The defendants left her on the side of the road and she went immediately to the police.

While the defence counsel argued that she agreed to perform fellatio, she argued that she was threatened and forced to do so. Bruising indicated that she was punched, but the degree of intimidation and violence were contested. The defence counsel attempted to discredit Sasaki, arguing that (a) she was not a virgin and had slept with a few men, (b) she had been drinking and therefore missed her train, (c) she willingly entered a stranger's car and (d) she enjoyed driving around for a long time after her friend had been dropped home. In addition, the defence counsel successfully argued that the defendant's confession was invalid due to police coercion.

Although the defendant was found guilty of attempted rape, largely because Sasaki resisted, the defence arguments were taken into consideration in the sentencing. Summing up, the judge emphasised that forcing Sasaki to perform fellatio amounted to an injury to her character (*jinkaku*), he did not admit his guilt or offer an apology, Sasaki requested a severe sentence, the incident took place while he was on a three-year suspended sentence, and he had a previous conviction for forgery. On these grounds, the judge stated that normally the defendant would be imprisoned. However, the following points had to be considered: Sasaki had 'invited the attack'; the defendant's desire to have sexual intercourse with Sasaki was understandable because young men have strong sexual urges; he gave up attempting to penetrate relatively quickly; the violence was not heavy enough to wound her; and although the fellatio caused her to feel humiliated, this act was considered beyond the boundaries of the judgment because the accusation in this case was attempted rape and the fellatio took place after the attempted rape. The defendant was, therefore, sentenced to two years' imprisonment suspended for four years.

Case 16: Fujiwara

Following an argument between her boyfriend and her father Fujiwara, an 18-year-old university student, ran away from home and then decided to wait in a bar until it was time for the first morning train. Fujiwara joined the table of three men including the two defendants (X and Y) and later agreed to drive with them to a family restaurant. After dropping the third man home at 3 a.m. Y drove to a love hotel instead where the rape took place.

The defendants withdrew their original confession made to the police[4] and argued that although they lied about going to the family restaurant, after some persuasion Fujiwara 'nodded consent' to going to the hotel, took a shower and consented to sexual intercourse. However, X had trouble penetrating and she commented that he was not erect. He then hit her. In contrast to their story, evidence of significant intimidation and violence inflicted on Fujiwara clearly indicated rape, but according to the judge this was complicated by the 'facts' that she accompanied two strange men to a hotel and then took a shower. The main points of argument were, therefore, whether Fujiwara consented to go to the hotel and whether the rape was premeditated. The trial focused particularly on whether Fujiwara's account of events leading up to and after the rape was trustworthy and, consequently, her testimony was scrutinised in great detail.

According to Fujiwara, she attempted to get out of the car when they stopped to drop the other man home, but the door was locked. X grabbed her and threatened that if she did not sit quietly they would drop her in a tank of cement (this took place around the time there was much media coverage of a case in which this happened to a girl who had been raped and tortured repeatedly over a month or so). In the hotel, Fujiwara could not ask for help because she was frightened. X told her to take a shower, which she did in order to 'steal time'. Although she locked the door, X somehow entered. He led her to the bed and tried to penetrate. Fujiwara said, 'Please stop, I'm a virgin', and resisted. He hit her twice, she hit back and he punched her in the face. Y then took X's place and responded to her struggle by threatening to burn her vagina with a lit cigarette. Finally, X and Y forced her to perform fellatio on each of them. Her wounds took seven days to heal and included a black eye and bruising on the left arm, knee, thigh and breast. The defendants stole her money and a telephone card and when they left the hotel, she called her mother and they went to the hospital.

According to the judge the whole story did not really add up:

> it is necessary to think about whether [Fujiwara] consented to go to the hotel. We could assume that under normal circumstances it is unlikely that an ordinary young woman would agree to such a situation. However, in this age of increasing sexual freedom, the idea of a woman consenting to go to a hotel to have sex with two men or of a woman consenting to sex with a man she has just met is conceivable. . . . The main problem is that in this case the victim was 18 years-old, a university student and furthermore, a virgin.
>
> (Case 16 Fujiwara: 241)

The judge resolved his dilemma by finding that, although under ordinary circumstances a virgin would be unlikely to consent to go to a hotel with two unknown men, her particular circumstances explained her transgression from the norm. The judge constructed a narrative of a woman in a desperate psychological state (*jibō jiki*) due to strained relations with both her boyfriend and her father, but who was nevertheless attracted to one of the defendants. Furthermore, she knew her behaviour was blameworthy and, therefore, she had no intention of filing a complaint. However, she was compelled to do so when her father reported the matter to the police. According to the judge, she consented to go to the love hotel and was, therefore, partially responsible for her rape. The judge accepted the defence story that because Fujiwara consented to go to the hotel they presumed she would be willing to have sex and, therefore, the rape was not planned. However, because there was clear evidence of physical injuries caused by the attempted rape, as in Sasaki's case, X was found guilty of rape resulting in bodily injury even though penetration did not take place – but the decision did not include the fact that Fujiwara was forced to perform fellatio on both X and Y.[5] Like Sasaki, Fujiwara's blameworthiness or partial responsibility effectively cancelled out the seriousness of the crime. X was sentenced to three years' imprisonment suspended for four years. Y was found guilty of attempted rape (because he threatened but did not physically injure her) and sentenced to 18 months' imprisonment suspended for three years.[6]

Case 17: Atsumi

Atsumi, an 18-year-old high-school student, and the defendant, aged 28, had been acquainted for several years and during this time the defendant had tried to date Atsumi. However, Atsumi said she neither liked nor trusted him because she thought he was a gang member. Eight days before the incident he had asked her out and although she agreed to meet him, she stood him up. On the day of the incident, he was waiting for her outside her home after school and he asked her to go with him to a café. Atsumi refused but he threatened her so she agreed. He told her to change out of her school uniform while he waited in his car. When Atsumi returned, she said she had to be back by 5 p.m., he agreed, took her bag, threw it in the back of the car and she got in. Instead of driving to a café, he headed out of town, and when she suggested they return as it was almost five o'clock, he parked the car and asked her to talk to him. She did so, thinking this might enable her to get away sooner. He fabricated a story about having a terminal illness and said before he died he wanted to have sex with her. He threatened her with a knife and raped her. Atsumi asked him to take her home, but he said he wanted another beer and told her to go and buy one. He then drove her to a railway station. Atsumi said she had no money so he gave her ¥4,000. She caught a taxi but asked to be dropped about 1 kilometre from her home and then began walking home in the rain. Her mother found her in the street and Atsumi filed a complaint on the following day.

At the first trial the judge determined that Atsumi had been raped but not by the defendant. Neither of their accounts was deemed trustworthy. The judicial account produced a narrative in which Atsumi had been raped by another man whom she wanted to protect by concealing his identity. Although the defendant confessed to the rape after initially denying the accusation, the judge accepted his argument that he made a false confession in order to end the interrogation. His innocence was supported by the following facts: he could not provide a detailed account of events and could not take police directly to the place of the incident; it was unlikely he would have been drinking and driving because he had a weak tolerance for alcohol and did not usually drink; at 28 years old he had much experience with women so there was no need for him to drink to relax in order to seduce a woman; it was improbable that he would allow Atsumi to go to the shop to buy him a beer because she might tell someone if she had just been raped; his story, told to the police, that he had to hurry to meet a friend and therefore had no time to take her home was a lie because Atsumi actually lived quite close to where he wanted to meet his friend and, therefore, he would have taken her if he had been with her. Furthermore, the story he told police about swapping his Japanese car for a foreign car was a lie because he could not tell police who the other party was and the police could not find the car. In short, the judge decided, 'his confession is illogical and unnatural. He made up a story which lacked credibility'.

The aspects of Atsumi's testimony found to be 'unnatural' and 'untrustworthy' were as follows: she said the defendant was driving a Japanese car but the police could only find a foreign car; although she remembered the style and condition of the car she had not checked the number plate; she changed from her school uniform into an 'attractive' black dress; she lied to her father saying she was going to meet friends; she left with no money; her statement that the defendant asked if she wanted to go to the police to report the rape is an unnatural conversation between rapist and victim but possible between two people on good terms; a rapist would not take two and a half hours to commit rape, 'if he wanted to rape her there would be no need to take so long. Therefore the situation was probably calm and thus not rape'. The most damning aspect was that Atsumi did not try to escape. It was emphasised that she did not attempt to escape despite opportunities both before and after sexual intercourse, and she not only failed to protest but, rather, talked with him and expressed regret about his illness. Furthermore, the judge reasoned that after such an incident it is likely Atsumi would want to be rid of him as soon as possible and that this opportunity arose when he suggested dropping her near the station. However, she was only anxious about how to get back home as she had no money. The judge thought it strange that Atsumi was dropped 1 kilometre from home by the taxi, reasoning that if she was really upset or suicidal, she would not be thinking about what her parents would think and would ask to be taken all the way home. The judge suggested that perhaps Atsumi was intending to lie to her parents, telling them she returned by train as the taxi dropped her near the station. Furthermore, if she was really upset there would be no room to think about ideas such as accusations of prostitution and nor would she be thinking about trying to make him feel bad by telling him she did not want to go home and see her mother. This was 'unnatural'.

However, after new evidence was found (his car, cigarette butts, tissue paper and beer can) an appeal was lodged and the defendant was found guilty and sentenced to three years' imprisonment. The car provided crucial and unambiguous evidence and the judges reinterpreted the 'facts' and found that: Atsumi usually wore good clothes and was careful about her image because she worked part-time as an actress and model; the defendant did drink a lot; Atsumi entered the car because he threw her bag in; her disturbed psychological state was indicated by the fact that she paid ¥4,000 for an ¥840 taxi fare and that she left her umbrella in the taxi despite the rain.

Case 18: Nishimura

The defendant and the complainant Nishimura, both aged in their twenties, married in 1981. After a history of violent abuse and attempts to leave the defendant, Nishimura ran away in 1984. On this occasion, the defendant and his male friend waited for Nishimura, dragged her into their car when she passed, and drove off. They parked the car and discussed raping Nishimura. She struggled, was threatened, assaulted and held down while both men raped her.

In the District Court, both men were convicted of rape and the defendant was sentenced to two years and ten months' imprisonment. The defendant appealed the judgment on the grounds that:

> the defendant and [Nishimura] were married when the incident occurred and a husband and wife have the right to ask each other for sex and it is their duty to comply. Therefore, even when a husband has sex with his wife using violence and coercion, only the violence and coercion are illegal, the sexual intercourse itself cannot be the object of punishment; the crime of rape cannot take place within marriage.
>
> (Case 18 Nishimura: 154)

The High Court, however, upheld the original decision on the grounds that the marital relationship had ceased to exist in reality (see Nakamori 1988: 216–218).

Case 19: Endō

At the time of the incident Endō, the plaintiff, was in her early twenties, married with four children, and she worked part-time in a fast-food outlet. Over a period of three or four months prior to the incident, the defendant, who was the store manager, had on a number of occasions attempted to touch and kiss Endō. On the night of the incident Endō remained in the shop after the other workers had left in order to talk to the manager about changing her shifts to accommodate her new schedule at a hairdressing school. The defendant did not really discuss the matter, but asked if she would stay on to do some paperwork. When Endō sat down, he tried to kiss and touch her, knocking her off the chair and onto the floor. They struggled for approximately 15 minutes before he gave up and walked out. This particular incident was more serious than previous advances towards her.

With no evidence, the case boiled down to his word against hers. Endō argued that after the initial shock, as they were both outside the shop preparing to leave, she became angry and demanded an apology. They began to argue and he suggested they go back inside. When they re-entered the shop he turned to Endō and yelled at her to get upstairs. She complied because she was frightened by the tone of his voice and demeanour and, despite her pleas to stop and attempts to resist, the defendant raped her on the storeroom floor. The following day she rang the defendant and demanded an explanation and apology.

The defendant argued that as he was walking to his car, she ran after him and pleaded with him to stay, that she tended to be rather fickle in their 'love affair' and so her change of heart was not unusual although it was difficult to understand. They kissed, he suggested going back inside to have sex and she nodded consent. He suggested they lie on a bench in the restaurant but she suggested going upstairs because it would be more private. Although she protested a little upstairs he was overcome with passion and they had consensual intercourse. He became confused when she then started crying and locked herself in the bathroom and so he was eager to leave. When she rang him the next day, he had had enough and told her their 'love affair' was over. According to the defence, Endō regretted the affair and became vindictive; she made a false accusation to cover up her adultery, which only came to the knowledge of her husband some months later when he realised he had contracted a sexually transmitted disease.

The case was rejected by the Prosecutor's Office and so it proceeded as a case for marital damage in the civil court. Endō's claim was dismissed at the District Court and in both appeals to the High and Supreme Courts. The 'love affair' scenario was accepted, largely because there was insufficient evidence of 'force and intimidation to the extent that the plaintiff's resistance was made significantly difficult'.

Case 20: Komatsu

The 16-year-old plaintiff Komatsu and the 28-year-old defendant attended the same external high school. On the night of the first of three alleged incidents of rape in August 1988 they had dinner together with two of his friends. At 8.30 p.m. the defendant's two friends were dropped home and then the defendant drove with her to a love hotel telling her he had a quick errand to do in the building and then he would drop her home. She followed him into the building, he opened a door, pulled her in and pushed her down on a bed. She screamed and verbally protested to which he replied, 'when women say no they mean yes'.

He forced her into a position where she could not resist, raped her then fell asleep. She sat on the sofa in shock until he awoke around 3 a.m. She told him she was in terrible pain and was bleeding and asked him what she should do. He was unhelpful and then raped her again as she struggled. They left the hotel and he dropped her at the station at 4 a.m. Komatsu sat in a phone booth for about two hours before returning home. She could not tell her parents what happened, they were angry she had not returned home that night and her mother ordered her out of the house. The defendant had told her to call him if necessary so she did and they arranged to meet later that afternoon to look for a place for her to stay. He found her a hotel and told her he would sleep in the car, however, she woke to find him in the room and he raped her again. The following morning he drove her to the station.

Komatsu requested compensation through her lawyer in August 1991. The defendant ignored the request and so the case proceeded to court. The defendant denied the charge of rape, arguing that they were involved in a 'love relationship' and she had consented to sex on each occasion. He supported his case by arguing that she had given him gifts in the past, she had stated she did not want to return home after dinner on the night of the first rape, she agreed to go to a love hotel, she had changed into a *yukata* (robe) in the room, and that she did not scream for help.

The judge decided that none of his evidence was believable and concluded that she entered the hotel because it was raining and hence visibility was poor, she had never been to a love hotel so she did not know what type of place it was, and the psychological injuries she incurred including an attempted suicide were extreme. The defendant was, therefore, ordered to pay ¥2.5 million compensation and ¥0.5 million legal costs.

Authorised violence and the license to rape: *yūkeiryoku*

One element in the establishment of the degree of violence and intimidation necessary to define an act as rape is to distinguish this from masculinist constructions of what constitutes the 'normal' amount of force involved in consensual sex (*yūkeiryoku*). This distinction was central to the acquittal of both defendants in the two cases that raised this issue (Watanabe and

Matsumoto). According to the High Court judgment in Matsumoto's case, although it was admitted that the sexual intercourse took place against Matsumoto's will, that she was screaming and pleading with him to stop and to take her home, nevertheless the degree of force could not be distinguished from that used in 'normal' sex (*tsūjō seikō*):

> regarding the extent of force used in consensual sex men generally pull women who are sitting up down to end with sexual intercourse, put their hands on women's shoulders and pull them near, push them down, tend to pull off their clothes then position themselves on top of the woman and so forth.
>
> (Case 13 Matsumoto: 113)

Consequently, the original conviction was overturned because there was insufficient evidence that the defendant had used sufficient force and threats 'to make resistance significantly difficult'. Emphasis was placed on the 'facts' that Matsumoto had not physically tried to escape, the defendant did not rip Matsumoto's underclothes, and she asked him to wait because the position she was in on the back seat of the car was painful. The judge described the events at the time of the sexual intercourse in great detail emphasising that the defendant had kissed her, he had made statements such as 'after carrying on asking to be taken home you must be pleased you stayed', sexual intercourse had been interrupted to wind down the window, they had moved positions, and so forth. Summing up, the judge interpreted the situation as 'calm' (*heion*) and, therefore, not rape.

However, even situations that do not appear to be calm may be discursively incorporated into 'normal heterosexual sex'. In a sexual harassment case involving a rape charge, the defence (unsuccessfully) argued that the woman's statement that she was hit over ten times was untrustworthy because she did not seek medical attention. The defence further argued that, 'even if there was some violence involved, consensual sexual relationships normally involve some refusals (*kyohiteki gendo*) and violence (*bōryoku teki kōi*), and therefore we cannot say that the sexual relationship was against her will only on those grounds' (Case 28 Kyoto: 74).

In Watanabe's case, the judge stated that:

> To establish the crime of rape it is necessary to examine the extent of violence and threats from the evidence and in this case such evidence was not found. In this case there is evidence of *yūkeiryoku*. That is, the defendant embraced her, pushed her down, pressed her right arm with his body and held her left arm, pushed off her underpants and so forth and lay on top of her. However, it can be said that . . . [this behaviour] may not only be part of rape but it also generally accompanies normal sexual intercourse.
>
> (Case10 Watanabe: 286)

The judge determined that the defendant had wanted to talk to Watanabe and then he gradually began to want to have sex with her and so there was no intention to rape. This case illustrates Duncan's observation that:

> Subtextually, the intention to commit non-consensual intercourse can be subsumed by the intention to have intercourse – the overwhelming urge, subsuming the possibility of *mens rea* creating permission for the male subject, disciplining the body of the female other. . . . Space is constantly created for the (hetero)sexuality of the male subject as it is contracted for the ontology of the female other.
>
> (Duncan 1995: 340)

The defendant, whom Watanabe had only greeted in the hotel, entered her room uninvited and refused to leave when asked to do so. Her consent or will could only be 'objectively' determined by complying with the narrow script of non-consent involving substantial physical struggle followed by immediate escape, preferably to the police or hospital. Outside the *tsūjō* rape scenario, a woman's non-consent can be registered only if it conforms to this culturally recognisable pattern. The questions of what positive indications of consent existed, or why a woman staying in a hotel with her husband would consent to sex with a stranger in her room while her husband was out, were not regarded as obvious ones to ask because a woman's consent is always already presumed. Her sexuality is perceived as the mirror image of male desire. Her subjectivity is denied, her body existing only as the object of male subjectivity and male sexuality. *Yūkeiryoku* clearly links normative constructions of 'heterosexuality' and rape through the positioning of the male as subject and the privileging of masculinist interpretations of rape. This is achieved through the denial or exclusion of female subjectivity, which makes it almost impossible for a woman to tell an alternative story of abuse and to have this understood and validated.

Suspicious stories of threats, intimidation and injury

The four cases focusing on the degree of force and resistance that resulted in a conviction (Sasaki, Komatsu, Nishimura and Fujiwara) involved unspecified threats and Fujiwara was also threatened with a lit cigarette. In none of the other cases were threats or intimidation regarded as significant enough to explain the women's lack of resistance or inability to escape. Atsumi was threatened with a knife, Nakajima was threatened with rape, having her clothes cut up and, like Takeda, with not being released. Non-specific threats were also made against Atsumi, Takeda and their families. In Matsumoto's case the defendant threatened double suicide (*shinjū*), which in this context would be more accurately described as murder-suicide.

It is reasonable to assume that a woman not engaged in a romantic affair might interpret a man's talk of committing *shinjū* as a serious threat to her life. However, *shinjū* is also a culturally significant sign of genuine romantic love and deep, albeit troubled, passion (Robertson 1999; Pflugfelder 1999: 107–108). Heterosexual *shinjū* stems largely from the practice of arranged marriages first introduced in the samurai class during the Edo period and is reinforced by Buddhist notions of reincarnation offering the possibility of being together in the next life (Lebra 1976: 195–198). *Shinjū* signals the 'pure' love between a couple who cannot marry or be together and thus resonates with the romantic narrative. The 'threat' of a double suicide is, therefore, not necessarily read as evidence of a life-threatening situation or as a threat at all, as was the case in Matsumoto's trial and in a case of indecent assault (Case 33).

Women's experiences of fear and intimidation are silenced by the definitional emphasis on force and physical resistance. The judge decided in Matsumoto's case that perhaps the defendant had threatened her 'but this did not make resistance impossible and there is insufficient evidence to say that she was frightened just because of these threats' (Case 13 Matsumoto: 335). In Takeda's case, the judge determined that because, '*he* liked her and wanted to stay with her . . . the threat was very minor' (emphasis added) (Case 11 Takeda: 378). The fact that the 'already sexually experienced' Takeda then spent ten days with the defendant was interpreted as reinforcing the argument that any initial force, intimidation and fear experienced by her were not serious.

The perceived insignificance of the harm caused to Sasaki is evident in the judge's statement that, 'the violence was not heavy enough to wound her' and the description of the defendant's behaviour (attempted rape and coerced fellatio) as 'imprudent' (*keisotsu*) (Case 15 Sasaki: 162). While the judgments in Sasaki's and Fujiwara's cases mentioned the 'humiliation' of being forced to perform fellatio, only in Komatsu's case and the High Court decision in Atsumi's case was the harm of rape emphasised. The fact that Sasaki and Fujiwara were considered blameworthy diminished the significance of the injury that could be recognised.

Not only is it difficult for women to project images of genuine fear, even when these are accompanied by bruises and damage to vaginal tissue, if the narrative does not accord with the stock story of *tsūjō* rape it is unlikely that such 'evidence' will be accepted. For example, in Takahashi's case the judge had a very clear image of how a man might open a woman's legs. Takahashi's story did not correspond and she was, therefore, perceived to be lying.

> [Takahashi] claims that he took off her underpants and when she tried to resist by closing her legs he punched her thighs in order to open them. However, if one wants to open someone's legs it would be normal to open them directly by, for example, wedging one's knee in

> between or order her to open them by slapping her face . . . to punch someone's thighs in order to open them sounds a little strange. It appears that [the complainant] found bruises on both her inner thighs and tried to find an explanation. This part of her testimony is clearly suspicious. (Case 14 Takahashi: 151)

Summing up, the judge stated that her injuries did not accord with those normally incurred by rape and that they were more likely to have been caused as a result of Takahashi's state of intoxication:

> she was very drunk so it is possible she hit her legs and arms and got the bruises when she went to the toilet or after the defendant dropped her home. Therefore it is not clear what caused the bruises . . . in truth she was probably very drunk, had some memory and used the little she had to construct a story.
>
> (Case 14 Takahashi: 153)

Evidence of bruising and damage to vaginal tissue was also rejected as evidence of rape in Nakajima's case because it could not be distinguished from that caused by 'ordinary' sexual intercourse or the 'rough' insertion of a finger. In Endō's case photographs of bruising were submitted as evidence, but these were rejected because the time the photographs were taken was not considered conclusive. Thus photographic or medical evidence of bruising or inflammation of vaginal tissue was dismissed in all three cases in which this evidence was presented (Nakajima, Takahashi and Endō).

These cases suggest that information concerning the use of force is compelling only if it fits with the judge's existing image of rape and appropriate victim responses. Very similar evidence may be accepted or dismissed on the basis of the constructed story that frames the case. Far from force being the 'objective' evidence on which the most reliable determinations of rape can be made, the cases suggest that evidence of force is interpreted by judges in the context of a range of other factors considered significant to the case. This analysis, therefore, lends support to the Experimentalists' theory, outlined in Chapter 1, that judgments are fundamentally the justification of the verdict and sentencing decisions rather than a clear statement of the way in which the decisions were guided by the rule of law. This is very clearly illustrated in the discussion of the contrasting District and High Court judgments in Atsumi's case.

Atsumi's 'sub-standard' conduct was reinterpreted in the appeal trial when new conclusive evidence provided by the car established that the defendant was the offender. The District Court's finding that her testimony and behaviour (failure to resist, attempt escape and seek help immediately after the rape) were 'unnatural' was found to be mistaken in the appeal. The High Court judge reinterpreted her behaviour as naïve and rash, but understandable responses to being threatened by a knife. The judge acknowledged her sense of fear and intimidation and stated that it is 'only natural for rape victims to think their assailant will seek revenge if they try to escape or that not escaping might lead to their earlier release when the assailant accomplishes his goal' (Case 17 Atsumi: 251). Furthermore, the judge was impressed by the 'particularly natural evidence' of the victim's testimony that she was probably careless – a risky admission in sexual assault cases[7] – in not seeking help immediately after the rape. In contrast to the narrative constructed by the original decision, the very different story of a foolish but innocent young girl that emerged in the appeal trial was convincing largely because it was framed by conclusive material evidence. Such evidence, however, is not available in the majority of cases.

Unheard screams and pleas to stop

In seven of the 11 cases (Takeda, Nakajima, Matsumoto, Sasaki, Fujiwara, Endō and Komatsu), the judgment noted that the woman pleaded with or asked the defendant to stop. However, verbal non-consent alone is regarded as insufficient evidence of resistance – explicitly dismissed in Nakajima and Takeda's cases. Drawing on the argument that the existence of rape can only be determined by the degree of threats and violence, the judge in Nakajima's case stated:

> Even though she said she did not want to kiss or caress and so forth we cannot find evidence of her attempting to escape or even of her feeling like wanting to escape. She argued with him about undressing and lying on the bed, but if we accept her testimony that she trusted him initially and therefore did not try to escape and in light of the fact that she states she was a virgin, when she realised he intended to have sex she should have done something to resist . . . she complied when he ordered her to touch his body and so her behaviour was co-operative. She did not resist, thinking only about her clothes being ripped and being kept until morning – neither of which he did. And if she really was a virgin, she would not care about these things when she saw the danger to her life and body.
>
> (Case 12 Nakajima: 336)

In Takeda's case, the judge decided that although she objected to the second defendant's behaviour she did so only verbally; she did not physically resist and, therefore, 'it cannot be said the defendants intended to be violent or threaten her and thus they had no intention to rape her and are therefore not guilty'. In effect, the judgment that she consented to sexual intercourse with one man under immoral circumstances meant consent to all. Takeda was scripted in much the same way as the prostitute who foregoes her right to say 'no' to any man (Case 11 Takeda: 378).

Interestingly, Komatsu and Fujiwara's cases, the two in which the defendants explicitly stated that a woman's 'no' means 'yes', resulted in a conviction. It is possible that when confronted directly, the 'logic' of this argument is unlikely to be convincing. Nevertheless, the assumption that a woman's 'no' means 'yes' is sustained by, and informs, the principle that a woman genuinely not consenting will physically resist. The centrality of the 'no' to the romantic narrative of seduction overrides the alternative explanation that the woman was not freely consenting to sexual intercourse. The majority of cases indicate that the power of the seduction narrative was more convincing than the narrative of the woman articulating non-consent. Komatsu's case is the notable exception. In Nishimura's case, the fact that there were two offenders and clear evidence of considerable violence left little room for images of seduction, and in Sasaki's and Fujiwara's cases the defendants were given suspended sentences because they could almost be forgiven for misinterpreting or being confused by the women's signals, given their earlier provocative behaviour (consenting to go to the hotel and to get into the car, respectively).

Screams may also be viewed as insufficient evidence of resistance and readily open to question if the context does not conform to a familiar script:

> according to [Takahashi] she screamed at least twice, but the defendant did not cover her mouth or threaten her, he just pushed her into the car. If this is true then it is likely the neighbours would have heard, and he would have covered her mouth but she did not say this and this is a questionable point.
>
> (Case 14 Takahashi: 151)

Similarly, in an indecent assault case the judge dismissed the woman's account that she screamed ten times or more because 'ordinarily if a woman was screaming the offender would cover her mouth to silence her, which he did not' (Case 32: 265). The High Court overturned the District Court's conviction because there was insufficient evidence of force and coercion and neither the defendant's nor the woman's account was trustworthy. The judge stated that:

> if the victim and the witness chased the defendant as they stated, then she is also likely to be the sort of person who would have resisted. However, she did not emphasise this, stating merely that she screamed again and again. . . . Because she did not really talk about her resistance, her statement is not enough to imagine a situation of indecent assault.
>
> (Case 32: 270)

It is clear that the woman must script her story in alignment with the dominant stock story if she is to be believed. These stock stories prevail, not necessarily because they are supported by material evidence but because they 'make sense' to those doing the judging – a key element in the construction and reception of a legal code. As Binder (1995: 297) notes:

> It is ultimately the failure of narrative, the absence of compelling imagery, which causes the crime of 'simple' rape to remain disembodied from the popular imagination. A woman's 'innocence', and thus a man's culpability, is inevitably judged by the power of her narrative.

In *fushizen* or 'simple' rape cases, threats may be read as either insignificant or as declarations of love. Verbal pleas to stop, and sometimes even screams, are not regarded as sufficient evidence of non-consent – in fact, non-consent is not always regarded as wholly relevant. To achieve a conviction for rape (and indecent assault and sexual harassment cases involving rape or indecent assault), when the scenario does not conform to the *tsūjō* rape narrative, women must demonstrate that they physically resisted in order to meet the force and coercion requirement. The focus of the trial, thus, shifts from an interrogation of the defendant's actions to the woman's behaviour. It is her conduct that comes to be judged as reasonable or substandard and, on this basis, whether or not the defendant acted legitimately (see Estrich 1987: 31).

Resistance

Rape cases differ from other crimes in that there is frequently little evidence to support the accusation other than the woman's own word. Witnesses are rare and injuries are often not physically visible, or are difficult to establish, especially if immediate medical attention was not sought. Given these difficulties and the constraints of Japanese legal discourse on rape discussed in the previous chapter, a woman's strong physical resistance is read as an important marker of truth, not merely because it is regarded as 'objective' evidence, but also because it is perceived as *the* natural or instinctive response to fear for women confronting a sexual assault. Much emphasis was placed on the fact that the responses of Watanabe, Takeda, Nakajima, Matsumoto and Endō were sub-standard – they did not adequately resist. Similarly, the judges stressed that Watanabe, Nakajima, Matsumoto, Atsumi (in the first trial) and Endō did not attempt to escape. In the only other case resulting in an acquittal (Takahashi) her claims of resistance, attempted escape and substantial bruising were dismissed.

In Fujiwara's case, the judge stated: 'though she was frightened, it was unnatural that she did not ask for help because she was a virgin' (Case 16 Fujiwara: 243). Similarly, at every stage of Endō's legal battle, her lack of resistance was regarded as unnatural and this was central to the dismissal of her allegations. The District Court judge concluded that,

> [Endō] was not positively willing to have sex (*susunde hikoku to seikō shiyō motsu kimochi niwa natte orazu*) and the behaviour of the defendant was a little too aggressive (*yaya seikyū na men ga atta koto ga ukagaeru*). However, although she refused and struggled against the defendant's aggressive sexual behaviour [prior to the rape], the plaintiff stopped the defendant outside the store as he was leaving in his car. She then went upstairs before him, she did not scream for help and there is no evidence that she tried to escape. Even considering their positions as manager and part-time employee, her attitude and behaviour are quite unnatural for a person frightened of the defendant's sexual violence and for someone with the clear intention to refuse him.
>
> (Case 19 Endō)[8]

These and numerous other judgments clearly indicate that constructing resistance as an instinctive or innate response normalises and universalises resistance as the only response to sexual violence that makes sense, the only response that can be readily recognised as credible in the courtroom. The following 1997 sexual harassment judgment is illustrative:

> If an indecent assault occurred as she insists, it would be normal for her to scream, ask for help or physically resist in order to escape . . . [however] up to the point where her shoulders were held against the bed she said nothing, letting the defendant do what he wanted . . . [then] she finally started to resist. Of course we cannot deny that there are occasions when women cannot say anything or resist because of their fear . . . but considering the relation between them [university professor and his part-time research assistant], and the age and history (*keireki*) of the plaintiff [middle-aged with two children] we cannot say that the plaintiff's responses mentioned above are normal responses to indecent assault. Furthermore, providing reasons for why she let him do what he did, the plaintiff says that she was surprised when she was pushed onto the bed and tried to stop him by grabbing his hands but she withdrew because his hands seemed so dirty (*kitanarashiku*). It is normal for victims of indecent assault to try to escape without thinking or to resist spontaneously. While it can be said that a victim may not resist at all due to fear, this does not apply to her state of mind . . . her attitude is based on rational thoughts (*reisei na shiko*) which is quite unlikely for victims of indecent assault.
>
> (Case 26 Akita: 49–50)

The normalisation of resistance silences alternative experiences, emotions and responses to sexual attack such as repulsion, guilt, rage, anger or lucid, rational decision-making regarding submission or negotiation (however problematic or ineffective these might be) to minimise further injuries.

Feminists responded to the constraints of this script, regarding appropriate responses to sexual violence and the pervasive silence surrounding sexual assault, by introducing alternative discourses of rape and fear – to extend the limited vocabulary with which sexual assault could be articulated. It was into this environment that the idea of the immobilising effects of fear on women, as a result of their socialisation, was introduced. The idea of the impossibility of resistance, of freezing in the face of fear, was a strategic response to the legal requirement to demonstrate resistance. The sexual harassment judgment above indicates that these (now not so very) new ideas are permeating the Japanese courts – albeit with limited impact in terms of achieving better outcomes for women. It is worth noting that for those feminists in the 1990s (e.g. Marcus 1992; Burton 1998) who look not to the law but, rather, advocate a more individualised approach – women taking greater responsibility for protection against sexual assault by achieving empowerment through re-socialisation including self-defence classes – the idea of involuntary immobilisation may be counter-productive. It can easily lead to biological understandings that reinforce women's vulnerability if the key role of socialisation is not emphasised.

Nevertheless, unlike the sexual harassment case above and numerous others (Case 24 Yokohama is the most notable)[9] where acquittal was largely based on the woman's failure to resist, there have been a number of sexual harassment cases that successfully introduced new arguments and the testimony of expert witnesses regarding a wide range of credible responses to sexual attacks (see Chapter 7). It is probably for this reason that Tsunoda Yukiko, Endō's Supreme Court lawyer, attempted to contextualise Endō's rape in terms of sexual harassment and to articulate the inconsistencies and contradictions in conventional understandings of appropriate responses to a sexual attack:

> Victims of sexual harassment respond in various ways to offenders and their circumstances, but accepted criteria and patterns of victim behaviour are not based on victims' actual behaviours . . . The judge in [Endō's] original trial states that it would be natural for her to leave as soon as possible, but what is this assumption based on? Perhaps it is the male fantasy that a woman should be chaste, and to avoid further sexual attacks she should flee rather than fight back. At the same time, however, it is said that women must fight back.
>
> It is not said that women should leave as soon as possible without a struggle. It is said that to prove rape . . . the woman's resistance must be overpowered . . . Therefore, it is said that a woman must struggle and then escape . . . If the woman does not leave then it is deemed that there was no sexual attack. So, should a woman struggle? If she struggled hard while being attacked, it should not be unnatural for her to keep struggling afterwards and to ask for an apology as [Endō] did.
>
> (Case 19 Endō: 60)

In no other area of law is consent so disputed and the victim required to corroborate her allegation with additional evidence of resistance. The underlying rationale is that women fabricate such accounts to seek revenge.[10] Such an argument, therefore, seeks to protect the heterosexual male from false charges by avenging women, despite the lack of evidence that women are more likely to make false accusations of sexual assault compared to other crimes. The cases discussed in this chapter demonstrate that in *fushizen* rape cases non-consent is registered overwhelmingly by physical resistance, although these may be the minority of cases coming before the courts, as suggested by Taniguchi. If the circumstances prior to the rape can be imagined as a context in which sex is a possibility, for example, a developing love affair, a social occasion in a bar or if the woman is construed as unchaste or drunk, it is more difficult to construct an alternative image of rape. As Martha Burt (1998: 130) notes, the problems are 'compounded by the perception that any interaction between a man and a woman is potentially sexual', and thus the romantic narrative tends to displace women's accounts of rape.

Hegemonic tales of heterosexuality

The construction of sexual desire as natural urges over which men have little control, reproduces the system of compulsory heterosexuality and this is sustained in the courtroom. In Fujiwara's case the defendant's awareness of her non-consent 'was too late and he could not restrain his sexual desire' (Case 16 Fujiwara: 237). The judgment in Sasaki's case constructs active sexual desire as a positive sign of healthy masculinity; the aggressive pursuit of sex with 'easy' or 'provocative' women as understandable, if not expected:

> it is not difficult to appreciate that he would attempt to have sex with her because young men have strong sexual desires . . . but when she resisted he tried to finish using force and his behaviour is blameworthy, but this must be viewed in the context of the particular circumstances surrounding the incident [that is, that she 'invited' the attack].
>
> (Case 15 Sasaki: 161)

Takahashi's story of rape was dismissed as incredible because the defendant did not have to rape her:

> according to [Takahashi's] testimony, while driving the defendant did not suggest sex saying only that he wanted to pick up a bag from his apartment, but when he saw her trying to escape he suddenly attacked her, pushed her into the car and forced her to have sex. However, this is an unnatural situation because before going to the apartment they had talked about sex and played a game with sexual innuendoes.
>
> (Case 14 Takahashi: 150)

It was assumed that any healthy man could have determined she was already a willing participant to casual sex – all he had to do (and would have done) was ask. These constructions of a natural uncontrollable sexual desire and of a degree of violence in (hetero)sexual intercourse (*yūkeiryoku*) serve to normalise violence against women under certain conditions and privilege the defendant's subject position. While space is created for expanding his power to define events, the space in which women can tell their stories is simultaneously contracted:

> The rape trial is a process of disqualification and celebration. It disqualifies women's experience of sexual abuse . . . the very spectacle of the woman's account and the pornographic narrative she must relate draws the rape trial firmly into the realms of uncertainty and doubt. . . . But at the same time it celebrates so-called natural heterosexuality. . . . Being a sexual predator is regarded as normal, even desirable, for men. Sexualising all women is equally regarded as natural; pressing a woman until she submits is regarded as a natural, pleasurable phallocentric pastime.
>
> (Carol Smart 1990: 18)

More specifically, a common defence argument is that any reasonable woman should be aware that men are slaves to their sexual desires and should, therefore, take appropriate precautions. If they do not, then either they are at least partially to blame for neglecting to protect their honour and virtue, or, they wanted and therefore consented to sex. The first argument is more common. For example, the defence counsel in the following uncontested case used this argument as leverage for a lighter penalty – as a relevant mitigating circumstance:

> the defendant is guilty, however, people are not perfect and they have sexual desires. When a person does not want to have sex they should maintain an appropriate environment to protect themselves from such desires especially if the woman lives alone. . . . The plaintiff should have known that the defendant was also the sort of person who might be overcome by sexual desires. Nevertheless . . . the plaintiff went to sleep in the same room [as the defendant]. Such action lacks prudence. This point should be seriously considered before determining the amount of compensation.[11]
>
> (quoted in Fukushima 1997: 270)

Sympathy for the defendant who 'could not help himself' can be invoked through the conceptualisation of sexuality as uncontrollable. The Defence Counsel in Fujiwara's case appealed for compassion for the defendant, an established Casanova who became confused when he failed in his attempted conquest: 'it is possible [the defendant] can pick up girls and when almost there she refused. This was a shock for him and we need to think about how he felt at the time'. The defence argued that the ordinary young man was confused by varying discordant signals, 'so when she said stop, the defendant didn't think she really meant it' (Case 16 Fujiwara: 248). Similarly, in Nakajima's case, the defence successfully delivered a story in which it became only natural to assume that the very normal defendant wanted sex due to difficulties with his wife and, therefore, the situation with Nakajima was about sex rather than violence and rape.

Judges rarely differentiate between sex and rape in terms other than the degree of force and resistance involved. The conventional understanding is that both rape and sex are motivated by (male) sexual desire. However, feminist research and criminological studies of offenders convincingly argue that rape often has less to do with serving sexual needs and more to do with the sexual expression of power and anger (MacKinnon 1987: 85–92; Lees 1993: 11–36; Groth and Birnbaum 1980; Vogelman 1990). Moreover, the construction of sexual desire as the primary motivation for rape often results in placing the responsibility for the rape on the target of that assault – his arousal must have been stimulated either deliberately or inadvertently by her provocative behaviour. The woman's sexual desirability also becomes central to the understanding of that motivation (see Binder 1995). Woman functions as a mirror reflecting male desire and male subjectivity, but woman has no subject position in this arrangement; she is visible and relevant to the extent of the sexual value placed on her body. 'Innate urges' lose their explanatory power in situations where the victim is perceived to be undesirable: 'an urge for something constructed as sexually undesirable cannot be constructed as innate' (Duncan 1995: 333). To illustrate, in a case where a young man raped and killed a 67-year-old woman, and the degree of his alcoholism was in question, the District Court judge stated that, 'if normal, a young person like the defendant, would not be interested in an old [read sexually undesirable] woman. He did not check to see if she was young or old.' Clarifying this point the High Court judge explained, 'it is possible the defendant had trouble visually focusing on the woman and so without verification of the woman's age he carried out sexual intercourse'.[12] The assumption is that a normal man would not desire/rape a sexless body, therefore, the defendant was not driven by normal innate sexual desire. The boundary between normal and abnormal sexuality was thus constructed in terms of the male heterosexual subject. On this basis both judgments determined that the defendant suffered from a pathological level of alcoholism and was, therefore, not criminally liable.

If uncontrollable frustrated sexual desires are perceived to be the motivation behind rape, then rape must necessarily be conceived of as a sudden, explosive and violent occurrence. Quiet calculation and more unimpassioned coercive control are not easily integrated into the stock story of rape. Consequently, it is often found that women's experiences of rape that do not fit the *tsūjō* rape scenario 'sound strange', do not 'add up' or are 'unnatural'. Atsumi's case is illustrative:

> They were together two and a half hours and if he had wanted to rape her there would be no need to take so long. Therefore, perhaps the situation was calm and thus not rape.
>
> (Case 17 Atsumi: 276)

The judge's reconstruction of events in Takahashi's case also demonstrates the ramifications of ignoring the power dimension of rape, of perceiving rape merely in terms of the forceful acquisition of sex motivated by innate urges:

> [Takahashi] stated that when the defendant tried to choke her, she vomited and immediately afterwards he raped her. However, if her testimony is correct, the smell in the car would be bad and it would be unnatural for him not to care about the smell and just rape her. According to the defendant's testimony, the car was new and belonged to his father and his claim that she vomited after having sex causing them to quarrel is more believable.
>
> (Case 14 Takahashi: 151)

Under 'normal' circumstances of sexual intercourse a particular act or conversation – or in this case response to a bad smell – may evoke a conventional pattern of behaviour. Yet, the response may acquire a different significance under conditions in which the exercise of power, rather than the gratification of sexual desire, is paramount. Similarly, it 'makes sense' within the 'woman as rational actor model' for a woman to fight off her attacker, attempt to escape and make an immediate complaint when rape is constructed as a sudden attack by a stranger. However, this is not the typical scenario; this kind of attack occurs only in a minority of cases. Groth and Birnbaum argue that there are three basic patterns of rape and while some rapists may be deterred by resistance, others may be excited by such responses, possibly endangering the woman's life. The three patterns of rape are: '(1) the *anger* rape, in which sexuality becomes a hostile act; (2) the *power* rape, in which sexuality becomes an expression of conquest; and (3) the *sadistic* rape, in which anger and power become eroticised' (Groth and Birnbaum 1980: 21).

These patterns of rape indicate an array of motivations and rape behaviours that complicate simplistic conceptions of rape based on the stereotypic scenario of a sudden, physically brutal attack. The recognition of different types of rape and rapist also complicates the expectation and wisdom that women must necessarily respond by screaming, attempt to escape and physically struggle. A study of convicted rapists found that in response to a question about the way they reacted to their victim's resistance, one rapist replied, 'When my victim screamed, I ran', while another explained, 'When my victim screamed, I cut her throat' (Groth and Cohen 1976: 222, quoted in Adler 1987: 114). The different motivations for rape problematise Sharon Marcus's (1992) argument that women should resist the victim status into which they are socialised by fighting back. Marcus's proposition that women learn to be vulnerable and passive and, therefore, this can be changed, is important in terms of formulating a transformative politics for women. However, the 'fight back' solution Marcus proposes may not only endanger the lives of some women but it also reinforces the stereotype that rape is frequently impossible if a woman struggles hard enough. Marcus's proposal, therefore, has limited political purchase. While there are many credible reasons, as Marcus suggests, to move beyond the law and think about how to become agents for change outside existing social institutions, it is also necessary to subject the law to close scrutiny and to draw attention to the ways in which it constructs particular 'realities' and excludes women's voices.

6 Markers of truth

Silencing women in the court

Stories of sexual assault are assessed and evaluated according to a number of particular standards or benchmarks, which are assumed to be valid indicators of truth and blameworthiness. The primary markers of truth are: strong physical resistance as discussed in the previous chapter; the purity of the woman, primarily assessed in terms of sexual inexperience; evidence of significant shock and distress; promptness in reporting the sexual attack; and a consistent, comprehensive and clear description of events before, during and after the sexual assault. These markers of truth, however, are mediated by the stock stories of *tsūjō* rape. In other words, they take on particular significance and meaning in cases of *fushizen* rape when corroborating evidence is minimal. In such cases, the legal argument is not merely concerned with the question of whether the woman consented to sex or not. In order to adjudicate and sentence 'appropriately', the moral blameworthiness of the woman must be interrogated. Former Supreme Court Justice Taniguchi provides the rationale:

> victims themselves may easily respond to the criminal's seductions (*hannin no sasoi*) and create opportunities for crime, or even though victims could easily escape they do not seriously attempt to do so. It may be said that a sex crime is an extension of sex play (*momoiro yugi*) and for this reason defence lawyers say that when it comes to fighting cases in court, rape cases focusing on the question of consent are the easiest to win.
>
> (Taniguchi 1970: 6)

What are these 'opportunities for crime' that women may create and, thus, be held accountable? The cases analysed indicate that the primary markers of blameworthiness are: consenting to go to the site where the offence took place; consuming alcohol; previous sexual experience; and provocative behaviour, language and clothing. This chapter focuses on the way in which judgments consider these standards of truth and blameworthiness to produce what Sheila Duncan refers to as 'mythological constructions of woman as Other'. These mythological female figures are:

the virgin whose purity and innocence serves as a standard by which all women must be assessed; the fallen angel who regrets the loss of her virginity; the vindictive woman who seeks revenge by making false allegations of sexual assault; and the provocative woman whose character and behaviour determine that she deserved, or asked for, what she got – her punishment (Duncan 1994: 16). These are the figures largely constituting the stock stories of *tsūjō* rape. Their discursive performance displaces individual woman's identity and thus makes it difficult for women – even those who believe they conform to dominant images of the blameless, sexually innocent victim – to tell their stories of rape in court and have them believed.

Purity and innocence

> Her innocent appearance in court, subdued dress at the time of the incident, and the fact that it was a quiet residential area . . . support the argument that she was forced to go to his apartment. And although it was argued that if she had been unwilling to go she would have resisted more than she did it must be considered that she was approached by a black man speaking broken Japanese. . . . she cannot be blamed. It is possible she was too scared and shocked to resist, and she was only 20 years old. It is true her evidence is not entirely consistent . . . but it also shows she sometimes acts compulsively. . . . It is unlikely that a woman would go to a man's apartment after just meeting him although of course there are some women who act like that, but it is quite rare and it is hard to imagine that the victim is that sort of woman. . . . the victim who is a young innocent woman . . . .The defendant is sentenced to one year and two months imprisonment with forced labour.
>
> (Courtroom observation, Tokyo District Court, 18 July 1997)

Like the High Court judgment in Atsumi's case, which 'forgave' or understood the young woman's 'rashness' once conclusive material evidence of the rape was produced, the judgment in the above indecent assault case found the basis for understanding the woman's 'compulsiveness' and 'inconsistencies' in the form of the black man. His 'foreignness', particularly his 'blackness' constituted material evidence of her fear. The racist sub-text informing the judgment suggests that in Japan the very presence of a black man is perceived to be threatening. Had the man been a young Japanese male acquaintance, would the judgment have been the same? Would more be made of her 'inconsistencies' and her apparent lack of resistance? This would probably be so, on the basis of other cases examined. Just as the above judgment makes it clear that a good woman or innocent victim does not visit a man's apartment, especially on first meeting, the following quotations from judgments in other sexual assault cases indicate the seriousness with which chaste women are to be protected and *tsūjō* rape viewed.

> the defendant is to be sentenced to ten years imprisonment. . . . the victim was pure (*seijun*) and had very little social experience. . . . The crime is outrageously shameful and vicious. She lost her virginity and even afterwards he disrespected her chastity several times.
>
> (Case 5: 150)

> the defendant committed these terrible crimes. . . . He just selected young girls he liked and forced his way into their apartments. . . . In all cases, the victims were unmarried young women . . . at no point had any of the victims made a mistake, and the fear, psychological humiliation and physical assaults inflicted on the victims is unfathomable.
>
> (Case 2: 303)

And in a case of robbery and attempted rape (not included in my sample):

> Because the victim was a virgin who lived alone and the fear and humiliation inflicted on her as a result of the criminal act in this case will not be forgotten for the rest of her life, the psychological pain she suffered is unfathomable . . . and it must be said that the defendant's criminal responsibility is grave.[1]

The fact that virginity and innocence are mentioned suggests that the rape of a virgin is considered more serious than the rape of a sexually experienced woman. The 'ideal' rape victim in Japan as elsewhere is configured as a blameless, young, sexually desirable yet virginal woman violated by a stranger in a public place. Right from the start of her legal battle, Endō's lawyer made her aware that she had to counter this image of the ideal victim but that the likelihood of success was negligible. According to Endō, her lawyer advised that:

> no one would believe me because I have five children, meaning that I have much experience in the sexual area. I was told that if I was a young girl people would believe me but with five children no-one would.
>
> (Endō, interview 10 December 1997)

Japanese cases are consistent with much of the English-language feminist research which has found that legal systems consistently divide women into categories of those who are rapable and those who are not (see NSW Department for Women 1996; Adler 1987; Burt 1998: 130–136). One of the primary determining factors of such decisions is (lack of) sexual experience. However, the adjudication of a woman's sexual innocence often depends on the context in which the sexual assault took place. In the *tsūjō* rape scenario the court is unlikely to have difficulty accepting a woman's status as virgin. However, in the *fushizen* rape scenario that could be imagined as a story of romance, a young virgin may well be constructed as seductress or liar and, therefore, blameworthy. The following statement by the judge in Nakajima's case illustrates the difficulty of establishing virginity or innocence once the woman admits sexual assault:

> Although [Nakajima] claims she was a virgin . . . we can only assume she has had sexual experiences because she was not particularly upset about the kissing and petting. If she was a virgin this would have frightened her. Alternatively we could assume that she was curious about sex and therefore accepted the defendant's behaviour. . . . If she was really a virgin when she saw the danger to her life and body she would not care about either her clothes [being cut up] or being kept until morning.
>
> (Case 12 Nakajima: 336)

The difficulty women have in claiming sexual innocence following a sexual assault reflects the discursive proximity of romance and rape. The pivotal link between the two is the lexical signifier 'no'. Drawing on Patricia Parker's definition of romance as 'that mode or tendency which remains on the threshold before a desired end', Nina Puren (1995: 21) argues that, 'that threshold in the romantic economy' is sustained through resistance – through the 'no'. A woman must continue to say 'no' to maintain the romance and to affirm her respectability but at the same time she 'must always have as a signified, a desiring [and thus "culpable"] body'. Woman in the romantic narrative is scripted as wanting sex but necessarily says 'no' and thus she is also scripted as deceitful: her 'no' really meaning 'yes'.

Puren illuminates the process by which allegations of rape are transformed into romantic narratives. She uses the idea of the hymen which, she argues, is first and foremost a 'hegemonic phantasy', to explain that the intact hymen 'codes the female subject as "respectable and legitimate" and the "potential producer of *true statements*"' while the broken hymen signifies deception and 'disqualifi[cation] from that group of bodies which can signify as injured' (Puren 1995: 16–17). The moment an allegation of rape is made the woman is thus signified as having a broken hymen and therefore potentially deceitful. Her privilege to truthfulness and protection is therefore, at least temporarily, suspended. The body of the woman claiming innocence in terms of virginal status becomes suspect. She is situated with all sexually experienced women who are suspected of inherent untruthfulness and therefore her account of rape must be subjected to particular scrutiny. Moreover, she must tell a story about a sexual encounter, providing graphic details of which body parts were where and when and this story resonates with narratives designed to sexually titillate and give pleasure, those found in soft-porn, romance novels and tabloid newspaper stories (Smart 1989: 39–40). She must tell the story in person, her body exposed to the imaginative exercise of others who attempt to reconstruct the sexual scenario. Her body becomes necessarily and unavoidably sexualised as it 'brings the story to life'. However, if her story arouses, she loses credibility: her story will sound less like rape and more like a 'standard sexual fantasy' which, Carol Smart (1990: 17) explains, constitutes 'the imagined substance of *other people's sex lives*' – plausible because they hold such wide social currency. In such cases the court must distinguish between the 'no' of rape and the 'no' of romance, sexual fantasy or pornography.

If the romantic narrative renders sexually experienced women as untrustworthy, or inherently suspect, how then do women construct persuasive narratives of rape? What are the specific constraints they face and how are these negotiated in the courtroom context? First, we need to address the specific constraints in terms of judicial expectations and what 'makes sense'.

Evidence of significant shock

According to conventional understandings, the shock or trauma of sexual assault is so significant that a woman becomes too distressed to continue her normal daily habits such as going to work or school. Komatsu's story, for example, could be imagined partly because after the incident she attempted suicide, ran away from home, and experienced a change in her personality. The prosecution in Takahashi's case also attempted to use the argument that failure to go to work indicated distress caused by the rape, however, in this case it was found to be less convincing. Similarly, in the Sapporo sexual harassment case, the woman successfully advanced the argument that she responded to the sexual harassment in a socially recognisable way – leaving work immediately and not returning on the following day.

If a woman does not demonstrate *familiar* signs of psychological disturbance or conform to the social script for female victim responses this may be used against her as evidence that she is fabricating a story. In the Kanazawa sexual harassment case, the judge found it 'unnatural' that the woman went to work the day after she was indecently assaulted. Similarly, in the Kumamoto sexual harassment case, the defence argued that the plaintiff, a professional sportswoman:

> never skipped training and from [her coach's] point of view there was nothing wrong with her attitude, so she was working and training

> normally. After rape it takes time to recover from the shock and therefore, the fact that she could live normally from the next day on indicates that she was not raped.
>
> (Case 31 Kumamoto)

This case, discussed further in Chapter 7, is interesting because the defence argument failed despite their familiar 'avenging woman scorned in love' narrative and on the night of the rape she was drunk, could not resist, she failed to report the incident and continued to have sexual relations with the defendant for three years. In contrast, the defence strategy, emphasising the failure to conform to normative modes of response to a sexual attack as evidence of deceitfulness, was more persuasive in Endō's case.

The defence stressed the 'unnaturalness' of the fact that Endō returned to work on the following day. The judge also asked her if she had missed work or arrived late following previous occasions when the defendant had allegedly sexually harassed her. Although she replied that she had, on further questioning she could not provide specific dates. Not only does this conventional expectation that women do not return to work after being sexually attacked constrain or limit alternative responses to sexual violations, but it serves to deny women a fully fledged worker identity. This case suggests that women's sexuality precedes their position as workers. Married women, particularly those employed part-time are frequently constructed as idle pleasure seekers who work for amusement (see Broadbent 2003) – an argument put forward by Endō's boss. Tsunoda's counter-argument invoked the single male standard as a rule to argue for equal treatment, thus situating Endō as worker (gender neutral) first and foremost:

> Many women come to work after experiencing physical or emotional hurt as a result of sexual discrimination. If they do not they may lose their income and job which would mean a double violation of their human rights. Similarly, men who are unreasonably harassed at work by their superiors still go to work the next day. Furthermore, it is important to recognise that no-one would argue that because a male worker went to work the day after being harassed that the unreasonable treatment against him could not have occurred.
>
> (Case 19 Endō: 12)

These cases suggest that the legal arena provides space for a very limited, clearly gendered, yet contested repertoire of acknowledged 'normal' responses to the shock of sexual assault. While recent sexual harassment cases indicate a broadening understanding within the judiciary (discussed in Chapter 7), demonstrating a familiar performance of shock remains significant in terms of registering 'truth'.

Promptness of reporting the incident

Many women do not report a sexual assault immediately or do not report it at all, for a variety of reasons. These reasons, or at least some of them, are acknowledged by the court and therefore failure to file an immediate report cannot formally be considered evidence of deceit or lack of credibility. However, the fact that this issue is raised at all suggests that the promptness of the complaint is regarded as a significant marker of truth despite any following judicial commentary to the contrary. In the judicial imaginary the horror of a sexual assault is so traumatic that a 'genuine' victim is compelled to report the attack immediately and to seek medical attention and supporting documentation. In short, as articulated in both the Akita and Kyoto sexual harassment judgments, an early complaint is considered the 'normal' response to a sexual attack. Sasaki's immediate complaint, in addition to evidence of violence and resistance, constituted compelling imagery that contributed to the conviction of the defendant despite a great deal of emphasis on her immoral character and reckless behaviour.

A prompt complaint suggests truthfulness only in the context of supporting evidence. Early complaints in the cases of Nakajima, Matsumoto and Atsumi were mentioned in the judge's narrative of events but no weight was accorded to this point. In Takeda and Fujiwara's cases it was noted that their fathers first reported the rape to the police and this served to undermine their credibility to some extent. Failure to make a prompt report was considered relevant or persuasive enough to mention in Takahashi, Fujiwara and Endō's cases and in three sexual harassment cases (Akita, Kyoto and Kumamoto), summoning the mythic fallen angel and the vindictive woman. In Takahashi's case, the judge stated:

> if she had really wanted to report the defendant she would have gone to the hospital sooner . . . and although clothes worn at the time are an important piece of evidence she took them to the cleaners, so it appears she did not plan to file a report. . . . no good reason can be found in [Takahashi's] explanation for taking considerable time to report the incident to the police.
>
> (Case 14 Takahashi: 152)

According to the 'Experimentalist' explanations of judicial decision-making, when the defendant is found not guilty, the onus is placed on the judge to produce a narrative that explains the inconsistencies in the case. Failure to file a prompt complaint provides fertile grounds in which to construct an explanation for false allegations. In Takahashi's case, the judge constructed an image of a humiliated woman trapped into covering up her indiscretion:

> it is possible that she felt bad, her pride wounded and she felt humiliated because after sexual intercourse took place, according to the

> defendant's testimony, he was angry with her because she vomited and he dropped her off only after she appealed to him to do so. Considering [Takahashi's] character it is natural for her to tell her friends about her anger but it would have been humiliating to admit she had consented to sex. In truth, she was probably very drunk, had some memory and used the little she had to make up a story. She wanted to pressure the defendant into apologising but he did not and so when her friend suggested she file a report she felt she had no alternative but to do so.
>
> (Case 14 Takahashi: 153)

A similar narrative was put forward in Fujiwara's case:

> It is necessary to consider how and when [Fujiwara] went to the police. She did not go on the same day. She . . . went to the hospital, but did not ask for the papers detailing the extent of her injuries . . . she filed a written complaint three days later. Even though in ordinary cases many rape victims are too embarrassed to go to the police, they go soon after the event, but in this case her father went the following day and she went the day after that. This is a problem. Perhaps . . . when her father asked what happened, she could not tell the truth . . . so she told a story in which she was totally innocent. On hearing this story her father went to the police and so it became difficult for her to admit the truth or to change her story. And in the three days before filing the written complaint she had time to make up a story in which she was blameless.
>
> (Case 16 Fujiwara: 242)

It virtually goes without saying (the basis for any powerful argument) that 'fallen angels' making 'false' accusations of rape tell lies to cover up their loss of virtue – understandable, if not expected behaviour given the emphasis on chastity (at least in the judicial imagination). Somewhat differently placed and usually older women who lay 'false' allegations of sexual harassment are more likely to be constructed as bitter women full of vengeance. In the Kumamoto sexual harassment case involving an initial allegation of rape followed by a forced sexual relationship lasting three years, the defence argued that it was months before she spoke of the incident to anyone and:

> it took about three years to file a complaint against the defendant. It is doubtful that such a thing is possible. Our assumption is that she started to resent the defendant because she had to stop seeing him and stop the relationship in which she was a willing participant.
>
> (Case 31 Kumamoto)

The fact that Endō filed a complaint the day before the expiry of the six-month time limit to report rape (abolished in 2000) was not raised in court, but it was raised at the pre-trial stage by the prosecutor who rejected her case. According to Endō, the prosecutor argued that she made a false accusation in order to defend her muddied reputation. Yet, the defence did attempt to suggest that she was deceitful and untrustworthy because she did not immediately confide in her husband. According to Endō:

> I caught a sexually transmitted disease . . . that's when my husband realised something had happened, but in the court they argued that it was strange that I couldn't talk about it with my husband. . . . The judge at the trial said that it was normal to speak about something like this with your husband . . . no-one at the court could understand the difficulty I had in talking about it. They just think that rape is the same as other crimes like robbery.
>
> (Case 19 Endō, interview 10 December 1996)

These cases suggest that although a woman is not required to file a complaint immediately after the attack, despite judicial comments to the contrary, a prompt report can act as a marker of truthfulness. However, perhaps more importantly, failure to do so facilitates the space in which the judicial imagination can compose an alternative narrative around the mythical figures whose appearance displaces the identity, experiences and stories of women who have been the targets of sexual assault.

Comprehensive, consistent and clear accounts

Providing a consistent detailed account of the incident is important to the construction of a persuasive narrative in any sort of legal case. Consistency and clarity are particularly important in sexual assault cases because it is assumed that horrific events are inevitably and indelibly marked in one's memory. It can, therefore, operate as a significant marker of truth as illustrated in Case 7: 'from the very beginning, [the complainant] repeated a consistent and clear statement of events . . . especially given its consistency, details and clarity we cannot deny the reliability of [her] statement' (Case 7: 160).

Tsunoda's Supreme Court appeal therefore emphasised Endō's consistent account of the actual rape, 'in such detail it is difficult to imagine creating such a scenario in the mind' (Case 19 Endō: 84).

However, in certain cases the usual emphasis on consistency and clarity may be overlooked: in Case 4 involving the rape of a 12-year-old girl by three US marines, the judge stated that, 'after the first rape the girl was understandably confused and hurt so although she cannot clearly remember if [the defendant] hit her, this does not constitute evidence that he did not' (Case 4: 148). In this clear case of *tsūjō* rape, the requirement of a consistent story and clear memory is thus mitigated by the circumstances including her very young age and the fact that there were three foreign defendants.

Nevertheless, most trials placed a lot of emphasis on women's inconsistent accounts of 'what happened' and even the most seemingly insignificant detail can impact on the case:

> [Fujiwara] said she was strangled, but first she said he put his right arm around her throat and then she said he used both hands. The defence counsel pointed out the discrepancy and she replied, 'what the police say is right'. If she really was strangled, it would undoubtedly have shocked her so her memory would be clear.
>
> (Case 16 Fujiwara: 244)

As a result of this apparent change in her story – or lapse in memory – the judge reasoned that Fujiwara probably fabricated the story about not consenting to go to the hotel. The judicial assumptions concerning reactions to a traumatic situation or incident are based on 'common-sense' ideas of victim response. These were challenged through the use of expert witness evidence in only the Ikebukuro case (discussed in the Prelude) and two sexual harassment cases (Kumamoto and Utsunomiya). As a result, the limited repertoire of appropriate victim responses that constitute the dominant narrative are sustained as the legal standard against which individual cases are measured.

The failure to remember details and dates is typically interpreted as a sign of untruthfulness in legal proceedings. The District Court judge noted that Endō could not remember the dates she came to work late due to sexual harassment by the defendant. In the Kumamoto sexual harassment case, referring to the exact date of the rape three years earlier, the defence emphasised that 'it is unnatural she could not remember [the date of] such a shocking occurrence' (Case 31 Kumamoto). Similarly, Matsumoto's testimony was dismissed because she could not remember certain points and was led in her responses by the prosecutor. To illustrate, the following example was considered significant enough to reproduce in the judgment:

Prosecutor: It's some time ago now, but there was talk of the defendant killing you. At what point in time or at what stage was this said? Was it before he grabbed your shoulders with his hands or after?

Matsumoto: I don't remember.

(Case 13 Matsumoto: 113)

In Matsumoto's case, the defendant's narrative of a desperate attempt to proclaim and consummate his 'love' achieved the required images of familiarity which frame the convincing story and he was acquitted. His story was axiomatic and thus did not require that he prove his claim by remembering details and dates. Against such an ordinary story there was little space to consider Matsumoto's alternative account.

While a woman's poor memory generally signals untruthfulness in *fushizen* rape cases, it is frequently interpreted to mean something quite different for the defendant. It is reasonable to assume that defendants have a lot to gain by avoiding or minimising their punishment and are therefore potentially unreliable sources of information. Their interests are protected to an extent by their right to remain silent and they do not have to swear an oath that they will tell the truth like other witnesses, but of course considerable weight is generally placed on their version of events.

While inconsistencies in the defendant's testimony are, as would be expected, often interpreted as possible signs of untrustworthiness, a critical approach to his testimony is generally evident only when the evidence is already significantly weighted against him. In *fushizen* rape cases and other cases where the legal question boils down to his word against hers, the defendant's inability to provide appropriate details or contradictions in his evidence is frequently interpreted as evidence of his innocence, psychiatric disorder or some other cause. For example, in Case 6 a low IQ accounted for the contradictions and inadequate detail in the defendant's confession, which was therefore rejected and the defendant acquitted. In Endō's case, being 'too excited', consumed by passion, was accepted as a reasonable explanation for the defendant's poor memory and inability to provide a detailed account of the sexual act in question. In a case involving rape and murder police coercion was central to the rejection of the defendant's confession, which was found to be 'not completely natural or logical' and lacking sufficient detail.[2] In another rape and murder case alcoholism was found to be the cause of the defendant's poor memory and sketchy confession, contributing to his acquittal.[3]

Alcoholism was also central in a classic 'his word against hers' case in which the 24-year-old 'sexually experienced' door-to-door saleswoman alleged that following a quarrel the 52-year-old defendant, a customer and friend, threatened her with a knife, attempted anal sex and other forms of indecent assault. When she screamed a neighbour heard and called the police. The defendant argued that following their quarrel as they tried to patch things up 'one thing led to another and the mood changed'. However, when he could not achieve an erection he became upset (and spoke of committing a double suicide) and she became angry. Deciding between these conflicting accounts the judge dismissed the woman's story partly because she failed to produce a detailed account of what actually happened. The judge speculated that she was probably surprised when the police arrived and she came out to meet them quite slowly because she 'needed time to think up a story'. The inconsistencies in the defendant's confession were attributed to his alcoholism. There were substantial problems in both their testimonies, but while she was represented as a woman of questionable virtue and a liar, he was represented as a man with an affliction (or two) who deserved some sympathy (Case 33).

In many of these sorts of cases judges do not tend to assume that the defendant was lying to protect himself, in a manner consistent with the common assertion that women make false allegations. There are two key reasons for this. First, judges assume that the investigation process is capable of extracting the truth in the form of a confession as long as the details conform to other evidence. Second, the defendant is presumed innocent until proven guilty. The procedural scales are thus tipped in favour of the defendant. Although a confession alone is insufficient evidence to convict, it is granted considerable weight. However, it is also recognised that defendants frequently make 'voluntary false confessions' due to police coercion at the interrogation stage. Such allegations are likely to be believed because the interrogation process inevitably involves an element of coercion. Thus, the lack of an adequate account is often perceived as an understandable response to coercion. Therefore, these defendants are also less likely to be construed as deceitful than tends to be the case for women alleging a sexual assault.

Based on arguments of police coercion, confessions were revoked by the defendant in the cases of Sasaki, Fujiwara and Atsumi. In the first trial of Atsumi's case, the judge accepted that the defendant had confessed in order to end the police investigation and that his innocence was supported by the fact that he did not (interpreted as *could not* – because he was not the offender) provide important details or take the police to the location of the offence. When new material evidence was introduced at the appeal stage, the defendant was found to be lying. Similarly, in a case of murder and rape resulting in death, the defendant was acquitted in the first trial because his confession was contradictory and changeable. The court decided that if he had really raped and killed the 7-year-old girl he would have remembered the incident in greater detail. However, the High Court rejected this argument stating that 'just because he contradicted himself does not mean he did not commit the offence'.[4] These cases indicate that while a 'lapse of memory' is likely to signal lack of credibility in a woman claiming sexual assault, under certain circumstances, it may signal the defendant's innocence or reasonable response to police coercion.

Going to the site of the offence

Cars and love hotels were the most common locations of rape in this study. Love hotels, numbering 35,000 throughout Japan and 4,000 in Tokyo in 1984 (Bornoff 1991: 18), indelibly mark the urban Japanese landscape with erotic fantasy – often ablaze with neon lights and sporting façades of towering Disney-style castles, ships and dungeons or quiet Japanese-style architectural structures blending into the local surroundings and offering greater sophistication and discretion. The love hotel and the car are two familiar settings for stories of romance and lust. They are not ordinarily associated with the terrain of rape, more likely to be imagined as ditches, dark streets and deserted parking lots. The site of the alleged offence can perform a significant role in the production of a persuasive tale of romance or of rape. In Endō's case, the image of romance was reinforced by the defendant's statement that he could not afford a love hotel. Endō strengthened her story of rape with images of dirt and impurity, emphasising that the offence took place 'on the storeroom floor – where people walk with their shoes' (interview 10 December 1996). In the Supreme Court appeal, Tsunoda argued that his car would have been a more natural choice if they had, indeed, been a 'loving couple'.

In addition to contributing to the overall picture of the romance scenario, consent to going to the location where the alleged offence took place offers the defence two strategies: first, to imply that the woman consented to sexual intercourse, and second that she is partially responsible for the offence, placing herself at risk and failing in her duty to protect her body. These strategies are not unique to Japan. A US study of rape by Holmstrom and Burgess (1978: 177 cited in Adler 1987: 112) found that conviction is less likely in cases where the woman was perceived to have consented to go to the place where she was allegedly raped. Although Adler's British study did not find a similar direct correlation to the verdict, she argued that this factor may take on central significance when other factors are considered (Adler 1987: 113). Similar statistical methods were not carried out in this study, but the Japanese cases presented here clearly indicate the importance placed on this factor in terms of verdict and sentencing.

The defence argument that the woman consented to, or was negligent in, being in the location where she was allegedly raped, was influential in seven of the eight cases in which these arguments were raised. These arguments contributed to the decision to acquit in five cases and to minimise penalties in two of the three cases achieving a conviction. The exception was Komatsu's case in which the judge rejected the notion that the woman consented to go to the hotel and argued that even if she had this could not be construed as consent to sex. It was argued that Nakajima, Fujiwara, Komatsu and, to a lesser extent, Takeda, willingly entered the love hotel, implying consent to sex. Similarly, it was argued that Takahashi, Sasaki and Atsumi willingly climbed into the cars and consented to a drive with the defendants prior to the assault. Although convictions were achieved in Sasaki and Fujiwara's cases, the women were found to have consented to be in the location of the offence and were, therefore, partially responsible. It was then argued that this warranted light sentences for the defendants (suspended sentences for all three defendants). Conventional legal wisdom asserts that the defendant should receive a degree of leniency in accordance with the extent of the woman's blameworthiness or responsibility in provoking the attack. In other words, men may be absolved of their responsibility for rape to the extent that women are construed as 'precipitating' the attack. Legal discourse thus legitimises and perpetuates the idea that a woman may 'ask' to be raped and, likewise, deserve to be punished.

The danger for a woman of getting into a car with a man alone 'goes without saying'; it is widespread common-sense knowledge imparted to girls in the 1974 Ministry of Education booklet (mentioned in Chapter 2) and elsewhere. Takahashi, Sasaki and Atsumi were, therefore, clearly marked as foolish, naïve and asking for trouble. Consequently, they, rather than their rapists, were held accountable. Women were also viewed with suspicion, or regarded as negligent and therefore partially responsible, when they failed to lock the hotel door (Watanabe) or bathroom door (Fujiwara) and were out late at night (Takeda, Takahashi, Sasaki, Fujiwara, Endō and, to a lesser extent, Matsumoto) and, of course, especially if they were in a bar (Takahashi and Fujiwara).

Consuming alcohol

Sasaki's consumption of alcohol, resulting in her missing the train home and hitch-hiking, was raised to suggest that she was irresponsible, putting herself at risk and creating the impression that she might be a woman of easy virtue willing to participate in casual sex. This theme was discussed more directly in relation to Takahashi. Takahashi's drinking in this case was used to suggest two things: that alcohol lowered her 'inhibitions' contributing to her decision to have consensual sex with a man she had just met and that it diminished her memory of events, thus rendering her an unreliable witness. The judge determined that her sense of guilt or shame in engaging in a casual sexual encounter led her to make a false accusation to cover up her embarrassment:

> How much she drank is important in this case. She lied about the amount because she wanted to deny that she consented to sex. If she was drunk, her chastity would be weaker and her memory would not be so clear and we cannot trust such a memory.
>
> (Case 14 Takahashi: 149)

The judge also determined that the complainant's state of intoxication was a more likely explanation for her injuries than rape:

> she was very drunk so it is possible she hit her legs or arms and got the bruises when she went to the toilet or after the defendant dropped her home. Therefore it is not clear what caused the bruises. . . . So in truth she was probably very drunk, had some memory and used the little she had to construct a story.
>
> (Case 14 Takahashi: 152)

The defendant's drinking in this case was interpreted entirely differently. No suggestion was made that alcohol may have affected his memory and although it was accepted that the defendant was sober enough to drive, he was considered too drunk to lift the woman, who was about his size, up onto the back seat of the four-wheel drive car. The issue of the defendant's alcohol consumption was also raised in Atsumi's case. Challenging Atsumi's story, in the first trial the defence argued he was unlikely to have been drinking because he had a weak tolerance for alcohol (rejected in the appeal) and 'at 28 years of age, he had much experience with women so there was no need for him to drink in order to relax to seduce a woman' (Case 17 Atsumi: 278). These cases suggest that alcohol consumption is a gendered phenomenon. For a woman it signals irresponsibility, a loosening of morals and poor memory. For a man it signals diminished physical strength but not memory, and a normal, recognisable social lubricant in the game of seduction.

Sexual experience

Many countries have introduced 'shield' laws to prevent or restrict the woman's sexual history being questioned in court because advocates argue that it is usually irrelevant to the particular offence in question, it is raised primarily to discredit the complainant, and it can cause further trauma. Raising the question of a woman's sexual history serves no purpose if it is assumed she is a freely consenting subject who exercises her free choice every occasion and with every partner (Duncan 1994: 18). However, despite the 'shield' laws the woman's sexual past is still frequently found to be relevant and admitted as evidence by the presiding judge (Lees 1993: 11–36; Edwards and Heenan 1994: 213–236).

In the Japanese courtroom, any evidence that contributes to an understanding of the details and background of the case may be admitted. A woman's sexual history may be raised to bolster or deny assertions regarding her character and credibility. However, as it is not an adversarial system it is possible this form of questioning may not be as gruelling as it is under the adversarial systems. The cases in this study indicate that, wherever possible, the prosecutor uses the complainant's virgin status to establish her as a respectable, ordinary young woman whose social and sexual naivety explains any seemingly irrational or compulsive conduct that does not conform to social expectations of appropriate victim behaviour (Nakajima, Fujiwara, Atsumi and Komatsu). Conversely, the sexual experience of Takeda, Takahashi and Sasaki was used to malign their moral character, drawing on assumptions that sexually active women are less likely to be discriminating in terms of sexual partners and because this behaviour defies social convention she is more likely to lie about it. The judge found that Sasaki 'invited the incident', integrating evidence that she was 'not a virgin and had slept with a few men', she had been drinking, had entered a car with two men and driven around with them for quite a long time. Her culpability diminished the judge's perception of the significance of the harm:

the defendant's behaviour, including attempted rape and forcing her to perform fellatio was described as 'imprudent' (*keisotsu*) and 'the violence was not heavy enough to wound her' (Case 15 Sasaki: 161–162). Takahashi's sexual history was also raised as part of a very deliberate character assassination, which will be discussed in the following section.

The cases reveal that judges tend not to mention a woman's sexual history as evidence of untrustworthiness unless additional factors are also perceived to raise doubts about her moral character. Endō's case revealed that while judges may be sensitive to attacking a woman's morality and character in a public space such as the courtroom, which may be closed during the woman's cross-examination, police and prosecutors use this information to decide whether a case is worth pursuing (similar to the issue of making an early complaint). Although her sexual history was not directly raised in any of the trials, the police asked her questions regarding how many sexual partners she had had, whether she was a virgin when she married, and about her husband's sexual experiences. While Endō stated she was uncomfortable answering the police questions, it was the prosecutor's trivialisation of the assault that she found the most traumatic:

> the doctor and police gave no bad impressions, but the prosecutors were totally different. They didn't think at all about women's problems; they just judge if she is a woman who should be protected or a slut – that's their only criteria. . . . I had to stay in bed to recover from the shock and humiliation . . . I felt so bad that I almost had a nervous breakdown . . . all these things which had nothing to do with what I wanted to talk about. There was no chance to discuss with them – from the beginning they didn't listen and had decided they wouldn't take the case to the court.
>
> (Endō, interview 10 December 1997)

Given that the Prosecutor's Office is likely to dismiss cases not conforming to *tsūjō* rape scenarios, including those in which the woman's sexual history can be used to discredit her testimony, it is surprising that some of these cases actually do reach the criminal courts. It is likely that Takeda and Sasaki's cases made it to trial because there were two offenders. Gang rape (*rinkan*) is a more serious crime than rape and not limited to the provision of prosecution only on complaint (See Appendix 1, Article 180, section 2).

The existence of a sexual double standard is no surprise: sexual experience signals deceit and blameworthiness in a woman, while for men it is considered part of healthy heterosexual masculinity. As a result, sexual harassment is still regarded by some as trivial. For example, in the Kanazawa case, the judge described the defendant's offer of money to his employee for sex, and trying to touch and fondle her, as 'acting carelessly' (Case 29 Kanazawa). Thus, many of Law's assumptions regarding sexuality and gender privilege and protect the male subject from strong social sanctions even when a conviction is achieved.

Provocation

Dress and behaviour may signal either femininity or provocation depending on the context (e.g. wearing a nightgown in the bedroom as opposed to the streets) and on the perceptions of those involved (see Sterling 1995). To some extent, differing interpretations of the same behaviour may be the result of a gap in perceptions, as discussed in Chapter 2. In this study, women were perceived to be provocative, regarded with suspicion, or to have expressed a sexual interest in the defendant on the basis of the following: taking a bath when forced to stay overnight at her employer's home due to heavy snowfalls (Case 29 Kanazawa);[5] changing into an attractive black dress, not checking the car's number plate, lying to her father about where she was going and leaving home without money (Atsumi); staying after work to talk to her boss when she knew they would be alone, and lending an 'erotic' video (*Betty Blue*) to her boss (Endō); giving the defendant a pencil case and address book for his birthday (Komatsu); consistently staying out late at night in the company of boys (Takeda).

In some cases it is not merely a perceptual gap that is the problem, but the judicial imperative to weave all elements of the complex social reality surrounding the case that are made known in court and the recognised 'facts' into a tight persuasive narrative that unambiguously articulates and justifies the judges' overall conclusion. This is best illustrated in Takahashi's case. Her character and moral behaviour were subjected to an extraordinary level of scrutiny and she was crafted into a provocative, deceitful and untrustworthy vixen in the final judgment. She was condemned as not the kind of woman the law of rape was intended to protect. The judgment barely mentioned her perception of the attack but, rather, as a proxy for the issue of consent, interrogated her character and behaviour leading up to and following the alleged rape. The judge's narrative focused on Takahashi's untrustworthiness and immorality:

> she lacks integrity because even though it was a game she talked about sex with strangers and at the very least she took off her stockings and waved them around which is very provocative behaviour. . . . She lied about the amount she drank because she wanted to deny that she consented to sex . . . the victim and her friend made up the story about asking the second car to follow in order to make herself appear chaste (*teiso*).
>
> (Case 14 Takahashi: 148–149)

The judge's dismissal of Takahashi's claim to chastity was 'substantiated' by the following five points, which were elaborated at considerable length:

1 After high school she worked as a fashion model, actress and a 'party companion', which is much the same as a hostess, 'so it must be said that she has more of an exhibitionist's (*hade*) personal history than the ordinary person'.
2 The clothing she liked to wear to night clubs was 'flashy' (*hade*) and she enjoyed going out to night clubs, contrary to her claim that she goes to study social behaviour.
3 'Perhaps one of her hobbies is watching adult videos although she claims it is her boyfriend who likes these and rents them with her card. Her boyfriend said sometimes he used her card but checking the dates he said some of them were rented before he met her. Even during this case on May 27 when she was thinking about whether to report the incident he rented a [pornographic] video and she did not object. It is even possible she watched the movie at that time.'
4 Her ex-boyfriend denied her claims that they were engaged to be married and stated that the reason their relationship ended was not because of the incident as she suggested, but because their personalities were incompatible. Furthermore, regarding her sense of chasteness (*teiso kannen*), according to her boyfriend's testimony, they had sexual intercourse on the second time they met 'so her chastity is questionable'.
5 'During her cross-examination, she spoke like a gentle person but sometimes she used slang and crude expressions revealing her true character'.

The judge concluded on the basis of these points that, 'It is apparent that [Takahashi] is far from chaste' and her testimony was deemed 'irrational and illogical', including 'lies and exaggerations'. The judge also condemned her because she did not accept any responsibility and was unrepentant:

> Even though they were strangers whom she had just met only a matter of two or three hours earlier, she played a game with blatant sexual content and drove alone with him to his home. In addition, she was drinking until 3 a.m. and so she is at fault. However, she does not admit her mistakes and says her behaviour is blameless. Moreover she told her lawyer that she wants the defendant to get the death penalty or life imprisonment. She lacks common sense.
>
> (Case 14 Takahashi: 146)

The judge appears barely able to constrain his/her indignation and contempt for Takahashi and her every action is interpreted as a transgression of conventional codes of feminine behaviour. The court silenced Takahashi's experience of rape and her non-conformity was unambiguously disciplined through character assassination.

Allocation of blame

This chapter has identified the importance of allocating blame in order to seek 'just' decisions in the Japanese courtroom. According to social and legal conventions a dispute almost invariably involves an element of responsibility and blameworthiness on both sides and reaching a 'fair' decision demands that each party's role in the deterioration of the relationship must be investigated. Of course, in *tsūjō* rape scenarios, factors such as no prior relationship, use of a weapon or involvement of multiple offenders clearly tips the scales of responsibility towards the defendant and it becomes unnecessary to investigate the complainant's possible responsibility for the crime.

The assumption that some women 'invite' or share responsibility for their abuse, and the lack of understanding of responses to fear which do not conform to the 'fight or flight' model, are often clearly articulated in divorce cases involving allegations of domestic violence and rape. These sorts of cases place particular emphasis on according blame to both sides because it is recognised that marital relations are complicated webs of emotion, rights and obligations. However, problems often arise in recognising the seriousness of acts regarded as criminal outside the family, when they occur between husband and wife (see Fukushima 1997: 2–99). For example, in a 1967 divorce and compensation case in which the couple had been separated for five years, the judge accepted that the husband was repeatedly violent towards his wife including hitting her in the head, kicking her with his boots on, and causing her injuries which on one occasion required medical treatment over ten times in the following two months. While the divorce was granted, her request for compensation was denied because she was seen as partially responsible:

> she decided to leave him too early and it would have been better for her to try a little harder. . . . the direct cause of the separation was the husband's behaviour but the destruction of the marriage was not only the husband's fault, the wife lost her love towards him. Therefore, it cannot be accepted that the wife is solely entitled to compensation so her request is denied.
>
> (quoted in Fukushima 1997: 59)

In a similar 1983 case, a woman's request for divorce was granted and the court ordered the husband to pay compensation for her share in their property. However, the wife's compensation request for violence was rejected because the judge determined they were 'equally responsible' and despite 'facts' accepted by the court which, according to lawyer Fukushima, clearly indicated criminal grounds for a charge of rape. The judge found that as a result of the wife's 'retiring' (*keppeki*) attitude to sex, the husband, who had strong sexual desires, became frustrated and tried to accomplish his purpose with force: he pushed her down, beat, kicked and threw furniture at her. This was not an isolated incident. The judge determined that:

neither of them have a deep understanding of marital life and they do not have the kindness to care for each other. Both acted selfishly, engaged in repeated physical confrontations and started to lose love and trust towards each other. Therefore the essential cause and responsibility for the destruction of the marriage, as seen above, is shared equally between them.

(quoted in Fukushima 1997: 54)

Consider the following 1985 divorce case involving an allegation of rape in which the judge stated that except under particular circumstances:

marriage means the sexual union between the sexes, therefore the husband's request for sex by force is not illegal and wives do not have the right to refuse. . . . When a wife's complete refusal to engage in sexual relations is a cause of her husband's behaviour, his behaviour cannot be called an inhumane invasion of human rights because if a healthy man in his forties has a wife with such an attitude for no apparent reason, then it is likely he will become sexually frustrated and we cannot stop him doing such things to his wife. The defendant behaved roughly but it was within the degree of a normal domestic argument (*fūfu genka*) and it cannot be considered a special problem.

(quoted in Fukushima 1997: 33)

These decisions assume that women provoke and frustrate men sexually and emotionally and are, therefore, to some extent deserving of their consequent victimisation. The avoidance of allocating blame solely to one party serves to deny and trivialise behaviour recognised as criminal outside marriage. The violence is naturalised through the construction of male sexuality as uncontrollable and also, in these cases, through the construction of naturally volatile marital relations, *fūfu genka*. The failure to condemn this type of behaviour and name it as domestic violence and rape in marriage serves to legitimate and perpetuate male violence as an expression of patriarchal control in the home.

Outside the home, the stock stories of avenging women scorned in love and deceitful angels covering up their mistakes flourish as *fushizen* rape victim-survivors are placed on trial. All their moral choices in life, before, during and after the rape may be used as a proxy for consent (Bumiller 1990: 132). In order to succeed in the difficult task of establishing sexual assault in such cases it is necessary to claim total innocence or blamelessness – appropriate victim status. This strategy requires that the description of 'what actually happened' is narrated in such a way that grey areas are white-washed. The story must, in effect, be sanitised. Kristin Bumiller puts it well:

the innocence of a female accuser is lost with her initial charge that she has been sexually violated – and it is further eroded as her moral

> purity becomes an issue in court . . . The accuser is forced into the role of an ‘angel’ who must defend her heavenly qualities after her fall from grace.
>
> (Bumiller 1990: 127)

However, as the above cases indicate, defending one’s virtue or blamelessness is no easy task. The stock stories of rape dominate and discipline those whose experiences do not correspond with the dominant insider perceptions. In trying to communicate what has happened to them, women take into account the imagined judgements of others in narrating their experiences and the strength of their stories boil down to their ability to invoke images which conform to those insider perceptions of innocence and *tsūjō* rape.

7 Subversive stories and feminist strategies

> The operation of law involves a continual use of strategies, in which one is constantly balancing the possibilities against the probabilities. Again, let us be clear – in general, it is a more than uneven fight. As law is constituted in a society which still privileges sections of that society in terms of gender, race, class and socially defined standards of ability, so it is by no means a 'free space' for equal engagement. But neither is it closed space which we must continually struggle *against* rather than *within*.
>
> (Bottomley and Conoghan 1993: 3)

The previous chapters suggest that the courts are a hostile place for some women claiming sexual assault, the experience often constituting a form of 'second assault'. For this reason some feminists – academics and grass-roots activists – have been reluctant to engage with the law at all. The Tokyo Rape Crisis Centre (TRCC), for example, is primarily concerned with empowering women who have been victimised and therefore does not attempt to persuade women to pursue legal channels, although this option is discussed and feminist lawyers are available for legal advice.[1]

After almost two decades of debate concerning sexual assault and the implementation of feminist-inspired law reforms in numerous countries, by the end of the 1980s much of the feminist literature, particularly radical feminist writing, was sceptical if not completely dismissive of law's potential to effect meaningful change. Not only was it clear to most that law reforms were not going to stop men from committing rape, but there was increasing evidence that despite the range of law reform adopted in Anglo-European countries there had been a general lack of success in achieving higher rates of conviction and more sensitive legal procedural practices (Los 1992; NSW Department for Women 1996). The British 'school' of feminist criminologists, in particular, began to argue that law reform was dangerous territory for feminists:

> If reforms are geared only to curbing the more obvious excesses of men's violence and to protecting women the police define as deserving of male protection, then women's demands will only shore up the

> existing relations between men and women rather than secure the feminist aim of autonomy for all women irrespective of class, race, and relationship to heterosexuality.
>
> (Hanmer *et al.* 1989: 5)

Carol Smart (1989: 160) also argued that feminists should avoid strategies focusing on the law because of the law's ability to resist and subvert feminist-inspired reforms and its power to regulate daily life. The power of the law, according to Smart, is affirmed and enhanced through attempts to change it. Feminists should therefore focus on de-centring the law by deconstructing its fundamental premises and by seeking transformative change through alternative avenues.

From the early 1990s a number of feminists returned to the fundamental question of preventing rape. Marcus (1992) for example, wrote a provocative paper also suggesting that women could not afford to wait for adequate legal responses to rape. She advocates a focus on disrupting the ways in which the dominant discourse on rape, or rape script, ascribes the feminine body as vulnerable and powerless thereby disabling that body and the feminine subject. She suggests two related ways women can disrupt this process. The first method, focusing on physical resistance, has found a number of advocates who argue that women can learn to become empowered and self-defence training is critical to this process (see Burton 1998). They argue that there is little evidence to support the assertion that fighting off an attacker increases the risk to the woman and, in fact, physical resistance can, and often does, succeed in foiling rape. While this may be the case in some situations, it is a dangerous strategy to promote, not only because it may be life-threatening but also because it reinforces the existing expectation that women in Japan must resist and failure to do so will be read as consent. Thus, the strategy consolidates the subjugation of women's explanations of alternative responses to rape.

More promising is Marcus's suggestion that women can imagine female sexuality in alternative ways that do not reflect ideas of sexuality as object or property and re-imagine the masculine body in ways that detract from its current representation as overwhelmingly powerful. She suggests focusing on 'the fragility of erections and the vulnerability of male genitalia' (Marcus 1992: 400). In some respects this approach corresponds with Smart's (1996) more recent work in which she attempts to deflate 'the phallic penis and its power'.[2]

Other feminists such as Sheila Noonan (1996) argue that Smart overdraws the 'power of law' in the very move to de-centre it. The law is not monolithic, unidimensional or undifferentiated but, rather, a fractured site containing contradictions and gaps that may be exploited. In other words, there is space for alternative argument and resistance and, thus, law contains the potential to attain at least small, concrete gains for particular women. As such, the law is not an area feminists can afford to ignore. Rather, what is required are new ways of looking at the law and its responses to sexual assault. To some extent this has motivated much of the feminist legal narrative work that seeks to explain and dislodge the hegemony of ideas underlying the conservative approach to rape and its stock stories, the rape script.

Law reform in Japan is likely to be an effective strategy in Japan, for two reasons. First, law has an important symbolic function signalling to the community that particular acts, attitudes or behaviours are unacceptable and no longer condoned. This is particularly important when a society is at a turning point in criminalising a behaviour previously regarded as normal or inevitable such as sexual harassment, stalking, *chikan*, and domestic violence. In this situation, law is placed in the position of having to choose between contesting social positions and to respond to the most forceful outside pressure. Law, then, plays a role in establishing new social standards.[3] Second, through the public and media attention they can attract, trials provide an authoritative forum in which to challenge the rape script. The power of this script has been reinforced by its virtual exclusion from social discourse as a subject of serious discussion because of its inherent unsettling 'unpleasantness', but at the same time, through the commodification of eroticised violence, it has attained a very high level of visibility as harmless private fantasy. Silence, therefore, surrounds the rape script as private fantasy and as taboo subject, sustaining its virtual hegemony and claim to truth in popular and legal discourse. Narratives that break this silence to articulate an alternative 'reality' are, by Ewick and Silbey's definition, 'subversive stories' and as such constitute an important form of resistance (see Olson and Batjer 1999: 141). Subversive stories, articulated both in the courtroom and around the trial, provide the social and legal pressure to which judges must respond.

In the courtroom, subversive stories may be those put forward to disrupt the rape script in order to better articulate the particular woman's experience. Feminist lawyers may also be motivated by long-term goals to use the trial as an opportunity to 're-educate' judges about the broader context of gendered power relations which contextualise the case. Endō's case is discussed below at some length to demonstrate the possibilities and the significant constraints of attempting to articulate an alternative vision within the existing legal framework. Through Endō's case Tsunoda in particular attempts to challenge patriarchal ideology and dominant interpretations of rape and to reconfigure the nature of heterosexual relations and the issue of consent. Given the unlikely chance of achieving a favourable outcome at the Supreme Court level, Tsunoda's strategy appears to have been designed as an explicit challenge to legal orthodoxy. In other cases, this orthodoxy is also being challenged with some success through the introduction of expert opinion which seeks to present a counter-narrative of the harm of sexual violation and, in so doing, expand the range of 'appropriate' responses to sexual violence.

Important strategies of resistance are also developed around and outside the trial. Feminist lawyers in Japan are particularly aware that achieving a successful outcome is often closely tied to demonstrating broad social support – and social interest and debate can be generated around trials. Legal battles have, therefore, been used very effectively in Japan as the focal point for organising and publicising feminist demands for change, and support groups that organise around particular cases are central to this process. Fundamentally, all these strategies are concerned at one level with changing the judicial community's attitudes and this leads to the question of whether or not adding more women to the bench might make a difference. Can women socially situated in a masculine position speak in a feminist voice?

The sanitisation strategy

Particularly given the pervasiveness of blame-the-victim narratives in Japan women are often compelled to tell a story that attempts to completely erase any possible reading of their actions that could be construed as blameworthy. Sanitising the woman's character, behaviour and representations of 'what really happened', is relatively uncomplicated in *tsūjō* rape scenarios. However, this strategy is more problematic in *fushizen* rape cases. Beyond the immediate goal of proving rape, the tactic is deeply flawed because it essentially works within the dominant discourse and reinforces the limited construction of female subjectivity in terms of the dichotomy between ordinary/non-sexual/victim and sexual/non-rapable/Other. However, manoeuvres such as this must be assessed within the broader context of the cultural and legal constraints placed on articulating alternative narratives.

The sanitising strategy is employed because the legal framework within which the woman's story must be constructed constrains the way her narrative can be told. However, the strategy often fails because the woman consequently loses credibility (for a discussion of Australian cases see Kaspiew 1995: 361). 'Sanitised' accounts sometimes result in contradictions, ambiguities and proposals that quite simply sound implausible or absurd. However, statements that appear contradictory, naïve or even highly improbable are not necessarily lies – although they could be. Therapist Janine Roberts notes that trauma victims' contradictory statements may reflect the process of trying to understand what happened in broad social terms, particularly when confronted with stock stories which do not relate a reality that seems familiar (Roberts 1994; see also Espinoza 1997: 913–917). Reinterpretations of one's behaviour and events in retrospect may also reflect the process of coming to an understanding of oneself in relation to what occurred (a process very much emphasised in Japan although this usually is oriented towards identifying one's own responsibility or blameworthiness, that is, *jiseki no nen*). The need to construct stories of total blamelessness, the lengths to which victims go to convince themselves and others that their behaviour was not at fault, is testimony to the strength, constraints and consequences of the blame-the-victim myths that are central to the stock stories of rape.

The failure of the sanitisation strategy to produce a persuasive account of 'what happened' was most clearly expressed in Takahashi and Endō's cases. Because Takahashi's narrative failed to conform to the judge's notion of 'common sense' she was presumed to be lying and deceitful and the judge responded to her with considerable disdain and hostility. Takahashi attempted to resist the implication that her character and behaviour were immoral or sub-standard by offering alternative explanations for why she went to bars, her 'provocative' behaviour in the bar on the night in question, and getting into a car alone with a man she had just met. To counter the narrative that she was frivolous, lacking responsibility or looking for sex, she attempted to construct her identity as a serious woman of good character arguing that her main purpose in frequenting bars was 'studying social behaviour' (*shakai benkyō*) – typically understood as students' experiences in part-time jobs and other forms of social activities and interaction. However, contextualising her activities in terms of this social convention not only sounds quite improbable it was further complicated by the fact that Takahashi was not in her early twenties but, rather, 28 years old.

Takahashi attempted to reinforce her narrative of sobriety, arguing that she generally tries to avoid being drunk, sometimes making herself vomit, but on the night of the rape, to end her part in the drinking game – a form of 'strip poker' – she took off her stockings. Although drinking games are popular in Japan especially among young people, participation places young women in a compromised situation. Such arguments are not unique to Japan (see Young 1998: 451). Conservative social conventions associate drinking, or at least drunkenness, with clearly inappropriate and unfeminine behaviour, implying sexual wantonness and immorality. At the very least, drinking is believed to lead to those ends and should, therefore, be avoided. Takahashi's explanation, therefore, failed to neutralise the defence attorney's compellingly vivid imagery of her waving her stockings around her head.

Aware of the social conventions warning women and girls against getting into a car with a man, Takahashi stated that she agreed because she believed her friends were following in a second car. Takahashi also attempted to support her argument that she exercised reasonable judgement by arguing that she knew the defendant worked at a well-known company and so she thought he must be a 'good person'. The assumption that social status equates with good character has particular social currency in Japan and it is not uncommon for women to mobilise this argument in their defence when their credibility is in question. Similarly, Endō stated that she had believed she could trust her manager because he had graduated from a reputable university. Takahashi's attempts to explain her behaviour as rational or reasonable were not merely interpreted as self-serving lies, but as evidence of her lack of repentance and failure to accept partial responsibility. As a result, her behaviour was interpreted as all the more insidious and morally reprehensible. In short, the sanitisation strategy did not simply fail, but contributed to the condemnation she received.

In Endō's case, the defence narrative constrained and shaped the space within which she could tell her story. The defendant mobilised the familiar narrative of a female temptress inciting men's uncontrollable sexual desires. In order to advance such an argument, the defence had to demonstrate that Endō was not genuinely frightened of the defendant as indicated in the following section of Endō's cross examination:

Defence counsel: Didn't you think that it was dangerous to be left alone with the defendant after him pressuring you for two months?
Endō: I didn't think he would do anything like that.
Defence counsel: Weren't you on your guard (*keikaisuru*) against the defendant?
Endō: That's why I kept fighting him off until then.
Defence counsel: Didn't you think it might be dangerous to go into the store?
Endō: I trusted him because he was a human being as well.
Defence counsel: . . . you said you thought that in the store there would be a discussion about why the events took place or talk of marriage. Did you think the defendant would talk about marriage?
Endō: I thought it was strange to do such things with no meaning.
Defence counsel: Had the defendant ever asked you to marry him before that?
Endō: No.
Defence counsel: What made you think that way?
Endō: Because he suddenly pushed me with such strong force I thought he was overwhelmed by some idea.
Defence counsel: What do you mean by 'the soul is shaken' in this note? [the note is a letter written by Endō to the defendant after the incident]
Endō: Shaking means my fear in softer expression.
Defence counsel: That fear, isn't it fear of the immorality (*haitoku*) of having an affair?
Endō: No, it's not.

(Case 19 Endō)

The defence counsel's questions framed only two possible explanations for Endō's behaviour. First, if the defendant was a real rapist, a reasonable woman (one who is always on guard to protect her body from men's uncontrollable sexual urges) would have been frightened and her natural instinct would be to flee. By not doing so Endō was negligent or foolish. Second, Endō was not merely a compliant actor in the romance narrative but a temptress/adulterer, and her fear related not to the defendant, but to the public exposure of her immorality. This defence strategy of offering a choice between two possible explanations for her behaviour, both serving to undermine Endō's credibility, contracted the space in which she could offer a viable counter-narrative.

The scaffolding on which Endō built her narrative consisted of a sanitised version of her own character and an idealised version of sexual relations within the context of 'pure' love. Every aspect of the case was placed within this framework, even the spatial context of the rape: the floor represented the 'impurity' of the act reinforcing it as rape not romance. A cast of figures were mobilised to represent Endō's essential morality: battler, Christian, wife and mother. At the first trial, the image of a struggling hard-working mother, too busy for love was emphasised:

> with four children . . . and trying to get certification to become a hairdresser, a woman who needed as much money as possible . . . it is difficult to believe that she tearfully confessed she was in love with him. . . . Even if we temporarily put aside the question of whether she could even think about men or love, it would be impossible to have someone else's child while living with her husband so we cannot believe she told the defendant she wanted to have his baby.
>
> (Case 19 Endō)

In the Supreme Court appeal, Tsunoda argued that Endō's interpretation of the defendant's initial attack – his overwhelming love and possible desire to marry – made sense in the context of Endō's Christian faith, which prohibits sex outside marriage. Implicit in this statement are the ideas that angelic purity distances the moral woman from any thought of male lust, and her sexuality (if it exists at all) is located solely within monogamous, heterosexual, legally sanctioned marriage.

Tsunoda attempted to consolidate this characterisation of unambiguous morality by drawing on the quintessential good wife, wise mother. Endō testified that the defendant requested a number of sexual services as if 'he was talking to a prostitute'. Tsunoda argued that 'a normal housewife with four children' could not make up such expressions because they are not part of female vocabulary. While it is true that the particular expressions are generally not used by women, it is more problematic to argue that women have no knowledge of them. All traces of female sexuality were excised from the terrain of the wife and mother. To counter the defence suggestion that Endō lent the defendant the 'pornographic' video *Betty Blue* as a means to seduce him, Tsunoda argued that this could not be construed as consent to sex. She also went to considerable lengths to demonstrate that the video was not pornographic but a very popular French 'art film' which, in any event, Endō did not watch. In addition, it was argued that because there was no love relationship, Endō (as a normal housewife and mother) would not consent to sex and therefore the act must be regarded as rape. The inference, however, is that women *only* consent to sex in the context of love. Why was such a seemingly erroneous argument put forward?

The strategy makes sense in terms of the assumption that to disrupt the dominant discourse of rape it is necessary to draw on an equally familiar and therefore persuasive narrative, which in this case is Japan's powerful discourse on motherhood. The strategic strength of appealing to the context of love pertains to representations of the high social value attributed to motherhood, as woman's fundamental social role and primary source of morality, rather than to ideals of romantic love in the 'Western' sense. The power of such images exists primarily in the domain of discourse or narrative convention rather than in 'reality' or lived experience. The image conveys a sense of women's value in terms of devotion and self-sacrifice rather than sexuality or female sexual pleasure. While the dominant Western image of love signals primarily (hetero)sexual relations, in Japan love is likely to be idealised in the form of the (non-sexual) mother and child relationship. The defendant's 'proof' of Endō's love, that is, her alleged claim to want to have his baby, is testimony to the strength of the link between love and motherhood.

However, the emphasis on contrasting rape with 'pure love' meant that Tsunoda had to interpret the defence argument of a 'relationship' to mean 'love affair'. Yet, the defence argued that the defendant merely responded to Endō's love (expressed as indirect advances) in a direct and understandably sexual manner. In other words, lust (*sukebei*-ness) rather than love was the sub-text of the defence argument. Tsunoda's argument, or at least aspects of it, appears to have inadvertently consolidated the defence position that the driving force in 'their relationship' was the defendant's 'natural' sexual desire, not love.

At all stages of Endō's legal battle, the defendant's story was found to be convincing largely because the sanitised counter-narrative failed to disrupt the dominant narrative of seduction and understandings of male sexuality as natural and uncontrollable. The strength of the seduction narrative is sustained by the lack of social or legal understanding of women's experiences of fear and responses to an attack. More broadly, the legal framework could not accommodate the extent of Endō's experience; she felt there were no words to express and explain her story and so she struggled to find a voice within the existing 'language' of the courtroom. Referring to Western legal systems, but equally applicable to Japan, Nicola Lacey (1998: 116) notes that:

> the language of embodied existence – of pain, shame, loss of self-esteem, the sense of violation and objectification – find no place within formal legal categories: nothing in those categories invites the victim

> to construct her testimonial narrative in the terms which empirical research suggest would best relate her experience. . . . Rape victims giving evidence in court are effectively silenced, caught between the equally inept discourses of the body as property, framed by legal doctrine but incapable of accommodating their experience, and the feminine identity as body, which pre-judges their experience by equating it with stereotyped and denigrating views of female sexuality.

The assessment of such legal constraints, in terms of the dominant narratives and categories informing rape law, frequently indicates to feminist lawyers the necessity of employing the largely unsatisfactory strategy of reproducing dominant essentialist representations of woman in order to achieve the immediate goal of conviction. However, given the limited range of alternatives, 'collusion' is one potential and pragmatic means of achieving success in the trial because the narrative that most conforms to 'common sense' is likely to be the most convincing. The danger, realised in Takahashi and Endō's cases, is that the story just 'doesn't add up' and the woman loses credibility.

Challenging patriarchy: constructions of heterosexuality and rapists

Another challenge to the rape script in Endō's case was based on the argument that dominant discourses construct rape within the parameters of the social institution of heterosexuality. Rape, narrowly defined in terms of the penetration of the vagina by the penis, privileges the male experience of heterosexual sex. Other forms of sexual violation are excluded from the legal definition of rape even though they may be experienced in terms no different from or no less abusive than forced penile–vagina penetration. These acts may constitute *kyōsei waisetsu* (indecent assault), but this crime is regarded as less serious than rape as indicated by the sentence (see Appendix 1). Tsunoda attempts to link rape with dominant expressions of heterosexual relations and demonstrate the difficulty in differentiating between the two within the patriarchal framework:

> The fact that after the first incident of sexual harassment she did not try to avoid him . . . was interpreted as forgiveness or submission. This amounts to convenient male logic. . . . In society, 'no' is interpreted to mean 'yes' which denies women's sexual freedom. It is difficult to understand what the court expects of her, that is, what more must she do besides saying 'no'? If he does not stop after saying 'no', she could kick or punch him, but women are not educated in this way and so in reality few women can do this.
>
> (Case 19 Endō: 25)

However, Tsunoda infers that the defendant exhibited a normal or general 'male mentality', that is, not something peculiar to an image of a cruel sadistic rapist. Putting the question of the validity of the argument aside, it may well be that articulated here such arguments might have been counter-productive. The challenge to the image of the pathological rapist was too subtle or too abstract to make an impact and, therefore, Tsunoda's argument may have been read as a further endorsement of the story constructed by the defence. The cases analysed in this study suggest that the accused are not always, and perhaps rarely, constructed as pathological deviants – that this is only the case in extreme *tsūjō* rape scenarios. More frequently, men who rape are constructed as normal healthy young men who cross a fine line between the use of acceptable and unacceptable degrees of force and coercion, and in many situations the mistake is regarded as understandable.

Similarly, Suzuki, Endō's lawyer in the first trial, argued that the defendant's subsequent regret and unstable emotional state was evidence of his sense of guilt, 'proving' the act was rape. However, the rapist with a conscience is not part of the familiar narrative. If the use of coercion or force is acknowledged and causes guilt, the act cannot be rape, but that perpetrated by a man who succumbed, albeit over-excitedly, to his natural instincts, and his sense of regret may be read as evidence of his fundamental humanity. Suzuki also pointed out that in explaining the lack of conversation, the defendant stated that while he was 'doing it with the plaintiff' he was 'excited and not thinking'. Suzuki interpreted his response as an indication that he had no consideration for the plaintiff's feelings and that he was captive to his sexual urges. However, this is the very point of the seduction narrative. The argument, therefore, fails to resonate with images of rape and reinforces the 'ordinariness' or naturalness of the defendant's conduct.

It is clear that Tsunoda used Endō's appeal as an opportunity to challenge the *tsūjō* rape script and educate the judges about the impact of rape trials on women:

> The original judgment says her statement was not trustworthy which means she was lying about the rape. In Japan today, is there any woman who willingly says she has been raped and tells superiors and colleagues about the incident in order to take a man to court? What has she to gain? . . . The social and legal situation in which the victim is accused and the rapist walks free is common. Given this reality, she has nothing to gain by lying about being raped. Unfortunately it is the reality that the victim is humiliated a second or third time through the court process. This may be invisible to male eyes but many women know it and therefore victims remain silent.
>
> (Case 19 Endō: 95)

Perhaps because of the confrontational style in which Tsunoda phrased her arguments and, perhaps, because other challenges to patriarchal discourse were framed in rather abstract terms, the strategy failed to disrupt conventional images of 'the rapist' and *tsūjō* rape. Moreover, it is possible these images were augmented and consolidated in the attempt to challenge them.

De-centring force and resistance: reconceptualising consent

Endō's case also presented the opportunity to extend the challenge to patriarchal ideology and its construction of heterosexual relations by reconceptualising the issue of consent. The liberal theory of rape (outlined in Chapter 4) focuses on the issue of an abstract right to property in one's body devoid of social context. However, as there is no gender-neutral body and rape is overwhelmingly perpetrated by men against women (and the legal precondition for rape in Japan), the liberal position assumes that consent (or not) is expressed by a feminine body – inscribed as passive – in response to an act assumed to have been initiated by a masculine body – inscribed as aggressive. Consent within this framework, therefore, serves to legitimise the power relations underlying the dominant discourse on rape. Moreover, because in many cases consent is not easily ascertained (since female sexuality is perceived as culpable), interpretations of rape law in Japan focus on the degrees of force and resistance. The issue of consent is, therefore, subsumed by the requirement of the woman to demonstrate adequate resistance to prove force was used. To determine rape, the focus of the trial therefore shifts from an examination of the defendant's behaviour to the woman because she is seen as responsible for granting or denying sexual access. The difficulty in proving lack of consent is compounded by the narrative of romance and seduction in which sex obtained by force or coercion can be redefined as consent in the form of submission.

Based on their critique of heterosexuality and the exclusion of women's experiences of rape, Suzuki and Tsunoda attempted the ambitious project of using the framework of love grounded in notions of motherhood to propose a reconsideration of rape law, constructions of heterosexuality and ideas about consent. They attempt to place the issue of consent at the centre of the law of rape and to construct that consent in terms of mutuality which assumes an empowered female role in heterosexual relations and a relationship of responsibility between women and men (see also Ehara 1995: 111–116; Lacey 1998: 118–124). This redefinition of (hetero)sex thus incorporates a sense of relational autonomy and integrity for women. Their approach to consent is, thus, significantly different from that assumed in the liberal theory of rape, because it contextualises consent within a perspective of embodied autonomy which highlights the relational aspect of sex. The project, therefore, serves to reshape power relations in terms of an alternative vision of sexuality and subjectivity. The implication for rape law is that space is constructed for women to convey their consent (or not) to sex as mutual partners in an equal relationship while, at the same time, placing emphasis on men's responsibility to confirm consent.

Endō's narrative assumes that sexual access would be denied by a good mother under any circumstances other than a relationship of mutual respect and love. The onus is thus placed on the defendant to provide evidence of love and affirmation of consent. Negotiating this redefinition of rape within the discourse of motherhood and pure love, reinforces the understanding of woman as citizen with legitimate social rights (such as freedom and bodily autonomy) which the state has an obligation to protect. As such, the legal argument gains legitimacy and thus makes considerable strategic sense.

Suzuki positioned the issue of Endō's lack of consent as the fundamental element of rape, arguing that the manager was the initiator of all sexual activity and he was only concerned with achieving his own sexual gratification and, therefore, Endō could not have consented because there was no love between them. Suzuki went to considerable lengths to establish this point emphasising the defendant's expression '*yarinige kana*?' ('root and run?')[4] was an unlikely expression between a loving couple, confirmed by the defendant's confusion and inability to adequately explain why he used the expression. The lack of conversation between them before and after sexual intercourse, and the defendant's sense of regret following sexual intercourse were also tendered as further evidence that theirs was not a loving relationship. Similarly, Tsunoda argued that the defendant treated her as a 'mere sex object' and attempted to redefine rape and complicate masculine constructions of 'normal' heterosexual relations:

> [the defendant] did not ask why she entered [the office], but as soon as she did he kissed and embraced her. He did not ask if this was acceptable or not . . . he just assumed she would not refuse him, probably thinking it was not necessary to ask. This behaviour illustrates the particular male mentality towards women that does not respect women's sexual freedom . . . this does not respect the foundation of male and female relations.
>
> (Case 19 Endō: 42)

Tsunoda's construction of consent invokes a form of liberal feminist ethics in terms of emphasising the individual responsibility to respect and not harm others. In the legal context of rape the expectation is that the defendant must demonstrate that the woman actively consented to sex, thus precluding the possibility of submission (which conveys no suggestion of free will) being interpreted as consent (see Smart 1989: 33–49, 1995: 113; West 1996: 233–251). The argument is reinforced by an appeal to liberal democratic notions of rights and freedom through an analogy to theft:

> if a man takes a woman's purse and she screams 'give it back, don't steal it', but she does not hit him, could he argue that she gave it to him before he ran away? The reason no-one would accept that the purse was given with consent is that it is obvious that the possessive right to the purse must be clearly surrendered verbally. . . . women's sexual freedom which is the right to make decisions about whether and how to engage in sex . . . requires the clear expression of consent and it cannot be said a woman accepted a relationship only because she did not refuse it by using force.
>
> (Case 19 Endō: 23)

The difficulty in disrupting the seduction narrative, which pivots around the idea of submission, by drawing an analogy with theft is partly that both arguments are premised on the same contradictory idea that female sexuality is regarded as both an inalienable object owned by an individual and something that can be taken from her or given away. Moreover, the idea of sexuality as a possession situates the harm of rape primarily as something that has been taken illegally. This idea limits the possibilities of framing rape in terms of alternative experiences of harm such as the infliction of shame, humiliation and degradation, feelings of worthlessness and guilt, violation of trust, stigmatisation, objectification and exploitation. In line with the argument, presented in Chapter 2, that rape constructs the feminine body as pre-victim, Sharon Marcus (1992: 399) succinctly states that, 'the horror of rape is not that it steals something away from us but that it makes us into things that can be taken'.

Expert witness evidence

The primary goals of feminist legal strategies are to achieve more convictions, to have sexual violence taken more seriously by expanding the understanding of the harm caused by sexual violence and, more importantly perhaps, the empowerment of women who have been victimised. When introducing a strategy to win a case all these factors need to be taken into consideration in conjunction with balancing the short-term goals of achieving a conviction and the broader long-term goals of achieving feminist-inspired transformative social and legal change.

Even a cursory examination of sexual assault trials in Japan clearly indicates that the judicial imagination accommodates only a very limited repertoire of responses to fear and women's stories of fear are frequently rejected because they sound 'unnatural', 'illogical', 'untrustworthy' or 'suspicious'. In Atsumi's case the judge inferred that if a woman is truly upset (read 'truly raped') it is unnatural to think of trying to make the offender 'feel bad' (Case 17 Atsumi: 277). In Nakajima's case the judge considered it illogical that a woman could feel anything but hatred for a man who had raped her (Case 12 Nakajima: 336). In the Sapporo sexual harassment case it was argued that to calm down soon after an indecent assault is unnatural (Case 23 Sapporo: 14). In the Akita sexual harassment case, a woman's 'rational' question after an indecent assault was considered unnatural and suspicious (Case 26 Akita: 49–50). In Endō's case failing to flee after the first sexual assault was seen as unnatural.

Although research in the field of trauma in Japan has developed significantly in the last decade, this body of knowledge has rarely been used in criminal cases involving a sexual assault and has only recently been used in civil cases of sexual harassment. Tsunoda stated that a few years earlier, when working on a marital damages claim involving a charge of rape, she could not find an expert witness to explain 'rape trauma syndrome'. She, therefore, translated and submitted US articles on the subject (interview Tsunoda 8 April 1997). It is possible that some judges, like some of their British counterparts, tend to resist the introduction of evidence by experts in newer fields of human behaviour whose knowledge might contest the conventional wisdom of legal expertise (see Smart 1989: 47). Nevertheless, some judges in Japan are now accepting expert evidence and, as in other countries, this has resulted in some successes in disrupting dominant rape scripts. Expert witnesses have challenged conventional understandings of the very limited range of 'normal' victim behaviours during and after a sexual assault by introducing ideas about the psychological injury caused by rape and explaining the woman's response in this light. The emphasis on *shakai tsūnen* (see Chapter 3) implies that judges and lawyers must remain in touch with influential debates taking place in the social environment within which law operates and this can be facilitated by expert witness evidence (see Mossman 1998: 33).

As noted in the Prelude, expert testimony was central to the success of the Ikebukuro appeal case. However, according to Tsunoda the persuasiveness of that evidence had much to do with the reputation and respect for the expert witness, psychologist Professor Fukushima Akira of Sophia University. This leads to the question of who gets to claim 'expert' status. Are prominent academics necessarily more knowledgeable or in a better position to speak for victimised women than rape crisis centre workers for example? The Ikebukuro case also suggests that professionals such as the psychiatrist quoted in the magazine, may well be used to subvert feminist claims about the nature of sexuality and the harm of sexual violence. Carol Smart (1989: 47) warns that introducing expert witnesses to speak for 'victims' fundamentally affirms their victim status and thereby achieves the empowerment not of women but of what she calls the 'psy' professions: 'women would be saved from the law, only to be surrendered to the "psy" complex' (see also Breckenridge 1999). Georgina Feldberg (1997: 89–114) is also sceptical about the use of expert witnesses. Her examination of the role of medical evidence (of penetration, semen, physical and/or emotional trauma) in sexual assault cases in Ontario found that the use of medical evidence not only failed to achieve more convictions, but complainants frequently stated that the expert testimony led to feelings of 'being an exhibit'.

However, the introduction of the concept of 'rape trauma syndrome', which explains women's inability to resist due to fear, does appear to have had some success in disrupting the dominant discourses of rape and victim response in Japanese sexual harassment cases (see Weatherfield 1995a, b). Presumably, this is because sexual harassment is a relatively new area of civil complaint. Many of the earlier Japanese sexual harassment cases were interpreted on the basis of the dominant legal discourse on rape, requiring evidence of force and resistance. However, more recently two of these decisions (the Akita and Yokohama cases) have since been overturned in the appeal on the recognition that women are not compelled to resist.

Expert evidence of rape trauma syndrome was also central to the successful outcome of the Kyoto sexual harassment case which involved rape and a coercive sexual relationship lasting seven years between a notable university professor and his research assistant (Tsunoda interview 8 April 1997). In the similar Kumamoto sexual harassment case, involving a professional badminton player raped in a hotel by a director of the Badminton Association, there were many elements of the *fushizen* rape scenario: prior to the rape they had been drinking and having dinner together, she did not report the rape immediately, she could not remember the exact date of the rape, and she continued to have a sexual relationship with the defendant for approximately six months. The defence put forward the familiar narrative of a woman scorned in love seeking vengeance. Nevertheless, the frequency with which the judgment referred in detail to Inoue Maiko's expert evidence (but not her profession or basis for her expertise) is testimony to its centrality in convincing the judge of the woman's experience of trauma.

Inoue Maiko explained that the trauma of rape can cause victims to subconsciously block their memory of the incident, that the plaintiff's seemingly 'normal' behaviour after the incident is common and that the fact that she remained in a sexual relationship with the defendant was understandable:

> When the defendant said he wanted to marry her she knew she could not deny the fact of the rape, but she thought that at least the reason for the rape was his love and not mere violence and this made her feel a little better. As a result, she tried to trust what he said by continuing the sexual relationship.
>
> (Case 31 Kumamoto)

Expert witness testimony was also used in the Utsunomiya sexual harassment case which began in December 1992 and was finally settled out of court in December 1997. Communication scholars Eric M. Kramer of Oklahoma University and Ikeda Richiko of International Christian University in Tokyo, submitted expert evidence (*kantei ikenshō*) regarding a 'gendered communication gap' as a cause of sexual harassment. It is difficult to gauge how influential the expert evidence actually was in this case as the parties came to a private settlement before judgment. Nevertheless, on the basis of the judge's pressure the company agreed to virtually all of Kikuchi's demands and according to Hikaru Koichi, a member of Kikuchi's legal support group, she considered the outcome an overwhelming success (personal communication, 30 December 1997).

While it is necessary to heed the warnings of feminist critiques of the use of expert opinion, given the Japanese procedural emphasis on evaluation of documentary evidence outside the courtroom rather than during the trial, it may be possible to use expert evidence in a manner that facilitates rather than displaces women's voices. In addition, given the general social deference to authority it may well be necessary to frame alternative narratives in 'expert' terms. Also, as noted by Endō, it may well be that the legitimation of victim status, in itself, is a significant gain for some women despite valid feminist reservations about the term. In an environment that systematically denies the harm of rape and discrimination against women, the validation of such harms, albeit in problematic 'victim' terms, may well be perceived as an important victory. Therefore, although it is by no means a solution, the claim to victim status has significant advantages in a context of limited alternatives.

Moreover, in the case of Japan where the law of rape remains focused on the standard of force and resistance, it is crucial to challenge judges' assumptions regarding responses to sexual attacks. It is possible that increasingly successful outcomes in sexual harassment cases, due partially to expert opinion evidence, may lead to an increased understanding of women's experiences of sexual assault and challenges to legal processes. One clear example of this took place recently in Osaka when, on 13 December 1999, after only two hearings in an uncontested case, the Court found the governor of Osaka (and former comedian), 'Knock' Yokoyama, guilty of sexually harassing a 21-year-old woman who worked as part of his campaign staff. Yokoyama was ordered to pay a record ¥11,000,000 (*The Japan Times*, 13 December 1999). Although the case was, in many respects, a victory for the woman, his failure to apologise or resign prompted her to file further criminal charges of indecent assault. It is widely believed that strong public opinion was instrumental in pushing the Prosecutor's Office to act (cited in Kenzo 1999) and on 10 August 2000, Yokoyama received an 18-month prison sentence, suspended for three years (*The Japan Times*, 21 March 2000).

It is likely that the Yokoyama case has made its biggest social and legal impact at the symbolic level, particularly given the significant media attention it has attracted. The case opens up a space in which to challenge the civil/criminal distinction in legal process, which reinforces the conventional idea that violence against women in the family (and in the broad sense this has included companies and their employees)[5] is distinct from, and less harmful than, violence against non-family members 'on the street' – the accepted public arena of state intervention and control.[6] Taking a case of sexual harassment to civil trial certainly challenges the discourse that links ideas of company, family and privacy. But to then take the same case to the criminal court reinforces the challenge to the public/private distinction, provides a space in which to challenge conventional understandings of the nature of male sexuality, power and the role of law, and amplifies the message that sexual violence is a serious matter wherever it takes place (see Roth 1999). The boundary between the public and the private is disrupted by highlighting the occurrence of sexual, hence 'private', conduct in public space such as work, education and transportation, and also the significance of gendered social power relations in defining and defending that privacy. These cases resist the dominant social narrative that women must simply accept and put up with men's sexual incursions by redefining that activity in terms of harm. The Yokoyama case may encourage or give confidence to other women who wish to proceed with criminal rather than civil proceedings. Whether this is a more satisfactory option for women is another question. Nevertheless, there is evidence that cases involving sexual violence are being approached with greater sensitivity in the broader community, at least in terms of public debate, and this has been reflected in recent public policies on issues relating to victims of sexual violence (discussed further on).

Law reform: reconfiguring rape as assault

In contrast to many Anglo-American countries, rape law reform has not received a great deal of attention in Japan. Some feminists have argued that criminal procedures need to be changed to ease the difficulties of women testifying in court and that sentencing in rape cases should reflect the seriousness of the crime and therefore be stiffer than that for robbery (see Tsunoda 1991; Miya 1984: 186–198). However, there has been little attention to the actual wording of the rape law, partly because its interpretation is regarded as the major problem.

Nevertheless, there has been some discussion on redefining rape as an act of violence, and assault. Kinjō (1990: 34–35) and Hayashi (1990: 28–31), for example, argue that rape may be taken more seriously if a single standard of morality and equal treatment can be implemented. Given the relative success in implementing formal equality reforms since the mid-1980s in Japan and the government's strict equality approach to labour reforms,[7] it is understandable that feminists have proposed reforms to rape law within the sex-neutral equality framework.[8] It is possible that if an act can be identified as discriminatory, the government may be obliged to address the issue on the basis of the Constitutional guarantee of equality between the sexes. Kinjō (1990: 32), for example, argues that:

> Concerning acts that violate sexual freedom . . . the Criminal Code treats people differently according to their sex. Rape pertains only to acts of sexual violation of women (with a minimum of two years imprisonment). Outside this, (where penetration has not occurred and the sexual violation of men) a lighter penalty is incurred (maximum seven years imprisonment). While these are the same acts of sexual violation, the heavier penalty for acts of violation against women stands in opposition to the Constitution that guarantees equality under the law.

The redefinition of rape as assault has several merits, not least that it can be incorporated quite readily into existing systems (for NSW reforms see L'Orange and Egger 1987: 12–38; for reforms in Canada see Los 1992: 160–171). More importantly, because consent is irrelevant to the law of assault, redefining rape as violence theoretically avoids the difficulty of having to prove non-consent, particularly important given the emphasis on the force-resistance standard. Theoretically, redefining rape as assault also precludes any justification for raising the issue of a woman's sexual history. In addition, emphasising the violence of rape may encourage legal administrators to take the offence more seriously and (male) judges who are unlikely to have experienced rape may deal more effectively with such cases if they can empathise with the victim (of assault) rather than the defendant (as men with 'naturally' aggressive sexual urges) (Scutt 1990: 471). Some feminists also argue that if rape is perceived in terms of violence it is possible more convictions would result because the social stigma of rape is avoided (Hayashi 1990: 30; Scutt 1990: 471). Presumably, (male) judges are reluctant to convict a man for an act that, given the acceptance of *yūkeiryoku*, looks similar to 'normal' sex and with which they can easily identify.

However, this difficulty in distinguishing rape from sex is not adequately addressed by the proposal to redefine rape as sexual assault, emphasising the violent nature of rape rather than the sexual component. Contrary, perhaps, to the cases that come before the courts, most rapes do not involve extensive violence leaving visible physical evidence and establishing rape is most difficult in these sorts of cases.[9] Thus, emphasising violence may make it even more difficult to prove rape and it also serves to downplay the psychological harm of rape, an issue that has only recently begun to be recognised in Japan. Tsunoda (1990: 46) notes that in compensation claims courts tend to gauge the extent of injury largely on the basis of whether or not the woman was a virgin, while little attention is paid to the psychological impact of rape. Moreover, privileging violence obscures the sexual component of rape, which fundamentally distinguishes it from other forms of assault:

> the individual women rape victims who prosecute their cases were marked by the threat of rape – simply because they were women –

> long before their bodies were actually violated, and that their experience of rape is not exhausted (although it is certainly dominated) by the one particular incident which commands the court's attention.
> (Cahill 2000: 59)

Rape as assault silences fundamentally important questions concerning gendered power relations and the social construction of heterosexuality.

Manipulating the rhetoric of rights

Japanese legal arguments that aim to disrupt dominant narratives of rape draw on rights rhetoric, however, this has had little impact on shifting the thinking on rape. Tsunoda notes that while it is now commonplace to acknowledge that the appropriate *hogohōeki* of rape law is women's human rights rather than chastity, there has been little discussion of this issue and, therefore, the meaning of women's human rights has not been clarified sufficiently to impact on the dominant interpretation of rape law (Tsunoda, interview 8 April 1997). Nevertheless, more success has been achieved in recent sexual harassment cases where the woman's position can be framed more forcefully using legally recognisable gender-neutral categories of citizen and worker. New legislation banning sexual discrimination and harassment at the workplace is incorporated into the revision of the Equal Employment Opportunity Law (hereafter EEOL), which took effect on 1 April 1999. Prior to the legislation, feminist lawyers succeeded in some cases in demonstrating that sexual harassment was a violation of women's human rights and sexual freedom and, as such, a form of sex discrimination violating Article 709 of the Civil Code and/or Article 14 of the Constitution (see Appendix 1).[10]

The first legal victory for the plaintiff in a sexual harassment case contested in the Japanese courtroom was the Fukuoka decision handed down in 1992.[11] The decision by the plaintiff and her lawyers to take the case to court as a case of sexual harassment rather than slander was partially motivated by the desire to bring about social and legal change beyond the case itself. Tsunoda, who was part of the legal team representing the plaintiff, states that the case provided the opportunity to guide social and legal attitudes towards the understanding that sexual discrimination is a violation of women's fundamental human rights and to use the law to prevent sexual harassment. The presumed preventative effect of law was based on the observation that US companies spend much time and money on the education of workers to prevent sexual harassment, due to the high costs incurred in a law suit (Tsunoda 1991: 191). How effective this strategy has been in the US or Japan is a question beyond the scope of this study, but the general question of whether law reform has a 'prophylactic effect' (Thornton 1991: 460) is a central and difficult one for feminist law reformers.[12]

Pragmatic use can be made of rights rhetoric because claims phrased in this way draw on established discourse associated with the ideals of democracy and freedom. They give the claim legitimacy and can draw the state's attention to a particular problem (Rhode 1993). However, rights discourse is problematic for feminism in a number of ways. Like most reform strategies, rights claims do not provide solutions to problems, partly because they tend to oversimplify complex power relations. As Smart (1989: 144) notes, they 'transpose the problem into one that is defined as having a legal solution'. Moreover, the rhetoric of rights can be easily appropriated by any group because, as Catharine MacKinnon (1983: 658) argues, law's propensity to define the world in male terms under the guise of objectivity and neutrality means that '[a]bstract rights will authorize the male experience of the world'. However, while MacKinnon's insight and rhetorical style are inspiring, her analysis often over-determines the nature of law and gender relations, thus foreclosing possibilities for feminist interventions. Mileage has been made out of using rights discourse in Japan and elsewhere and, in a situation of limited alternatives or an acceptance that change is going to be gradual, it might be unwise to dismiss the utilisation of rights rhetoric out of hand. Certainly, rape law in Japan has not been particularly receptive to this type of strategy but the same cannot be said for claims of sexual harassment. Moreover, the idea of rights is useful as a mechanism for inspiring political mobilisation.

Mobilising strength: support groups as resistance

Trials are not always only about achieving individual outcomes. In Japan (and elsewhere) trials are an important resource from which to generate political mobilisation, to register resistance to dominant discourses and to produce subversive stories. The effectiveness of using trials as a political strategy involves a process of mutual reinforcement between the woman at the centre of the trial, those who lend her their support, and her lawyers (see Olson and Batjer 1999).

Of course, some cases are more likely to foster interest and popular support than others. Endō had only a small support group, but a rape case is unlikely to generate the same amount of public interest as a sexual harassment case, for the same reason that the Ikebukuro case failed to gain support beyond a group of women explicitly involved in feminist activism. Women do not want to identify with prostitutes or rape victims – the two having too much in common. In popular discourse 'ordinary' women's status and 'protection' from sexual violence lies in the demarcation between themselves and those guilty of sexual transgression, both prostitutes and women who have been raped. Sexual harassment, in contrast, is now widely recognised as a common experience among women in a broad range of socio-economic circumstances and employment situations. It is, therefore, more likely to unite women as sex-neutral 'workers' than to divide them.

However, this may not be the case for women in 'elite' (usually male-dominated) professions, who generally benefit from equality legislation that provides them with the same advantages as similarly situated men. A 1997 survey of female lawyers in Japan, for example, concluded the elite status of women lawyers prevented them, particularly those under 30 years of age, from recognising gendered discrimination and the problems of differently situated women. For example, '32 per cent thought that "the claim of sexual harassment is an over-reaction on the part of the women involved"' (Kaminaga and Westhoff 2003: 478). Nevertheless, Tsunoda (interview 8 April 1997) notes that, among lawyers, while the general level of interest in sexual violence is still not particularly high, it has increased as a result of UN conferences that legitimise the seriousness of these issues.

Ironically, the current social support demonstrated around sexual harassment trials started with two cases in the mid-1980s involving a prostitute and a stripper. These two cases galvanised feminist interest in sexual violence and signalled a shift in thinking about gender relations. In the first case, known as the 'Nishi Funabashi case', the woman pushed a drunken man who was sexually harassing her and he fell off the railway station platform and was killed by an on-coming train. The woman was arrested for murder and, during the 18-month trial ending in 1986, a group mobilised to provide support. The woman's lawyer commented that their assistance had probably contributed to the woman's eventual acquittal (cited in Ikeda 1995: 184). The second case was the very similar 1987 Ikebukuro case discussed in the Prelude. An article published in the women's journal *Femin Fujin Minshu Shinbun* garnered support for the woman and the resulting group provided her with assistance, conducted discussions on issues of gender and prostitution, and organised a petition. The group thus contributed to raising awareness of gender issues within the community. It was also the group who in the appeal sought the assistance of Tsunoda Yukiko, then advisor to the Tokyo Rape Crisis Centre, and the team of lawyers succeeded in having the woman's sentence suspended.

These early support groups consisted primarily of committed feminist activists, many of whom continue their involvement in this area. However, support groups of more recent cases include a much broader cross-section of women and a few men. The lawyers involved in these cases play an important role in sustaining and mobilising these groups. This form of resistance is used in almost all sexual harassment cases and the significant numbers of participants indicates shifting social attitudes in this area.[13] It is also notable that defence parties appear to be concerned with the influence of these groups. At one of the hearings towards the end of the Utsunomiya case, so many people arrived at the courthouse that 'straws' had to be drawn to determine the observers allowed into the courtroom.[14] Once in the courtroom there were quite a number of vacant seats indicating that the defence had probably enlisted the defendant company's employees to subvert the woman's attempt to fill the room with her supporters. Court attendance is widely believed to influence judges in terms of demonstrating significant social interest in the issue (Miya 1989: 15; Yunomae 1989: 45–53). Public expressions of concern are particularly important in Japan where legal personnel tend to view the role of law as necessarily following, rather than guiding, social opinion (Goodman 1986: 27–28). For this reason, the Utsunomiya support group consistently tried to gain media coverage of the trial and they held a strategically timed symposium on sexual harassment on 5 July 1997, shortly before the anticipated judgment of the case.

Members of support groups attend trial hearings and a meeting after each hearing in which the lawyers explain the proceedings and their thoughts on the direction of the case. This is usually followed by a general discussion and then at least part of the group moves on to relax and, importantly, to buoy the spirits of the complainant, at a coffee shop or restaurant. Some members participate in a more politically active role such as writing articles to be published in the *mini-komi* to keep a broader audience up to date with the progress of the case and related issues. It is often difficult to identify patterns in decision-making, actions and power relations, partly because the judicial process isolates or individualises each case (see Olson and Batjer 1999: 140). *Mini-komi* is, therefore, a vitally important forum to formulate ways to link seemingly disparate phenomena and thereby think about new ways to conceptualise sexual violence and its impact on women's lives. It is only through this process of listening to alternative accounts of sexual violence and producing new ways to think about the effects of sexual violence that it is possible to disrupt the privileged knowledge produced in judgments. The *mini-komi* also constitute a fundamental means of sustaining and extending political mobilisation. Support groups, thus, play a crucial role in the resistance strategies formulated around the law, at the broad level of shifting social attitudes and, more specifically, in influencing judges in individual cases.

Re-educating judges

Many issues of the newsletter *Women in Japan Today*, published by the Office for Gender Equality, include a small section on the increasing numbers of female professionals in the criminal justice system. Reaching equivalence in terms of numbers may be read simply as the achievement of equality, but the underlying assumption is that the representation of women in powerful positions will serve to advance the interests of women as a group. Thus, increasing the numbers of women in the legal professions aims to correct any 'male bias' within the judiciary and elsewhere in the criminal justice system and to make the system more responsive to women's experiences, such as sexual victimisation. However, rather than waiting for this assumed process of gaining 'knowledge by osmosis' (Keeton 1988) to take place, Fukushima (1997: 296) recommends training programmes about sexual assault for judges and law students, following the government-funded US and Australian examples. Although lawyer Hayashi Yōko (interview 12 December 1996) is sceptical of the extent to which judges would be shifted in their thinking, training programmes may not be difficult to implement as judges regularly participate in courses on current legal issues, mostly sponsored by the Supreme Court. This sort of training has also begun in the police force with lectures given by lawyers working with the Tokyo Rape Crisis Centre.

Strategies to shift judicial perceptions are based on the recognition that 'judicial bias' or the lack of understanding of women's experiences of sexual assault is due, at least partially, to judges' limited life experiences. While the particular process of legal education and training of the judiciary in Japan exacerbates this problem, the paucity of judges' life experiences is not unique to Japan. Canadian judge Maryka Omatsu notes that judges do not:

> set out to twist laws and misrepresent facts prejudicially to advantage institutions and individuals with whom they identify on class grounds (though this may sometimes happen). Rather, their lack of experience of the daily lives of working-class people and the circumstances and functioning of specifically working-class institutions, such as trade unions, deprives them of potentially relevant information on which to make impartial judgments. This lack of experience will especially be apparent regarding findings of fact and judgments of motive, but perhaps it may also sometimes create blind spots affecting findings of law as well.
>
> (Omatsu 1997: 7)

The significance of judges' life experience leads Omatsu to argue that female judges are better placed to fully appreciate all aspects of sexual harassment. While this may well be the case, it does not mean that female judges can easily transform those experiences into more sympathetic hearings, or that they are likely to convict more readily. Endō's initial trial and a number of sexual harassment cases in which the defendants were acquitted, including the first trials in the Yokohama and Tokyo cases were heard by female judges. Tsunoda (interview 8 April 1997) suggests that the female judges in these cases seemed to want to distance themselves from the complainants, indicating that the judicial demands of objectivity requires women to deny a female subject position, their elite status depending on their identification with the socially masculine position (see also MacKinnon 1987). Similarly, Schultz (2003: iv) summarises findings from a range of countries that suggest female judges are no more likely than their male counterparts to be sympathetic to victims of sexual violence.

For the *Minshohō* school and others who accept a positivist account of adjudication, those who argue that judicial decision-making is a rational logical process based on the application of objective rules and 'facts', the gender of the judge must be inconsequential to the judicial findings. For a judge to speak as a woman, to draw on and acknowledge her personal experience would represent bias, to defy the objectivity and neutrality of law – the very basis for which law claims the ability to know 'truth' and hence claim authority. If a judge was to speak as a woman it would, therefore, be in defiance of law and the woman judge would lose credibility. Female judges are thus constrained by, and victims of, both the 'violence of law' and of patriarchal society (Berns and Baron 1994).

Nevertheless, Sandra Berns and Paula Baron suggest that it is possible for a female judge to express an alternative 'feminine voice' – by this they mean someone who is located outside the historically constituted male interpretive legal community and one who is prepared to speak out of 'otherness'. To do so, they argue, situates such judges closer to the goal of achieving justice. However, to speak out and maintain the authoritative position of judge is only possible by working surreptitiously within accepted legal conventions. Women judges, they contend, can work 'the gap between legality and justice' by ensuring decisions are represented as just and enforceable by law. This is achieved by constructing the judgment in such a way that the decision appears inevitable:

> the feminine. . .must make its appearance, not on the face of the text, but through the inevitability of the narrative of the text, so that the decision seems, feels, as if it could not have been other than it is. The difference *différance* makes must be read, not as difference but as legality if the text is to become self-enforcing legal and legitimate (and inevitable). . . . While the text may, indeed, speak the feminine, it must be read as only speaking the law. . . . For the other to be heard at all, *différance* must be heard as force [the force of law], and that force become inevitable. The meanings of the author must become, somehow, self-enforcing, speak at a level at once beneath and beyond interpretation, so that to speak as a woman becomes to speak as a judge.
>
> (Berns and Baron 1994: 147–148)

Berns and Baron's proposal thus suggests that the task of the feminist judge is to mask and make invisible her attempts to produce an alternative vision of gendered power relations. In a sense the proposal draws on and uses the insights of poststructuralist or deconstructive theory to construct a narrative that mimics disembodied objective legal Truth. The potential pragmatic advantages of this strategy are clear, but from an epistemological point of view the problem with their argument is that it restores the privileged discourse of law and its power to define and normalise heterosexual and gender relations, albeit in a potentially more sensitive voice.

Thornton (1998: 170) extends the argument of Berns and Baron to some extent by similarly suggesting that as the number of women in the legal professions increases, the 'presence of a diverse range of "others" corrodes, although does not efface, the flawed presuppositions of the imagined masculine and the fictive feminine'. Thornton (1998: 148) insists that the cultural constructions of gender must be carefully deconstructed and de-centred for it is here that we can most adequately explain why, despite the now large numbers of women in the jurisprudential community (50 per cent of law students and almost 30 per cent of practising professionals in Australia), women are not fully accepted in that community and continue to be constrained in their ability to make a greater impact on transforming law's role in the production of social relations. In the Japanese context, deconstruction of *sukebei* masculinity and the discursive dominance of the rape script are critical.

Domestic and international pressure

There has been a significant shift in public awareness regarding sexual violence over the past decade, as indicated by Justice Minister Usui Hideo who stated that three recent bills were a response to increasing public demands (*The Japan Times*, 17 March 2000). These bills, approved in March 2000, aim to clarify the rights of victims and provide them with additional assistance. One of the bills enables a partition to be erected between the witness and the defendant in cases involving minors and sexual assaults (used for the first time in Yokoyama's criminal trial) or the use of video conferencing or videotape. The other bills include the abolition of the six-month time limit for victims of rape to file a formal complaint, allowing a support person to accompany the victim into the courtroom, and allowing victims to state their feelings as well as opinions in court (currently admissible only if they appear as a witness) although these statements will not be recorded as evidence.

These three bills may be partly attributed to the 1997 'Plan for Gender Equality 2000: Vision of Gender Equality' (*Danjō kyōdō sankaku 2000 nen puran: danjo kyōdō sankaku bijon*) which recommended the examination of laws and punishments relating to crimes of violence against women, the possibility of adopting additional legal measures, the training of legal personnel to protect women's rights and improve the treatment of women who have been victimised, and the need for public awareness to stop victim-blaming. The policy also emphasises the need to improve shelters for battered women (currently numbering about 40) and recognise the work carried out by their staff (Danjō kyōdō sankaku suishin honbu 1997: 31–34; for a more detailed analysis see Burns forthcoming).

This official recognition of some of the problems relating to sexual violence and women's work and research in this area stems partly from developments leading up to and following the United Nations' 1995 Fourth World Conference On Women in Beijing. At the conference, violence against women was re-affirmed as a priority issue and official delegates at the conference were pressured to improve co-operative measures with non-governmental organisations (NGOs) by those attending the concurrent NGO Forum, including around 5,000 Japanese participants. At the same time, the Japanese government (and other signatories to the United Nations Convention to Eliminate All Forms of Discrimination Against Women) were obliged to monitor and file a report on what the government had done to address the issue of violence against women. This pressure was also heightened, perhaps, by the Japanese government's concern to increase its profile in the United Nations and its general role in the international arena. Moreover, from the late 1980s, increasing international attention was paid to the 'comfort woman' issue, the Japanese government's responsibility and inadequate response. The government's broader interests, thus, coalesced to some extent with both international and domestic pressure to respond to the question of violence against women in Japan. As a result, dialogue between official bodies and some women's groups has improved and a number of issues relating to sexual violence are being addressed (Hayashi Keiko, Chief, International Affairs Unit, Office for Gender Equality, Interview 23 June 1997).

However, inevitable divisions remain between grassroots feminist groups, academic feminism and larger ideologically more conservative women's organisations. These tensions are exacerbated in the process of participating in the various committees set up to address the UN demands and to establish domestic reforms. Committee participants are perceived by some as unrepresentative, constituted by a privileged group including lawyers, Diet members and other 'elite' women. These committee members face the problem of all those who attempt to incorporate a feminist agenda into existing systems, institutions and frameworks. Compromise is inevitable and leads to perceptions, if not the reality, of lack of principle, weakness, self-interest and opportunism. It is not surprising, therefore, that the Plan for Gender Equality has been strongly criticised by some Japanese feminists as failing to adequately address the structure and causes of the gender discrimination in Japan (see Editorial Committee of 'Women's Asia 21' 1996: 51).

There are a large number of women's groups in Japan and networking between them has been critical to the mobilisation that has taken place to protest against issues relating to sexual violence or contribute support to particular cases. Often with great rapidity many of these groups emerge, dissolve or evolve into other groups focusing on relatively specific issues (see Khor 1999; Mackie 2003; Yokohama Josei Fōramu 1991; Yunomae 1990). In addition to conducting research and organising various protests, groups concerned with sexual violence have established Rape Crisis

Centres, shelters for women and children escaping domestic violence (initially established for immigrant women escaping enforced prostitution) and counselling centres. The vast majority of this work has been carried out autonomously, financed by subscriptions and donations rather than relying on government support and funding, partly because of the fear that official assistance would result in co-option and a compromise of principles and practices. While this has inevitably constrained their ability to provide services it has also been a source of strength in sustaining the integrity and commitment to advancing women's interests. Many of the achievements in terms of addressing the problems of violence against women are largely attributable to the strength of the informal feminist networking and their increasing opportunities to make use of international linkages to bring pressure on the government to respond to their concerns.

Given the long silence surrounding sexual violence, legal intervention plays a significant role at both the symbolic level and the level of addressing individual harms. Breaking this silence means placing these issues on the public agenda. Feminist lawyers and activists are contesting the dominant narratives produced in law, beyond the formulation of arguments designed to advance the interests of individual women in individual cases. Cases are used as opportunities to both mobilise public interest and to shift the thinking of judges. Efforts are directed at promoting public debate in order to reconceptualise sexual violence as harmful rather than a non-threatening masculine fantasy. This is not merely a necessary first step. The wisdom lies in creating the space in which to construct alternative narratives of rape. Legislation that does not significantly improve the court's receptiveness to hearing alternative accounts offers few benefits to women, as has been demonstrated in many Anglo-American countries. The focus, therefore, on shifting social and judicial attitudes within and around trials makes considerable strategic sense.

However, this is no easy task. The power of law to constrain, appropriate and dismiss women's stories is demonstrated by the sanitisation strategy that failed to provide the framework for the telling of a 'suspect' story within a conventional storyline. Another failed but potentially more promising strategy used in Endō's case was extending the logic of masculinist arguments to their limits to disclose internal contradictions and inconsistencies. This strategy is likely to have a greater impact over the long term as a means to gradually undermine the authority of the rape script. Articulating women's counter-stories in terms of rights rhetoric and through expert opinion are, similarly, part of the process of dislodging the dominance and legitimacy of the rape script. However, these approaches require considerable caution. Disrupting the privileged knowledge produced in judgments requires listening to women's (and men's) experiences of sexual violence and ensuring that these understandings do not disappear in their translation into professional discourses. Without careful consideration of the fundamental nature of the problem, achieving a more representational judiciary and implementing law reforms that do not adequately reflect or facilitate the telling of women's stories of sexual victimisation are unlikely to make much impact.

8 Conclusion

> If we could further our understanding of what judges know, how they know it, how this shapes the construction of reality in judgments – that is, how judges 'orient' their narrative – and how this is all affected by gender, then maybe things *could* change.
>
> (Graycar 1995: 269)

This book has aimed to take up Graycar's challenge, above. Analysing cases of sexual assault has revealed the extensive circulation of rape myths in the Japanese courtroom, which silence alternative narratives of sexual violence. Japan is anything but unique in this respect; much the same, certainly familiar rape myths continue to permeate the legal environments in Australia, Canada, Britain, the US and elsewhere. The significant difference, perhaps, is the popular perception in Australia, if not elsewhere, that legal and social approaches to rape have dramatically changed. It seems comments such as those made by Victorian Judge Bland are quickly forgotten:

> often, despite criticism that has been directed towards judges lately about . . . men acting violently to women during sexual intercourse, it does happen, in the common experience of those who have been in the law as long as I have anyway, that no subsequently means yes.
>
> (*The Age* 6 May 1993: 11; for other examples see Scutt 1992, 1994b)

The findings of numerous and extensive studies, most notably in Australia the study *Heroines of Fortitude* (NSW Department for Women 1996), clearly demonstrate the continuing circulation and influence of rape myths in criminal proceedings of sexual assault cases – despite various law reforms.

Judicial opinions reflect, and therefore make visible, dominant discourses and, at the same time, they play an important symbolic role in legitimising (or not) particular social conventions and behaviours. Judgments, therefore, have a significant role beyond the case itself, as authoritative in terms of precedential value and as powerful social discourse. This study found that the perceived need to demonstrate that force was used to commit rape is mitigated in certain sorts of cases where there is no evidence of a prior relationship between the woman and the defendant, where there were multiple offenders, multiple offences or the defendant had a prior conviction for a similar offence. These sorts of cases conform in a relatively unambiguous way to dominant or stereotypic perceptions of rape. They easily 'make sense' as rape scenarios and so it is usually deemed unnecessary to scrutinise the woman's integrity. Given the prosecutor's role in filtering out cases unlikely to win in court, it is probable that these are the sorts of cases that judges most frequently adjudicate. Their decisions, therefore, serve to reinforce the stereotypes of *tsūjō* rape cases. However, in cases that do not conform to the stereotype, those typically comprising *fushizen* aspects, the demonstration of utmost force-resistance becomes central to the judicial interpretation of rape.

It is in these sorts of cases that judges most clearly animate the discourse of compulsory heterosexuality, which denies women a space in which to indicate non-consent and a position of subjectivity. Underlying this discourse is a construction of rape as extreme sex, motivated by the same natural uncontrollable urges that drive *sukebei* sexuality and that render its practices 'harmless'. The power dimension of rape is subjugated and responsibility is shifted from the offender to the woman, thereby displacing or disqualifying alternative narratives of fear and violation. Moreover, the woman's enactment of gender is constrained and shaped by the legal standards of assessing her moral blameworthiness and by the sexualisation of her body, which takes place through the process of claiming rape. The alignment of women who have been raped with prostitute 'Others' impacts on women's reluctance to report a sexual assault and thus perpetuates the silence surrounding sexual violence.

But no discourse or discursive practice is totally hegemonic. Because the power/knowledge nexus is exercised in diffuse, multiple and localised forms (Foucault 1980) there are inevitable gaps and weaknesses that can be exploited to disclose these internal contradictions and inconsistencies. Recent shifts in legal and social awareness of sexual violence in Japan indicate that gradual but significant legal and social changes are taking place, at least partially, in response to feminist interventions in and around the law. As mentioned in the previous chapter, the Nishi Funabashi and Ikebukuro cases in the mid-1980s significantly contributed to feminist interest in sexual violence and gender relations in Japan. Although tried as murder cases they have, more recently, been interpreted by Japanese feminists as 'forerunner' sexual harassment cases. Analysing the connections between different sorts of cases or those differentiated in legal discourse has facilitated new understandings of the various ways in which patriarchal discourses impact on women's lives in fundamental and differing ways and in differing contexts. Thus, the courtroom stories sustain the 'fight' within the feminist 'movement' which, according to Breckenridge (1999), has been somewhat lost in the Australian context where the feminist–state alliance has inadvertently diluted public concern regarding sexual violence.

Demonstrating public concern is the first step to any form of legal reform and the role of feminist lawyers in mobilising public support and awareness around particular trials has been critical to this process. The question of what types of strategies to adopt is all the more imperative now that it seems the government and legal institutions are, at least, either partially listening or being forced to demonstrate that something is being done to address issues relating to sexual violence.

Perhaps the most problematic legal strategies in cases of sexual violence are those that seek to emphatically distance the complainant from the prostitute to reinforce the 'innocence' of 'ordinary' women. The counter-story insists that a mistake has been made, that the proper distinction between the two 'sorts' of women has been confused. The 'safety net' provided by prostitutes for the protection of 'ordinary' women raises difficult questions for feminist legal strategies. There is a need to think carefully about whether these strategies sustain and reinforce the ideology of sacrifice, which clearly affected the first trial of the prostitute in the Ikebukuro case. In this case, the woman's difficulties in telling a story of rape and assault were amplified by the fact that she was a prostitute, and the sexual contract between prostitute and client was seen to void her right to bodily autonomy. This interpretation is not unique to either Japan or the legal arena. A recent study found that violence towards prostitutes was prevalent worldwide and that they are beaten, raped and murdered (in the majority of cases by clients – men from ordinary social and family backgrounds) not simply because they are prostitutes, but because they are the most vulnerable women in our societies (Perkins 1991: 344). Law's power to construct prostitutes as Other to 'respectable women' not only contributes to their vulnerability, but it also sends a coded warning to 'ordinary women and children' that transgressions of normative constructions of gender and female sexuality exact a high price. The 'Othering' of the woman because she was a prostitute in the Ikebukuro case also served to obscure and silence, in the popular media and in the courtroom, linkages between male sexuality, gendered power relations and sexual violence.

However, sexual harassment cases appear to be generating new understandings of these linkages. This may well facilitate the process of displacing the pervasiveness of biological discourses of sex and gender by demonstrating not only alternative understandings of responses to sexual assault, but also of the ways in which the discourse of *sukebei* masculinity and its practices reinforce the power relations which produce an unnatural sexual hierarchy. The process of legal decision-making in rape cases needs to incorporate the idea that sex is a fundamental part of a larger system of sexual hierarchy and that the threat of rape constitutes women's lives in sex-specific ways. Sharon Marcus (1992: 397) suggests defining rape quite simply as 'a sexualized and gendered attack which imposes sexual difference along the lines of violence'. Broadening the definition of rape, which currently excludes, and thereby diminishes the seriousness or harm of, violations other than penile–vagina penetration including male–male rape and sexual assaults committed by women, not only disrupt the system of compulsory heterosexuality, but also challenge the hegemonic discourse of *sukebei* masculinity by recognising the harm of its material effects. Redefining rape may provide a useful means to continue the process of reconceptualising both rape and gender relations outside of law – for it is only outside the law that solutions can be found to prevent sexual assault. The recent work on the ways in which the body is inscribed as feminine suggests a potentially productive direction for resistance in terms of finding new ways to re-inscribe bodies with alternative ideas and values. Creating a space and new ways for women to define their own experiences and develop their own understanding of sexual abuse is also fundamentally important in terms of disrupting the power of law to define women's lives and experiences. However, it is also through law, through the narratives generated around particular cases, and through an examination of the social conventions employed in judicial narratives that opportunities for redefinition and the construction of new knowledges emerge. The legal arena is, therefore, a potentially productive site for the development of subversive stories that disrupt dominant narratives of rape, sexuality and gender, which must be at the basis of feminist intervention if transformative change is to be achieved.

Appendix 1

Legal definitions

Legal definitions of sexual assaults

Japan recognises five statutory sexual offences against the person: indecent assault (obscenity by compulsion), rape, constructive compulsory indecency and quasi-rape, attempted indecent assault and rape, indecent assault or rape resulting in death or injury. The following crimes are defined under the Criminal Code, Chapter XXII 'Crimes of Obscenity, Rape and Bigamy' (EHS Law Bulletin Series 1996: 53–54) as:

Obscenity by compulsion [*kyōsei waisetsu*, translated in this book as 'indecent assault']

> Article 176. A person who by violence or threat, commits an indecent act [*waisetsu kōi*] against a male or female person of thirteen years or over shall be punished with penal servitude for not less than six months nor more than seven years. The same shall apply to a person who commits an indecent act against a male or female person aged under thirteen years.

Rape [gōkan]

> Article 177. A person who by violence or threat, obtains carnal knowledge [*seikō*] of a female person of thirteen years or over shall be guilty of rape and be punished with penal servitude for a limited period of not less than two years. The same shall apply to a person who obtains carnal knowledge of a female person under thirteen years.

Constructive compulsory indecency and quasi-rape [*junkyōsei waisetsu* and *jungōkan*]

> Article 178. A person, who by taking advantage of loss of reason or incapacity to resist by causing such loss reason or incapacity to resist, commits an indecent act or obtains carnal knowledge of a woman shall be dealt with in the same way as provided for in the preceding two Articles.

Attempts [*misuizai*]

Article 179. Attempts of the crimes mentioned in Article 176 through the preceding three Articles shall be punished.

Crimes subject to prosecution on complaint [*shinkokuzai*]

Article 180. The crimes mentioned in Article 176 through the preceding Article shall be prosecuted on complaint.

2 The provisions of the preceding Article shall not apply to those crimes mentioned in Article 176 through the preceding Article which are committed jointly by two or more persons on the spot.

Compulsory indecency, etc. resulting in death or injury [*gōkan chisho; kyōsei waisetsu chisho*]

Article 181. A person who by committing any of the crimes mentioned in Article 176 through 179, kills or injures another shall be punished with penal servitude for life or not less than three years.

Relevant Articles of the Civil Code and Constitution

Article 709 of the Civil Code

A person who violates intentionally or negligently the right of another is bound to make compensation for damage arising therefore.

Article 715 of the Civil Code

A person who employs another to carry out an undertaking is bound to make compensation for damage done to a third person by the employee in the course of the execution of the undertaking; however, this shall not apply, if the employer has exercised due care in the appointment of the employee and in the supervision of the undertaking or if the damage would have ensued even if due care had been exercised. 2. A person who supervises the undertaking in the place of the employer shall also assume the responsibility mentioned in the preceding paragraph.

Article 14, paragraph 1 of the 1947 Constitution

All of the people are equal under the law and there shall be no discrimination in political, economic or social relations because of race, creed, sex, social status or family origin.

Appendix 2

The cases

Rape

Case 1 Case of blackmail, rape, attempted rape, Osaka District Court, 1990 H2 (wa) No. 444, H2 (wa) No. 620, H2 (wa) No. 1300, H2 (wa) No. 1358, Judgment 2 October 1991, *Hanrei Taimuzu* 770, 15 January 1992: 276–280.

Case 2 Case of rape resulting in bodily injury, attempted rape, indecent assault, escape, attempted indecent assault, Sapporo District Court, 1993 H5 (wa) No. 336, H5 (wa) No. 111, H5 (wa) No. 596, H5 (wa) No. 658, Judgment 14 March 1994, *Hanrei Taimuzu* 868, 1 April 1995: 296–303.

Case 3 Case of rape, violation of the cannabis control law, Tokyo High Court, 1988 SH63 (u) No. 1271, Judgment 25 January 1989, *Hanrei Jihō* 1318, 1 October 1989: 151–153.

Case 4 Case of unlawful arrest and confinement, rape and bodily injury, Naha District Court, 1995 H7 (wa) No. 293, Judgment 7 March 1996, *Hanrei Jihō* 1570, 1 September 1996: 147–154.

Case 5 Case of quasi-rape, constructive compulsory indecency, Tokyo District Court, 1986 SH61 (wa) No. 233, Judgment 15 April 1987, *Hanrei Jihō* 1304, 11 May 1989: 147–151.

Case 6 Case of rape, Osaka High Court, 1991 H3 (u) No. 692, Judgment 28 February 1992, *Hanrei Jihō* 1470, 12 May 1993: 154–162.

—— *Hanrei Taimuzu* 829, 15 January 1994: 277–286.

Case 7 Case of rape resulting in bodily injury, Kumamoto District Court, 1983 SH58 (ta) No. 1, Judgment 31 January 1989, *Hanrei Jihō* 1312, 1 August 1989: 158–161.

Case 8 Case of attempted rape, Urawa District Court, 1991 H3 (wa) No. 835, Judgment 27 February 1992, *Hanrei Taimuzu* 795, 15 November 1992: 263–265.

Case 9 Case of violation of Stimulant Drugs Control Act, break and entry, attempted quasi-rape, Osaka District Court, 1987 SH62 (wa) No. 2689, Judgment 1 October 1987, *Hanrei Jihō* 1256, 1 February 1988: 123–124.

—— *Hanrei Taimuzu* 657, 1 April 1988: 261–263.

Case 10: Watanabe Case of rape, Hiroshima District Court, 1968 SH43 (wa) No. 700, Judgment 26 March 1969, *Hanrei Taimuzu* 235, August 1969: 285–286.

Case 11: Takeda Case of rape resulting in bodily injury, Osaka District Court, 1969 SH44 (wa) No. 2261, Judgment 12 March 1971, *Hanrei Taimuzu* 267, December 1971: 376–378.

Case 12: Nakajima Case of rape resulting in bodily injury, Osaka District Court, 1970 SH45 (wa) No. 3611, Judgment 27 March 1972, *Hanrei Taimuzu* 283, January 1973: 332–337.

Case 13: Matsumoto Case of rape resulting in bodily injury, Hiroshima High Court, 1978 SH53 (u) No. 59, Judgment 20 November 1978, *Hanrei Jihō* 922, 1 June 1979: 111–114.

Case 14: Takahashi Case of rape resulting in bodily injury, Tokyo District Court, 1993 H5 (wa) No. 167, Judgment 16 December 1994, *Hanrei Jihō* 1562, 11 June 1996: 141–154.

Case 15: Sasaki Case of attempted rape, Urawa District Court, 1987 SH62 (wa) No. 1335, Judgment 3 October 1989, *Hanrei Jihō* 1337, 1 April 1990: 150–162.

—— *Hanrei Taimuzu* 717, 15 March 1990: 244–256.

Case 16: Fujiwara Case of rape resulting in bodily injury & larceny, Urawa District Court, 1990 H2 (wa) No. 452, H2 (wa) No. 539, Judgment 9 March 1992, *Hanrei Taimuzu* 796, 1 December 1992: 236–252.

Case 17: Atsumi Case of rape, Osaka District Court, 1986 SH61 (wa) No. 396, Judgment 20 February 1989, *Hanrei Taimuzu* 700, 1 September 1989: 270–279.

—— Osaka High Court, 1989 H1 (u) No. 534, Judgment 12 March 1992, *Hanrei Taimuzu* 802, 15 February 1993: 233–258.

Case 18: Nishimura Case of rape, bodily injury, Hiroshima High Court, 1987 SH62 (u) No. 4, Judgment 18 June 1987, *Hanrei Jihō* 1234, 1 August 1987: 154–156.

—— *Hanrei Taimuzu* 642, 15 October 1987: 257–262.

Case 19: Endō Compensation claim, Maebashi District Court, Takasaki Branch, 1993 H5 (wa) No. 338, Judgment 23 April 1995.

—— Compensation Claim, Supreme Court, H8, No. 492, Judgment 12 August 1996.

Case 20: Komatsu Compensation claim, Yokohama District Court, 1992 H4 (wa) No. 187, Judgment 23 March 1993, *Hanrei Taimuzu* 813, 10 June 1993: 247–251.

Sexual harassment

Case 21: Fukuoka Compensation claim, Fukuoka District Court, 1989 H1 (wa) No. 1872, Judgment 16 April 1992, *Hanrei Taimuzu* 1426, 21 September 1992: 49–65.

—— *Hanrei Taimuzu* 783, 1 July 1992: 60–77.

Case 22: Numazu Compensation claim, Shizuoka District Court, Numazu Branch, 1990 H2 (wa) No. 388, Judgment 20 December 1990, *Hanrei Taimuzu* 745, 1 March 1991: 238–240.

Case 23: Sapporo Compensation claim, Asahikawa District Court, 1992 H4 (wa) No. 296, H5 (wa) No. 28, Judgment 18 March 1997 (Judgment transcript).

Case 24: Yokohama Compensation claim, Yokohama District Court, 1992 H4 (wa) No. 2024, Judgment 24 March 1995, *Hanrei Jihō* 1539, 1 August 1995: 111–117.

Case 25: Utsunomiya Compensation claim, Utsunomiya District Court, 1992 H4 (wa) No. 636 (sections of trial transcript). Settled out of court in 1998.

Case 26: Akita Compensation claim, Akita District Court, 1993 H5 (wa) No. 516; Counter Compensation claim, 1994 H6 (wa) No. 334, Judgment 6 January 1997.

Case 27: Hachioji Compensation claim, Tokyo District Court, Hachioji Branch, 1993 H5 (wa) No. 2423, Judgment 15 April 1996, *Hanrei Jihō* 1577, 11 November 1996: 100–104.

Case 28: Kyoto Compensation claim, Kyoto District Court, 1994 H6 (wa) No. 2996, Judgment 27 March 1997 (Judgment transcript).

Case 29: Kanazawa Compensation claim, Nagoya High Court, Kanazawa Branch, 1994 H6 (ne) No. 98; H6 (ne) No. 103, Judgment 30 October 1996 (Judgment transcript); Kanazawa District Court, 1992 H4 (wa) No. 3, Judgment 26 May 1994, *Rōdō Hanrei* 650, 15 July 1994: 8–14.

Case 30: Tokyo Compensation claim, Tokyo District Court, 1994 H6 (wa) No. 4102, Judgment 25 December 1996 (Judgment transcript).

Case 31: Kumamoto Compensation claim, Kumamoto District Court, 1996 H8 (wa) No. 1178, Judgment 25 June 1997 (Judgment transcript).

Indecent assault

Case 32 Case of indecent assault, Nagoya High Court Kanazawa Branch, 1990 H2 (u) No. 27, Judgment 26 March 1991, *Hanrei Taimuzu* 786, 1 August 1992: 260–283.

Case 33 Case of indecent assault, Tokyo District Court 1989 H1 (wa) No. 551, Judgment 17 February 1992, *Hanrei Jihō* 1454, 21 June 1993: 154–162.

Case 34 Case of indecent assault resulting in bodily injury, Tokyo District Court 1987 SH62 (wa) No. 111, Judgment 16 September 1987, *Hanrei Taimuzu* 670, 15 September 1988: 254–257.

—— *Hanrei Jihō* 1294, 1 February 1989: 142–146.

Case 35 Case of arrest and confinement, indecent assault, violation of the arms control law, Fukuoka High Court 1984 SH59 (u) No. 22, Judgment 25 Oct 1984, *Hanrei Jihō* 1176, 21 February 1986: 160–162.

Case 36 Case of indecent assault, Osaka District Court 1980 SH55 (wa) No. 4567, Judgment 15 December 1980, *Hanrei Jihō* 995, 1 May 1981: 131–168.

—— *Hanrei Taimuzu* 450, 15 November 1981: 167–168.

Case 37 Case of indecent assault, Supreme Court 1988 SH63 (a) No. 130, Judgment 26 October 1989, *Hanrei Taimuzu* 713, 1 February 1990: 75–91.
—— *Hanrei Jihō* 1331, 11 February 1990: 145–161.
—— *Hanrei Hyōron* 380, *Hanrei Jihō* 1355, 1 October 1990: 231–238.

Case 38 Case of indecent assault, attempted indecent assault, Tokyo District Court 1995 H7 (wa) No. 545, Judgment 8 January 1996, *Hanrei Taimuzu* 933, 1 May 1997: 278–282.

Case 39 Case of indecent assault, Niigata District Court 1988 SH63 (wa) No. 225, Judgment 26 August 1988, *Hanrei Jihō* 1299, 21 March 1989: 152–154.

Case 40 Case of kidnapping for ransom etc., indecent assault, Yokohama District Court 1988 SH63 (wa) No. 2548, Judgment 21 December 1989, *Hanrei Jihō* 1356, 11 October 1990: 156–162.
Case 41 Compensation claim, Tokyo District Court 1994 H6 (wa) No. 19033, Judgment 16 May 1995, *Hanrei Taimuzu* 876, 1 July 1995: 295–303.

Notes

Prelude

1 Rosalind Coward's conceptualisation of pornography as a 'regime of representations' is useful in understanding how we learn to identify and apply codes of interpretations to particular images, texts or representations when they comply with certain modes of signification. She states that: 'The [representations] show bodies (usually naked) in a sexualised way, or people involved in the sex act, according to certain conventions which means they are interpreted as pornographic by society' (Coward 1987: 310).

2 I follow the Japanese convention of family name followed by given name in citing Japanese-language sources except in the citation of English-language references where the authors have followed English-language order.

3 Case of murder, Tokyo District Court, 1987 SH62 (wa) No. 67, Judgment 18 December 1987, *Hanrei Jihō* 1275, 11 July 1988: 45.

4 This point was central to both trials, but is most clearly stated in the appeal judgment. Case of murder, Tokyo High Court, 1988 SH63 (u) No. 155, Judgment 9 June 1988, *Hanrei Jihō* 1283, 9 June 1989: 57. In two recent Australian cases judges also invoked the myth that prostitutes are not as harmed psychologically as ordinary women by rape (see Scutt 1994b).

5 The practice of making a personal apology and offering a symbolic financial settlement (*isharyo*) is regarded as particularly significant in Japanese legal culture and usually results in greater leniency (see Johnson 2002: 202; Wagatsuma and Rosett 1986: 461–498; Haley 1986: 499–507).

6 Case of murder, *Hanrei Jihō* 1275, 11 July 1988: 45. For a more detailed analysis of the case see Burns (1997).

7 Marcia Goodman (1986: 27–28) argues that law in Japan explicitly seeks to reflect dominant social attitudes: 'According to official philosophy, it is impossible to establish rigid standards since the prosecutor must represent the national will (*kokka ishi*), and standards must therefore flow with the changing times and environment'.

1 Legal storytelling and sexual violence

1 In Tokyo, the groups *Kōdō suru onnatachi no kai* and *STON-Sei bōryoku to tatakau onnatachi no nettowāku '90* have been very active, tackling a wide range of issues relating to sexual violence in particular.

2 The first judicial statement on sexual harassment was made in the Numazu case in 1990. The judge stated that the sexual harassment in this case included an indecent assault and because the car door was locked the plaintiff could not

escape. Moreover, the woman's employer ignored her will and took advantage of his superior position. The defendant did not enter a defence and so the woman's testimony was accepted and she was awarded ¥1,100,000 including legal costs (Case 22 Numazu). Leon Wolff (1996) also discusses this case, but refers to it as the 'Shizuoka Sexual Harassment Case'.

3 Yamada (1999a and b) argues that sexual harassment cases are also increasingly recognising psychological damage and inability to work. He notes that the compensation awards should be higher, but he expects the current trend of gradual increase to continue. He provides details of the amounts of compensation awarded in the total 32 cases of sexual harassment that reached judgment between 20 December 1990 and 12 March 1999.

4 Japanese feminist scholars generally use the term *higaisha* (victims). A number of Anglophone feminists and therapists (see Kelly *et al.* 1996: 90–93; Burton 1998) offer valuable critiques of the term 'victim', particularly that it denies women the space for agency. There are, however, times when it is useful to contrast the positions of 'victim' and 'offender' and to emphasise that when confronting the legal system the complainant must conform to a limited repertoire of 'appropriate' victim behaviours. I am also guided by a conversation with Endō, a woman who clearly wanted to claim the status of victim. Because her experience of rape had been rejected at every level of the court system and thus her perception of victimisation had been denied, to be acknowledged as a victim meant the legitimation of her experience and an important aspect of her recovery. It is also possible that using the word 'survivor' (*ikinokorimono*), which is common among Anglophone feminists, might reinforce the expectation that women resist sexual attacks to the utmost of their abilities. For a discussion of the potentially productive ways in which the term 'victim' can be re-incorporated into a feminist analysis using the theoretical insights of 'radical victimology' see Anne McLeer (1998: 43). I also refer throughout this book to 'victims' or 'victim-survivors' as women. This is not to deny that men and boys are also sexually victimised, but to emphasise that the abuses that come before judges are overwhelmingly perpetrated against women and girls. This is due both to the gendered nature of sexual violence and the definition of rape, which excludes the possibility of recognising male victims. The complaints of men and boys who have been targets of sexual abuse are limited to the less serious charge of indecent assault (see Appendix 1).

5 This general position follows the argument of H.L.A. Hart. For a succinct synopsis of Hart's argument see, Ingleby and Johnstone (1995: 179).

6 I use the term to highlight the constraints placed on conforming to commonsense understandings of rape and the possibilities for deviation, being able to resist and to ad-lib. This idea draws on the work of Sharon Marcus (1992) who uses the term 'rape script' to develop the idea of rape as a grammar and John Gagnon and William Simon (1973: 19–26) who use the term 'sexual script' to emphasise the social construction of sexual meanings.

7 Amsterdam and Bruner (2000: 110–142) go on to explain in considerable detail the various components of the narrative form.

8 All cases are numbered. In addition, pseudonyms are attached to the cases that are discussed in most detail (Cases 9–20) and I follow Japanese legal convention in referring to sexual harassment cases by the name of the court where the case was heard.

9 Although approximately 40 sexual harassment cases had gone to trial in Japan by mid-1997, it is difficult to obtain an exact figure because some of the earlier trials in particular did not explicitly use or define the term sexual harassment (*seku hara* or *sekushuaru harasumento*). Legal scholar Yamada Shōzō (1999a: 43–45) lists 32 cases of sexual harassment that had reached judgment by March

1999. Moreover, one case included in the sample (Case 28 Kyoto) is a defamation suit involving allegations of sexual harassment including rape by a professor from Kyoto University. It is included here because the judge considered each of the allegations in detail.

10 The partial transcript of Case 25 Utsunomiya, a tower of paper about knee-high from the floor, was obtained with the permission of the complainant, Kikuchi Kiyomi – the first complainant in Japan to allow publication of her name.

11 Endō, the complainant, lent me copies of the full trial transcript of the court of first instance, and the following High Court and Supreme Court appeals.

12 *Hanketsu* refers to a judicial decision in cases tried to a verdict and, as such, differs from *kettei* (ruling), *handan* (adjudication), *meirei* (order), *saiban* (decision), and *shinpan* (adjustment). For a more detailed explanation see Dan F. Henderson (1980: 149).

13 In his study of rape in Chicago, Menachim Amir (1971: 259–276) developed the theory that a man should not be held accountable for rape if the woman could be construed as provocative (in terms of a seemingly endless list of circumstances and behaviours. Jocelynne Scutt (1994a: 135–138) provides a feminist critique of his work.

14 For a comprehensive guide to court procedure see Ministry of Justice (www.courts.go.jp/english/procedure/keiji2_e.html) and Davis (1996).

15 Ewick and Silbey (1995: 197–226) use the term 'hegemonic tales' to describe narratives that reproduce existing power relations and inequalities.

2 Hegemonic masculinity and guilty feminine bodies

1 The chief of the Police Bureau, fearing racial contamination warned that Japanese men should be kept from 'consorting with these prostitutes, who would serve as a hygienic buffer' (Garon 1997: 111).

2 Allison (1994: 72–73) notes that 'the sexual privilege accorded to male customers in hostess clubs institutionalizes the sexualization of male privilege' and that following the first successful sexual harassment case a fad among clubs emerged in which the hostesses dressed as OLs ('office ladies').

3 These industries, in fact, support mainstream work practices. For example, a company's interests are served by securing the maximum amount of time and loyalty possible from a worker. The 'distraction' of family can be partially ameliorated by providing services for sexual gratification free of responsibility outside the home (Allison 1994).

4 A survey of 204 women in Osaka in the late 1980s found that 95 per cent of the women had 'encountered *chikan*' (Ihaya 1990: 4). Shigematsu (1996: 79) also cites a number of more recent surveys which found extremely high levels of sexual violation in general; most if not the vast majority of cases can probably be attributed to *chikan*.

5 *Enjo kōsai* may involve sex for money, but not necessarily. The main concern is that the predominantly high-school girls are soliciting 'dates' and providing services to satisfy men's sexual pleasures for money to buy designer fashion items. The activity was effectively banned by legislation passed in May 1999, which prohibits the purchase of sexual services from a child under the age of 18. The law (*Jidō baishun/ jidō poruno kisei hōan*, 'Bill to Regulate Child Prostitution and Child Pornography') also prohibits the sale, distribution and transmission of child pornography.

6 The ordinance that formalised the regulation of 'voluntary' prostitution was *Naimushōrei dai 44 go*, so-called '*shōgi torishimari kisoku*' (Fujime 1997b: 91).

7 This was the only area of the new code, drafted by French lawyer Gustave Boissonade, that was completely rejected by Japanese lawmakers on the grounds that it did not protect Japan's traditional 'good morals and beautiful manners' (*jumpū bizoku*) (Mikazuki 1976: 455; see also Tanaka 1980: 622–623; Igeta 1978: 72–98).

8 Preserving the family line and wealth were paramount concerns in the Edo *ie* system, but this did not mean a woman's primary task was to bear and raise children. Motherhood was not necessarily defined biologically and women were frequently valued as workers, wives and daughters-in-law as much as mothers. The practice of substitute nursing mothers for babies was common particularly in wealthier families and childcare was frequently carried out by someone other than the mother. For an analysis of the considerable diversity and flexibility in women's lives and social roles in the Edo period see Kathleen Uno (1991). For two excellent discussions of constructions of sex and gender in the Edo period see Susan Griswold (1995: 59–76) and Jennifer Robertson (1991).

9 By 1890, working-class women had 'become the backbone of the developing Japanese industrial economy', comprising 60–90 per cent of the light industry labour force. The silk and cotton industries, dominated by female workers, provided the country with its chief export commodities on which Japan's industrial expansion was based. However, given that the ideology of *ryōsai kenbo*, which initially located women firmly in the home, was only directed at middle-class high-school girls, it was not a call for all women to leave their jobs and take up domestic responsibilities (Nolte and Hastings 1991: 157–163).

10 Chungmoo (1997: xiii) highlights the dichotomy between 'publicized domestic space and the privatized public space of prostitution'.

11 The state does regulate sexuality through the former licensed prostitution system and the current 1956 *Baishunboshihō* (Prostitution Prevention Law) and the *Fuzokueigyoto no kisei oyobi gyomu no tekiseikato no kansuru hōritsu* (Public Morals Law) which regulates the zoning of sex-related businesses. However, it is the prostitute and those who financially profit from prostitution, not the client, who can be charged for contravening the laws. As Nakayama (1990: 214) notes, the law's exclusion of the activities of the client of prostitution reflects the legal concern regarding 'police intervention to the private life of the citizens'. See also Veronica Taylor (1988: 99–114), Elmer H. Johnson (1993: 29–41) and Minoru Yokoyama (1993: 211–218).

12 In 1884 there were 28,432 licensed prostitutes in Japan and the number rose to 54,049 in 1916 (Garon 1997: 93). Thousands more were sold to, or worked in, brothels in China, Southeast Asia and the US. In 1909 there were 5,000 Japanese prostitutes in Singapore (Ichioka 1977: 3; Yamazaki 1975: 52–60).

13 However, when many of these 'filial' daughters returned home their prospects remained limited and they had no choice but to return to prostitution (Fujime 1997a: 150).

14 In the revised Civil Code the structure of 'the family' was significantly democratised. Choice of spouse, property rights, inheritance, choice of residence, grounds for divorce and so forth are now based on the principle of equality between husband and wife and between siblings. However, everyday practices rarely match legal provisions in Japan or anywhere else. Women in Japan face numerous forms of discrimination in varying shades of subtlety across a range of areas and government policies and employment practices that overwhelmingly privilege the heterosexual marriage in which the husband is the primary breadwinner (Buckley 1993; Buckley and Mackie 1986; Naftulin 1980; Smith 1987).

15 For example, both Filipino women in contemporary Japan and the naked Western female body featuring in 1970–80s' magazines and films catering to male sexual fantasies, are overwhelmingly stereotyped as sex workers (Kaneko 1995: 66–70).

16 A similar argument was made by Murase Yukihiro, professor of human sexuality at Hitotsubashi University, cited in Larimer (1999: 61). Miya Yoshiko (in Buckley 1997: 183) suggests that the popularity of *rorikon* among male university students may also be linked to the strong emotional attachment between mothers and sons, which is reinforced by the single-minded focus on educational achievement. Consequently, these sons remain in a state of immaturity, unable to psychologically separate from their mothers and are, therefore, terrified of mature women. Thus, Miya argues that 'the children of the *mazākon* (mother complex) generation graduate into the *rorikon* generation'.

17 Discussing the eroticisation of the child in late nineteenth-century European art, Bram Dijkstra traces the shift in the attraction of the innocence and purity of the child. Dijkstra (1986: 191) argues that many men sought pleasure in representations of the passive purity of the child because they could not find women who resembled their images of meek sexless mothers and who conformed to dominant ideas about women's childlike mentality. From the search for purity it was only a small step to rediscovering the 'enticements' of woman in the body of the child. Images of prepubescent girls 'suggested to the nineteenth century male not only innocence but also the absence of any resistance to the particulars of masculine desire'. Symbols of purity came to suggest sin and were thus deployed to titillate. Images of vulnerable woman–child suggested rape, 'a promise of unopposed carnal knowledge offered to the viewer – who became the sole proprietor of the innocence of the awakening woman – a fantasy of "love without fear"'.

18 This point was developed by Luce Irigaray who drew on Lacan's psychoanalytic theory of the 'mirror stage' in child development. Margaret Whitford (1991: 34) succinctly summarises Irigary's position:

> the male projects his own ego onto the world, which then becomes a mirror which enables him to see his own reflection wherever he looks. Women as body/matter are the material of which the mirror is made, that part of the mirror which cannot be reflected.

19 On this point, Marcus (1992: 387) notes that the association of rape as equal to, or worse than, death corresponds to the masculine ideology that implies rape can only be feared not fought. This, she argues, serves to produce a sense of futility that disempowers women.

20 McVeigh (1997: 155–163) also discusses these and other attributes and values at the centre of femininity training. Unlike Lebra I think that a closer analysis of 'moral training' would reveal a significant gendered pattern and certainly the consequences of this training are likely to be differently experienced by men and women. For example, Kinjō Kiyoko argues that the prevention of rape requires that women learn to act and speak more assertively (interview, in Miya 1984: 222).

21 Because rape has been a taboo subject and even the word itself was not used in the mass media, there is little public discussion or research in the area. Nevertheless, Keiko Higuchi (1985: 158–159) states, 'the greatest fear of young women and their parents is their being raped and killed' and that a woman born in the Meiji era told her daughter to bite off her tongue and die if she should be raped and lose her chastity. For a discussion of the difficulty and ultimate failure author Ochiai Keiko had in getting her book on rape published with the title *Gōkan* (Rape) see interview with Ochiai Keiko in Buckley (1997: 232).

22 Similar sentiments are expressed in letters to the editor of a major newspaper examined by Shibata (1999: 63).

3 Confronting the Japanese criminal justice system

1 In 1995, 464 women were murdered (36.4 per cent of total murder victims), 1,563 women were raped (including robbery and rape) (100 per cent of rape victims), 3,529 women were indecently assaulted (96.8 per cent of indecent assault victims) and 4,714 women were assaulted (19.8 per cent of assault victims). Indecent assault is the literal translation of *kyōsei waisetsu*. The figure for 'assault' includes *bōkō* (assault and battery/violence), *shōgai* (bodily injury), and *shōgai chishi* (bodily injury resulting in death) (Keisatsuchō 1996: 226).

2 The term domestic violence is translated as *kateinai bōryoku*, but in Japan this is generally understood as children's violence directed at parents. Perhaps for this reason thc term 'DV' (and 'domestic violence') has become popular, used in the media from the late 1990s.

3 Sasaki surveyed women in a government-funded Home for Single Mothers and Children, which provides dormitory type accommodation for an average of two years for economically disadvantaged single mothers with dependent children under 18 years of age. In 1987, there were 339 homes that were used by 6,843 families. The homes also provide employment counselling and childcare to both residents and the general public. Although many of the mothers are escaping violent relationships, generally the homes are limited in their capacity to provide emergency shelter, although some homes do have special rooms for this purpose. However, Sasaki noted that there was no special training for staff in crisis intervention for mothers and children in violent family situations (Sasaki 1989: 53–58; 204–205). Similarly, in 1981, 'husband's violence and/or drunkenness', at 31.6 per cent, was the most common reason for admission into the Tokyo Metropolitan Government's emergency refuge, popularly known as *kakekomidera* (Buddhist temples from the Tokugawa period or earlier that provided refuge and helped obtain divorces for women escaping forced or abusive marriages) (Tokyo Metropolitan Government 1983: 48).

4 The new law includes provisions for six-month protection orders and the removal of the spouse from the victim's residence for two weeks. Violations of the protection order are punishable – imprisonment of up to one year or a fine of up to ¥1,000,000.

5 Prostitution is one interpretation of the activity known as *enjo kōsai*, more accurately translated as 'compensated dating'. It involves typically junior high- and senior high-school girls dating older men for financial rewards. The 'date' does not necessarily involve sex. DAWN Newsletter (2003) provides data from a survey of high-school students' attitudes to *enjo kōsai*.

6 Rape is defined narrowly in terms of penile–vagina penetration, excluding penetration anally, orally or by an object. For this reason, I use the term 'sexual assault' to refer inclusively to rape, indecent assault, child sexual abuse and domestic violence.

7 The importance placed on maintaining the ideal nuclear family unit is illustrated by the reluctance of judges to grant divorce in contested cases, granted in only 40 per cent of cases (Bryant 1988: 226).

8 It is not uncommon for judges to argue that it is natural for a woman who has been sexually assaulted to confide in a family member and thus the failure to do so is interpreted as an indication that the complainant might be lying (see, for example, Case 16 Fujiwara).

9 A dominant assertion in the literature on law in Japan is that the state's reluctance to intervene in small communities reflects a cultural aversion to publicise disputes through litigation because this implies a failure of harmonious social relations (see Obuchi 1987: 83).

10 Andrew Green's analysis of the way in which cases are constructed in Western criminal justice systems also highlights the selectivity of 'information' to support investigators' 'preconceptions'. This takes place under conditions of 'low visibility' that mask the investigator's exercise of power and thus enable the evidence to 'masquerade as truth' (Green 1997: 17).

11 Johnson (2002: 108, 37) reminds us that the power to suspend prosecution is not, as is often argued, unique to Japan. Similar systems operate in Denmark, France, Great Britain, Holland, Norway and South Korea. This system is, nevertheless, central to Japanese criminal justice.

12 The Crisis Centre percentages are calculated on the basis of figures collected from September 1983 to December 1990.

13 For an analysis of these debates relating to two government policies, the 1987 'Shin Kokunai Kōdō Keikaku' [New National Plan of Action] and the 1997 'Danjo kyōdō sankaku 2000 nen puran: danjo kyōdō sankaku bijon' (Plan For Gender Equality 2000: Vision of Gender Equality) see Burns (forthcoming).

14 Courtroom observation, Judgment, 9 July 1997, Tokyo District Court, room 419.

15 The judge found that the defendant threatened the woman with a knife, taped her mouth, bound her wrists and intended to perform anal intercourse and sado-masochistic acts. Case of Indecent Assault, Robbery, Osaka High Court 1986 SH61 (u) No. 293, Appeal Judgment 7 October 1986, *Hanrei Jiho* 1217, 21 February 1987: 142–146.

16 Courtroom observation, Judgment, 15 July 1997, Tokyo District Court, room 419; Courtroom observation, Judgment, 30 July 1997, Tokyo District Court, room 424. An 18-month sentence was also handed down to a defendant (who had five previous convictions) in a case involving threats with a knife, confinement and indecent assault (Case 35).

17 The 99.9 per cent conviction rate in prosecuted criminal cases compares with 83 per cent in the US (Davis 1996: 100). However, if only cases where (a) the defendant did not plead guilty, and (b) partial judgments of not-guilty were passed are considered, the acquittal rate is 3–4 per cent (Horiuchi 1995: 78).

18 Itoh (1970: 775–804) provides a comprehensive analysis of Japanese debates concerning the nature of judicial decision-making and the incorporation of the concept of *stare decisis* since the establishment of the 1947 Constitution. The extent to which Supreme Court precedents, in particular, bind lower court decision-making is also discussed in works focusing more on the degree of judicial independence from the government (see Itoh 1990: 169–179; Haley 1995: 1–18).

19 Over 30 per cent of all Supreme Court appeals are dismissed within a year and without full comment on the merits of the case. The initial decision concerning which Supreme Court appeals are 'frivolous and should not receive complete review by a bench' are made by promising judges in their forties who act in the position of research judges (*chōsakan*) for 3–4 years (Davis 1996: 62–68).

20 There is currently a strong movement in Japan to reform the judicial system and the Ministry of Justice has responded by establishing the Judicial Reform Council. Proposals include the re-introduction of the jury system, increasing the number of legal professionals, encouraging more lawyers to become judges, reforming the legal education system, speeding up the trial process and improving access to courts. The consequent public debate has also triggered proposals such as the decentralisation of personnel administration, the abolition of assistant judges, and allowing judges more freedom to express opinions in public.

21 The average length of time for an 'ordinary case' heard in a District Court is approximately three and a half months and consists of three to four hearings about one month apart. However, cases may take considerably longer (2.1 per cent of cases took more than one year in 1992) (Horiuchi 1995: 100).

22 Margaret Thornton (1989: 122–123) notes that 'homogeneity is a central value of any organisational culture, since it is conducive to the maintenance of bureaucratic control and efficiency'. Thornton's discussion of 'homosocial reproduction' in the Australian academic context also resonates with practices within the Japanese judicial community.

23 In 1984, 58 per cent of applicants to the Legal Training and Research Institute graduated from Tokyo, Chuo and Waseda Universities (Chen 1989: 11). In 1996, Tokyo, Waseda and Kyoto Universities had the highest number of successful applicants to the Institute (Miyazawa 2000).

24 According to Abe (1995: 306) the examination favours those who memorise Supreme Court precedents rather than those who might adopt a critical approach. A mere 2–3 per cent pass the examination each year and so the vast majority of students succeed only after five or six attempts.

25 Margaret Thornton (1998: 147–170) provides a discussion of the very subtle but effective ways in which cultural constructions of masculinity, femininity and the female body undermine the position of women lawyers and 'others' in the Australian legal community.

4 Credibility in the court

1 The Japanese law's emphasis on force and intimidation by the offender and resistance by the victim may be moderated by the use of Article 178, which refers to cases where the offender causes or takes advantage of the victim's inability to resist. However, the cases analysed in this study suggest that the article is invoked only rarely and under very limited circumstances such as sexual assault obtained by fraud or where the victim was unconscious, asleep or disabled (see Appendix 1).

2 For a feminist analysis of the conservative and liberal theories of rape see Marcus (1992: 397–398) and Lacey (1998: 104–113).

3 LeGrand (1973: 924) asserts that many countries including France and Norway classify rape as a crime against society under categories such as 'Moral Offence' rather than as a crime against the person.

4 In 1958 an article was added to the law removing the necessity to prosecute only upon complaint (*shinkokuzai*) in cases of gang rape, and in 2000 the six-month time limit to report rape was abolished.

5 Although these ideas about the harm of rape are voiced in legal discourse there has been little discussion about the actual meaning of these terms (Tsunoda 1990: 46; Hayashi 1990: 31).

6 Taniguchi did not use particular terminology to categorise or differentiate the third and fourth approaches. The terms 'makes resistance difficult' and 'restrains resistance' seem to best capture Taniguchi's intended meaning in differentiating between the four positions.

7 These cases are referred to as numbers because they are not subjected to the same degree of scrutiny and do not provide comprehensive details regarding judicial opinion on subjects relating to sex, sexuality and gender as the cases discussed in Chapters 5 and 6. The reason is that the cases were either appeals that focused on legal questions not relevant to this study (e.g. legal necessity to verbally explain details of the evidence at the conclusion of the trial in Case 3, admissibility of the defendant's confession in Case 6, and the legality of the warrant used to arrest the defendant in Case 2) and/or the cases comprised uncomplicated stock stories of rape that did not require a great deal of deliberation. That is, the 'facts' were seen as unambiguous.

8 Pachinko is a form of Japanese pinball. Although cash prizes are prohibited, backstreet cashing shops exist to exchange prizes such as cigarettes and choco-

late for cash. Pachinko is, therefore, an accessible and very popular form of gambling.

9 Ten years' imprisonment is an extremely severe sentence for rape in Japan and reflects the defendant's recidivism.

10 Explaining this same observation in US society, Addeno Addis argues that segregation remains such a significant aspect of life that, 'the only sustained contact that whites and blacks have is through the media. Therefore, the media plays an important role in the construction of a national image of the criminal (transgressive) black' (quoted in Espinoza 1997: 930). It is likely that such perceptions of the criminal black man are also deep in Japan given that the US media is the most likely source of information on race relations and crime in the US. Similarly, Japanese media accounts of 'high rates of crime among foreigners' reproduce and reinforce such narratives.

5 Women subject to scrutiny

1 For example, in a sexual harassment case involving a rape allegation, the defence counsel argued that 'even though the first time [sexual intercourse] was forceful (*gōin na*) she submitted to it (*kanjushita*) to a degree' (Case 31 Kumamoto).

2 The case reporters identify both complainants and defendants using an English-language initial. However, for the purpose of clarity I refer to all women by a family name pseudonym and, where necessary, defendants are referred to by the identifying initial used in the case reporter.

3 Expensive housing means that young people frequently live with parents until marriage or share rooms with siblings or friends in apartments. Furthermore, thin walls between rooms add to the problem of finding an appropriate space for a discreet sexual liaison. Husbands engaging in extra-marital sex also need an appropriate space. For these purposes, love hotels in which rooms can be rented on an hourly basis abound in metropolitan Japan.

4 The confessions were ruled invalid due to the police coercion used to obtain them.

5 If an injury is caused during the course of an attempted rape then *gōkan chishō* (rape resulting in bodily injury) is deemed to have taken place because it is a crime of causing injury during the course of rape or attempted rape.

6 In 1983, 63 per cent of sentences for first-time offenders convicted of rape were suspended (Mayer 1984: 119).

7 Accepting partial responsibility is a very significant socio-cultural convention in understanding situations of conflict and dispute in Japan. It is, however, a double-edged sword for victims of sexual violence and a dangerous legal strategy for the prosecution given the wide social acceptance of blame-the-victim myths, which almost invariably work against the complainant. This problem is discussed in detail in the following chapter. The propensity for judges to allocate blame equally between husbands and wives in divorce cases often results in the denial or trivialisation of domestic violence and rape-in-marriage because the gendered power imbalance is ignored. Fukushima (1997: 33–98) discusses a number of such cases in some detail.

8 As noted in Chapter 1, some of the trial transcripts, judgments and materials submitted to the courts are not paginated. This is the case in Endō's District Court transcript, but not Tsunoda's Supreme Court appeal.

9 For a discussion of this and other cases see Weatherfield (1995a: 78–80).

10 According to lawyers Tsunoda (1991: 32) and Fukushima (1997: 251) the myth that women make false complaints of sexual violence due to vengeance is commonly accepted in Japan (as it is elsewhere) and informs policing practices.

11 In this civil case for compensation, the defendant was found guilty of rape and ordered to pay ¥1,710,000 compensation.
12 Case of rape resulting in death, murder, Tokyo High Court, 1981 SH56 (u) No. 625, Judgment 25 January 1984, *Hanrei Jihō* 1125, 21 October 1984: 166.

6 Markers of truth

1 The defendant's appeal that the sentence of five years' imprisonment was too severe was rejected in the High Court. Case of Break and entry, robbery and attempted rape, Tokyo High Court, 1993 H5 (u) No. 507, *Hanrei Jihō* 1495, 11 August 1994: 146.
2 Case of break and entry, rape, habitual theft, murder, abandoning a corpse, Tokyo High Court 1987 SH62 (u) No. 555, Appeal Judgment 23 April 1991, *Hanrei Jihō* 1395, 11 November 1991: 19–33.
3 Case of rape resulting in death, murder, Tokyo High Court, 1981 SH56 (u) No. 625, Judgment 25 January 1984, *Hanrei Jihō* 1125, 21 October 1984: 166.
4 Case of murder, rape resulting in death, attempted blackmail, Osaka High Court 1991 H3 (u) No. 822, Appeal Judgment 11 May 1994, *Hanrei Jihō* 1511, 21 January 1995: 170.
5 The judge argued that the woman was partially responsible for the situation because although 'it should have been easy to know what was really on the defendant's mind' she did not take appropriate precautions to avoid the defendant's sexual advances, and on more than one occasion she stayed over-night at the defendant's home (when it was snowing and dangerous for her to drive home) and took a bath on each occasion.

7 Subversive stories and feminist strategies

1 The Tokyo Rape Crisis Centre (TRCC) was established in 1983 and for many years it served the entire Japanese population. It is open three half-days per week, operates with two telephone lines, is staffed entirely by volunteers, and is financed primarily by subscriptions and donations. In 1989 the Centre received financial assistance from the Ichikawa Fusae Foundation. In 1993 four other rape crisis centres opened around Japan followed by another three in 1994. The TRCC publishes three newsletters per year, which include TRCC statistics and articles on a range of topics. In 1990 it also published a book on rape.
2 In this work Smart does not discuss law or sexual offences but rather feminist debates about heterosexuality. She argues that heterosexuality has been defined around the penis and penetration and is, therefore, largely perceived as inherently oppressive. Smart suggests the need to explore differences of meaning and experience, which may lead to more productive ways of looking at the idea of heterosexualities.
3 Frank Upham (1987) clearly demonstrates in his analysis of legal responses to four major civil disputes that law can, and does, influence the shape and direction of social change in Japan.
4 'Root' is an Australian colloquial expression meaning 'sexual intercourse'.
5 For a discussion of the Japanese cultural ideal of the company as 'one great family' (*daikazoku*) see Rohlen (1974). Dorinne Kondo (1990) provides a more nuanced discussion of the contradictions and resistance to the discourse and practice of 'our company' (*uchi no kaisha*).
6 Differences in legal rules and procedures that follow from this distinction are discussed in Susan Edwards (1992: 154–156). Jocelynne Scutt (1992: 441) also

highlights the 'irrationality' of the dichotomy, noting that the application for a non-molestation order against one's husband in Australia means that:

> the law will say to the man, through the order, that having once beaten her, harassed and molested her, he 'shouldn't do it again.' If he does, he will effectively be in contempt of court. . . . This means that women who are beaten and are thus the victim of *criminal* acts, have to go through a procedure which effectively decriminalises the abuse they have suffered.

7 The EEOL, for example, approximated the 'sameness' approach to equality within which women and men are assumed to be equivalent or, in all relevant respects, the same. Within this framework, harms can be addressed only if women can demonstrate that their grievances could be evaluated on the basis of a male standard. For a Western critique of debates on equality see Bacchi (1990). For critiques of Japan's EEOL and other 'equal rights' legislation see Kamiya (1995: 40–83), Kamio Knapp (1995: 83–137) and Brown (1988: 197–219).

8 The new sexual harassment legislation (which is based on the fundamental relevance of the sexual component of the act as integral to an understanding of the experience) might open a space within which feminists can negotiate reforms that do not demand sex-neutral frameworks.

9 A Canadian study, for example, found that unless a case involved violence it was unlikely to go to court and, consequently, 77 per cent of complainants were injured, threatened with a weapon or received serious harm (Yurchesyn *et al.* 1992: 67; see also Edwards and Heenan 1994: 233–236; L'Orange and Egger 1987: 14–15; Adler 1987).

10 However, law's power to resist re-interpretations and usage of law in novel ways and thereby thwart feminist challenges is illustrated by the Supreme Court's 1964 decision to construe Article 14 as a 'prohibition of unjustifiable discrimination, rather than a guarantee of absolute equality' (quoted in Kamio Knapp 1995: 97).

11 The Fukuoka case was, in fact, the third case to proceed to judgment in which the term sexual harassment (*sekushuaru harasumento* or *seku hara*) was discussed in the courtroom (although the word was not mentioned in the judgment). In both the first case (Numazu, or sometimes referred to as Shizuoka case or the 'New Fujiya Hotel' case) decided in 1990, and the second case settled in the Tokyo District Court in 1991, the defendant did not contest the charges and so there was no debate concerning the nature of sexual harassment (see Ikeda 1995: 222–233). For a discussion of earlier 'forerunner' sexual harassment cases see Miya (1989: 51–130, 151–206).

12 According to one report based on US data from the 1980s, only an estimated one per cent of sexual harassment victims take their case to court and of these only about one-third to one-half win their cases (Fitzgerald and Swan 1995: 123).

13 There was a core group of 15–30 members in both support groups in which I participated (the Yokohama and Utsunomiya sexual harassment cases) and thousands attended the 5 July 1997 symposium organised by the Utsunomiya group. For a discussion of the consciousness raising which takes place within these groups see Tsunoda (1991: 189).

14 The practice is not uncommon but it is usually only necessary for the trials of 'celebrities' such as Aum Shinrikyō defendants.

Bibliography

Abe, Masaki (1995) 'The Internal Control of a Bureaucratic Judiciary: The Case of Japan', *International Journal of the Sociology of Law* 23: 303–320.

Abe, Tetsuo (1998) 'For Criminalization of Child Sexual Abuse in Japan', paper presented at the 12th International Congress on Criminology, Seoul, Korea, 24–29 August.

Adler, Zsuzsanna (1987) *Rape on Trial*, London: Routledge.

Allison, Anne (1994) *Nightwork: Sexuality, Pleasure, and Corporate Masculinity in a Tokyo Hostess Club*, Chicago: University of Chicago Press.

—— (1996) *Permitted and Prohibited Desires: Mothers, Comics and Censorship in Japan*, Colorado: Westview Press.

Ames, Walter L. (1981) *Police and Community in Japan*, Berkeley: University of California Press.

Amir, Menachim (1971) *Patterns in Forcible Rape*, Chicago: University of Chicago Press.

Amsterdam, Anthony G. and Bruner, Jerome (2000) *Minding the Law*, Cambridge: Harvard University Press.

Anon. (1987) 'Hotetorujō no Hentai SM Otoko Koroshi: Bideo ga Miteita!', *Bishō*, 25 July: 52–53.

Anon. 'The Law for Punishing Acts Related to Child Prostitution and Child Pornography, and for Protecting Children'. Online, available at: www.npa.go.jp/english/index.htm (accessed 12 July 2004).

Arichi, Tōru (1987) *Rikon!? Suru Shiawase/Dekinai Fushiawase*, Tokyo: Yūhikaku.

Ariga, Chieko (1992) 'Dephallicizing Women in *Ryūkyō shinshi*', *Journal of Asian Studies* 51(3): 565–586.

Bacchi, Carol Lee (1990) *Same Difference: Feminism and Sexual Difference*, St Leonards, New South Wales: Allen and Unwin.

Barber, Lynden (1998) 'Teen Sex Story Rings True', *The Australian*, 7 August: 15.

Bartky, Sandra Lee (1988) 'Feminism, Foucault, and the Modernization of Patriarchal Power', in Irene Diamond and Lee Quinby (eds) *Feminism and Foucault: Reflections on Resistance*, Boston: Northeastern University Press.

Bayley, David H. (1976) *Forces of Order: Police Behaviour in Japan and the United States*, Berkeley: University of California Press.

—— (1984) 'Police, Crime, and the Community in Japan', in George DeVos (ed.) *Institutions for Change in Japanese Society*, Berkeley: University of California Press, Institute of East Asian Studies.

Bell, Vicki (1991) '"Beyond the 'Thorny Question'": Feminism, Foucault and the Desexualisation of Rape', *International Journal of the Sociology of Law* 19(1): 83–100.

Berns, Sandra S. and Baron, Paula (1994) 'Bloody Bones: A Legal Ghost Story and Entertainment in Two Voices To Speak as a Judge', *The Australian Feminist Law Journal* 2: 125–149.

Binder, Lisa A. (1995) '"With more than Admiration he Admired": Images of beauty and defilement in judicial narratives of rape', *Harvard Women's Law Journal* 18(Spring): 265–299.

Bornoff, Nicholas (1991) *Pink Samurai: The Pursuit and Politics of Sex in Japan*, London: Grafton Books.

Bottomley, Anne and Conoghan, Joanne (1993) 'Feminist Theory and Legal Strategy', in Anne Bottomley and Joanne Conoghan (eds) *Feminist Theory and Legal Strategy*, Oxford: Basil Blackwell.

Box, Steven (1983) *Power, Crime and Mystification*, London: Routledge.

Breckenridge, Jan (1999) 'Subjugation and Silences: The Role of the Professions in Silencing Victims of Sexual and Domestic Violence', in Jan Breckenridge and Lesley Laing (eds) *Challenging Silence: Innovative Responses to Sexual and Domestic Violence*, St Leonards: Allen and Unwin.

Brickman, Sarah (1986) 'Hush-hush topic but a good reason for jogging', *Far Eastern Economic Review* (1 May): 38.

Broadbent, Kaye (2003) *Women's Employment in Japan: The Experience of Part-time Workers*, London and New York: RoutledgeCurzon.

Bronitt, Simon H. (1992) 'Rape and Lack of Consent', *Criminal Law Journal* 16(5): 289–310.

Brown, Catherine W. (1988) 'Japanese Approaches to Equal Rights for Women: The Legal Framework', in John O. Haley (ed.) *Law and Society in Contemporary Japan: American Perspectives*, Dubuque: Kendall/Hunt.

Bryant, Taimie L. (1988) 'Marital Dissolution in Japan: Legal Obstacles and Their Impact', in John O. Haley (ed.) *Law and Society in Contemporary Japan: American Perspectives*, Dubuque, Iowa: Kendall/Hunt.

Buckley, Sandra (1991) '"Penguins in Bondage": A Graphic Tale of Japanese Comic Books', in Constance Penley and Andrew Ross (eds) *Technoculture*, Minneapolis: University of Minnesota Press.

—— (1993) 'Altered States: The Body Politics of "Being-Woman"', in Andrew Gordon (ed.) *Postwar Japan as History*, Berkeley: University of California Press.

—— (1997) *Broken Silence: Voices of Japanese Feminism*, Berkeley: University of California Press.

—— and Mackie, Vera (1986) 'Women in the New Japanese State', in Gavan McCormack and Yoshio Sugimoto (eds) *Democracy in Contemporary Japan*, Sydney: Hale and Iremonger.

Bumiller, Kristin (1990) 'Fallen Angels: The Representation of Violence Against Women in Legal Culture', *International Journal of the Sociology of Law* 18(2): 125–142.

Burgess-Jackson, Keith (1996) *Rape: A Philosophical Investigation*, Aldershot: Dartmouth.

Burns, Catherine (1995) 'Sexual Violence and Criminal Justice in Japan', in Vera Mackie (ed.) *Feminism and the State in Modern Japan*, Melbourne: Japanese Studies Centre.

—— (1997) 'Judicial Narratives on Trial: Constructions of Sex, Gender and Sexuality in the Japanese Courtroom', in Proceedings, 'International Conference on Women in the Asia-Pacific Region: Persons, Powers and Politics', 11–13 August, RELC, Singapore.
—— (forthcoming), 'Gendered Violence and the Criminal Justice System in Japan', in Vera Mackie (ed.) *Gender in Japan: Power and Public Policy*, New York and London: Routledge.
Burt, Martha R. (1998) 'Rape Myths', in Mary E. Odem and Jody Clay-Warner (eds) *Confronting Rape and Sexual Assault*, Wilmington: Scholarly Resources.
Burton, Nadya (1998) 'Resistance to Prevention: Reconsidering Feminist Anti-violence Rhctoric', in Stanley G. French, Wanda Teays and Laura M. Purdy (eds) *Violence Against Women: Philosophical Perspectives*, Ithaca: Cornell University Press.
Buruma, Ian (1984) *A Japanese Mirror: Heroes and Villains of Japanese Popular Culture*, London: Penguin.
Butler, Judith (1990) *Gender Trouble: Feminism and Subversion of Identity*, New York: Routledge.
—— (1993) *Bodies That Matter: On the Discursive Limits of 'Sex'*, New York: Routledge.
Cahill, Ann J. (2000) 'Foucault, Rape, and the Construction of the Feminine Body', *Hypatia* 15(1): 43–63.
Chalmers, Sharon (2002) *Emerging Lesbian Voices from Japan*, London: Routledge-Curzon.
Chen, Edward I. (1989) 'The National Law Examination of Japan', *Journal of Legal Education* 39(5): 1–26.
Chung, Chin Sung (1997) 'The Origin and Development of the Military Sexual Slavery Problem in Imperial Japan', *positions: East Asia cultures critique* 5(1): 219–253.
Chungmoo, Choi (1997) 'Guest Editor's Introduction', *positions: East Asia cultures critique* 5(1): v–xiv.
Clammer, John (1995) 'Consuming Bodies: Constructing and Representing the Female Body in Contemporary Japanese Print media', in Lise Skov and Brian Moeran (eds) *Women, Media and Consumption in Japan*, Surrey: Curzon Press.
Connell, Robert (1995) *Masculinities*, St Leonards, New South Wales: Allen and Unwin.
Coward, Rosalind (1987) 'Sexual Violence and Sexuality', in Feminist Review (ed.) *Sexuality: A Reader*, London: Virago.
Danbayashi, Kazue (1990) 'Gōkan Higaisha no Jinken to Keiji Tetsuzuki', *Hōgaku Seminā* 35(10): 40–43.
Danjo Kyōdō Sankaku Suishin Honbu (1997) 'Danjo Kyōdō Sankaku 2000 Nen Puran: Danjo Kyōdō Sankaku Bijon', Prime Minister's Office, Tokyo.
Davies, Margaret (1994) *Asking the Law Question*, Sydney: The Law Book Company.
Davis, Joseph W.S. (1996) *Dispute Resolution in Japan*, Den Haag: Kluwer Law International.
DAWN Newsletter (2003) 'Japanese Women Seen through Data'. Online, available at: www.dawncenter.or.jp/english/publication/edawn/9911/data.html (accessed 19 November 2003).
Delgado, Richard (1989) 'Storytelling for Oppositionists and Others: A Plea for Narrative', *Michigan Law Review* 87(8): 2411–2441.

Dijkstra, Bram (1986) *Idols of Perversity*, New York: Oxford University Press.

Duncan, Sheila (1994) '"Disrupting the Surface of Order and Innocence": Towards a Theory of Sexuality and the Law', *Feminist Legal Studies* 2(1): 3–28.

—— (1995) 'Law's Sexual Discipline: Visibility, Violence, and Consent', *Journal of Law and Society* 22(3): 326–352.

Dussich, John P.J. and Shinohara, Sugao (1997) 'Nonreporting of Sexual Assault in Japan', paper presented at the 9th International World Symposium on Victimology, 25–29 August, Amsterdam.

——, Paul C. Friday, Takayuki Okada, Akira Yamagami and Richard D. Knudten (2001) *Different Responses to Violence in Japan and America*, New York: Criminal Justice Press.

Editorial Committee of 'Women's Asia 21' (1996) 'Our Vision for the 21st Century: To Create the Society Based on Gender Justice, Ecological Sustainability and Global Democracy – Critique on the Japanese Government Vision', *Women's Asia 21: Voices from Japan* 2: 51–52.

Edwards, Anne and Heenan, Melanie (1994) 'Rape Trials in Victoria: Gender, Socio-cultural Factors and Justice', *The Australian and New Zealand Journal of Criminology* 27: 213–236.

Edwards, Susan (1992) 'Violence Against Women: Feminism and the Law', in Loraine Gelsthorpe and Allison Morris (eds) *Feminist Perspectives in Criminology*, Milton Keynes: Open University Press.

—— (1996) *Sex and Gender in the Legal Process*, London: Blackstone.

Ehara, Yumiko (1995) '"Sekushuaru Harasumento no Mondaika" wa Nani o Shitte Iru Koto ni naru no ka?', in Inoue Teruko, Ueno Chizuko and Ehara Yumiko (eds) *Sekushuaritii*, Tokyo: Iwanami Shoten.

Ehrlich, Susan (2001) *Representing Rape: Language and Sexual Consent*, London: Routledge.

EHS Law Bulletin Series (1996) *The Penal Code of Japan* 2 (2400).

Espinoza, Leslie G. (1997) 'Legal Narratives, Therapeutic Narratives: The Invisibility and Omnipresence of Race and Gender', *Michigan Law Review* 95(4): 901–937.

Estrich, Susan (1987) *Real Rape: How the Legal System Victimizes Women Who Say No*, Cambridge: Harvard University Press.

Ewick, Patricia and Silbey, Susan (1995) 'Subversive Stories and Hegemonic Tales: Toward a Sociology of Narrative', *Law and Society* 29(2): 197–226.

Feldberg, Georgina (1997) 'Defining the Facts of Rape: The Uses of Medical Evidence in Sexual Assault Trials', *Canadian Journal of Women and the Law/Revue Femmes et Droit* 9(1): 89–114.

Finch, A.J. (1999) 'The Japanese Police's Claim to Efficiency: A Critical View', *Modern Asian Studies* 33(2): 483–511.

Fish, Stanley (1980) *Is There a Text in This Class? The Authority of Interpretive Communities*, Cambridge: Harvard University Press.

Fitzgerald, Louise F. and Swan, Suzanne (1995) 'Why Didn't She Just Report Him? The Psychological and Legal Implications of Women's Responses to Sexual Harassment', *Journal of Social Issues* 51(1): 117–138.

Foote, Daniel H. (1992) 'The Benevolent Paternalism of Japanese Criminal Justice', *California Law Review* 80: 317–390.

Foucault, Michel (1977) *Discipline and Punish: The Birth of the Prison*, London: Penguin Books.

—— (1978) *The History of Sexuality: An Introduction*, (trans. Robert Hurley) London: Penguin Books.

—— (1980) 'Two Lectures', in Gordon, Colin (ed.) *Power/Knowledge: Selected Interviews and Other Writings, 1972–77*, New York: Pantheon Books.

Fujieda, Mioko (1989) 'Some Thoughts on Domestic Violence in Japan', *Review of Japanese Culture and Society* 3(1): 60–66.

Fujime, Yuki (1997a) 'The Licensed Prostitution System and the Prostitution Abolition Movement in Modern Japan', *positions: East Asia cultures critique* 5(1): 136–170.

—— (1997b) *Sei no Rekishigaku*, Tokyo: Fuji Shuppan.

Fujimoto, Tetsuya (1994) *Crime Problems in Japan*, The Institute of Comparative Law in Japan, Tokyo: Chūō University Press.

Fukushima, Mizuho (1997) *Saiban no Joseigaku*, Tokyo: Yūhikaku Sensho.

Funabashi, Kuniko (1995) 'Pornographic Culture and Sexual Violence', in Kumiko Fujimura-Fanselow and Atsuko Kameda (eds) *Japanese Women: New Feminist Perspectives on the Past, Present and Future*, New York: The Feminist Press.

Gagnon, John H. and Simon, William (1973) *Sexual Conduct: The Social Sources of Human Sexuality*, Chicago: Aldine Publishing.

Garon, Sheldon (1997) *Molding Japanese Minds: The State in Everyday Life*, Princeton: Princeton University Press.

Gatens, Moira (1996) *Imaginary Bodies: Ethics, Power and Corporeality*, London: Routledge.

Goodman, Marcia E. (1986) 'The Exercise and Control of Prosecutorial Discretion in Japan', *Pacific Basin Law Journal* 5(16): 16–95.

Goodstein, Lynne (1996) 'Sexual Assault in the United States and Vietnam: Some Thoughts and Questions', in Kathleen Barry (ed.) *Vietnam's Women in Transition*, London: Macmillan Press.

Graycar, Regina (1995) 'The Gender of Judgments: An Introduction', in Margaret Thornton (ed.) *Public and Private: Feminist Debates*, London: Oxford University Press.

—— (1996) 'Telling Tales: Legal Stories About Violence Against Women', *Cardozo Studies in Law and Literature* 8(2): 297–316.

Green, Andrew (1997) 'How the Criminal Justice System Knows', *Social and Legal Studies* 6(1): 5–22.

Griswold, Susan (1995) 'Sexuality, Textuality, and the Definition of the "Feminine" in Late Eighteenth-Century Japan', *U.S.-Japan Women's Journal* (English Supplement) 9: 59–76.

Groth, A. Nicholas and Birnbaum, H. Jean (1980) 'The Rapist: Motivations for Sexual Violence', in Sharon L. McCombie (ed.) *The Rape Crisis Intervention Handbook: A Guide for Victim Care*, New York: Plenum Press.

Hada, Aiko (1995) (trans. Kumiko Fujimura-Fanselow) 'Domestic Violence', in Kumiko Fujimura-Fanselow and Atsuko Kameda (eds) *Japanese Women: New Feminist Perspectives on the Past, Present and Future*, New York: The Feminist Press.

Haley, John O. (1986) 'Comment: The Implications of Apology', *Law and Society Review* 20(4): 499–507.

—— (1991) *Authority Without Power: Law and the Japanese Paradox*, New York: Oxford University Press.

—— (1995) 'Judicial Independence in Japan Revisited', *Law in Japan* 25: 1–18.

—— (1996) 'Crime Prevention Through Restorative Justice: Lessons From Japan', in Burt Galaway and Joe Hudson (eds) *Restorative Justice: International Perspectives*, Amsterdam: Kugler Publications.

Hanmer, Jalna, Radford, Jill and Stanko, Elizabeth (1989) *Women, Policing, and Male Violence: International Perspectives*, London: Routledge.

Hata, Ritsue (1990) 'Masumedia wa Gōkan o Dō Hōjiteiruka', *Hōgaku Seminā* 35(10): 48–51.

Hatarakukoto to Seisabetsu o Kangaeru Santama no Kai (1991) *Onna 6,500 Nin no Shōgen: Hataraku Onna no Mune no Uchi*, Tokyo: Gakuyō Shobō.

Hayakawa, Noriyo (1995) 'Sexuality and the State: The Early Meiji Debate on Concubinage and Prostitution', in Vera Mackie (ed.) *Feminism and the State in Modern Japan*, Melbourne: Japanese Studies Centre.

Hayashi, Yōko (1990) 'Gōkan o Meguru Hōjōkyō', *Hōgaku Seminā* 35(10): 28–31.

Heath, Mary and Naffine, Ngaire (1994) 'Men's Needs and Women's Desires: Feminist Dilemmas about Rape Law Reform', *The Australian Feminist Law Journal* 3: 30–52.

Helliwell, Christine (2000) '"It's Only a Penis": Rape, Feminism, and Difference', *Signs: Journal of Women in Culture and Society* 25(3): 789–876.

Henderson, Dan F. (1980) 'Japanese Law in English: Reflections on Translation', *Journal of Japanese Studies* 6(1): 117–154.

Henshall, Kenneth G. (1999) *Dimensions of Japanese Society: Gender, Margins and Mainstream*, London: Macmillan Press.

Higuchi, Keiko (1985) *Bringing Up Girls-Start Aiming at Love and Independence-(Status of women in Japan)*, (trans. Akiko Tomii) (English-language edition of *Onna no ko no Sodatekata*, 1978) Kyoto: Shōkadō Booksellers.

Hilsdon, Anne-Marie (1995) *Madonnas and Martyrs*, Sydney: Allen and Unwin.

Hirano, Ryūichi (1989) 'Diagnosis of the Current Code of Criminal Procedure', *Law in Japan* 22: 129–142.

Holmberg-Okubo, Susan Carol (1985) 'Criminal Justice and Social Control: A Japanese-American Comparative Study', unpublished PhD book, Rutgers: The State University of New Jersey, Dissertation Abstracts International 46: 1743A.

Hōmushō (1996) *Dai 109 Minji, Shōmu Jinken Tōkei Nenpō I Heisei 7 Nen, Annual Report of Statistics on Civil Affairs, Litigation and Civil Liberties for 1995, Vol.I.*, Tokyo.

Horiuchi, Kunihiro (1995) *Criminal Justice Profiles of Asia: Investigation, Prosecution, and Trial*, Tokyo: United Nations Asia and Far East Institute for the Prevention of Crime and the Treatment of Offenders (UNAFEI).

Hunter, Rosemary (2003) 'Women Barristers and Gender Difference', in Ulrike Shultz and Gisela Shaw (eds) *Women in the World's Legal Professions*, Oxford and Portland: Hart Publishing.

Ichioka, Yuji (1977) 'Ameyuki-san: Japanese Prostitutes in Nineteenth-Century America', *Amerasia* 4(1): 1–21.

Idrus, Nurul Ilmi (2001) 'Marriage, Sex and Violence', in Susan Blackburn (ed.) *Love, Sex and Power: Women in Southeast Asia*, Melbourne, Victoria: Monash University Press.

Igarashi, Futaba (1986) 'Forced to Confess', in Gavan McCormack and Yoshio Sugimoto (eds) *Democracy in Contemporary Japan*, Sydney: Hale and Iremonger.

Igeta, Ryōji (1978) 'Reform of Law in the Meiji Restoration', *ACTA Asiatica* 35: 72–98.

Ihaya, Manako (1990) 'Trouble on the Trains', *The Japan Times Weekly* 30 (32), 11 August: 4.

Ikeda, Richiko (1995) 'Changing Interpretations of Gender Relations in Japan', unpublished PhD book, Oklahoma University, Ann Arbor UMI.

Ikeuchi, Hiromi (2003) 'Domestic Violence', in *WOM: Japanese Women Now*. Online, available at: www.wom-jp.org/e/JWOMEN/dv.html (accessed 12 May 2003).

Ingleby, Richard and Johnstone, Richard (1995) 'Judicial Decision Making', in Rosemary Hunter, Richard Ingleby and Richard Johnstone (eds) *Thinking About Law: Perspectives on the History, Philosophy and Sociology of Law*, St Leornards, New South Wales: Allen and Unwin.

Ishimatsu, Takeo (1989) 'Are Criminal Defendants in Japan Truly Receiving Trials by Judges?', *Law in Japan* 22: 143–153.

Itoh, Hiroshi (1970) 'How Judges Think in Japan', *The American Journal of Comparative Law* 18: 775–804.

—— (1990) 'Judicial Review and Judicial Activism in Japan', *Law and Contemporary Problems* 53(1): 169–179.

Jackson, Stevi (1996) 'Heterosexuality and Feminist Theory', in Diane Richardson (ed.) *Theorising Heterosexuality: Telling it Straight*, Buckingham: Open University Press.

Johnson, David (2002) *The Japanese Way of Justice: Prosecuting Crime in Japan*, Oxford: Oxford University Press.

Johnson, Elmer H. (1993) 'Japan Reacts Against Street Prostitution: The Anti-Prostitution Law and Women's Guidance Homes', *International Journal of Comparative and Applied Criminal Justice* 17(1): 29–41.

Kaminaga, Yuriko and Westhoff, Jörn (2003) 'Women Lawyers in Japan: Contradictory Factors in Status', in Ulrike Shultz and Gisela Shaw (eds) *Women in the World's Legal Professions*, Oxford and Portland: Hart Publishing.

Kamio Knapp, Kiyoko (1995) 'Still Office Flowers: Japanese Women Betrayed by the Equal Employment Opportunity Law', *Harvard Women's Law Journal* 18: 83–137.

Kamiya, Masako (1995) 'A Decade of the Equal Employment Opportunity Act in Japan: Has It Changed Society?', *Law in Japan* 25: 40–83.

Kaneko, Ann (1995) 'In Search of Ruby Moreno', *AMPO: Japan-Asia Quarterly Review* 25(4)–26(1): 66–70.

Kaspiew, Rae (1995) 'Rape Lore: Legal Narrative and Sexual Violence', *Melbourne University Law Review* 20: 350–382.

Keisatsuchō (1991–1996) *Heisei [3–8] Nen no Hanzai*, Tokyo.

—— (2003) *Heisei 14 Nen no Hanzai*. Online, available at: www.npa.go.jp/taikei/index.htm (accessed 1 November 2003).

Keeton, Robert E. (1988) 'Legislative Facts and Similar Things: Deciding Disputed Premise Facts', *Minnesota Law Review*, 73(1): 1–72.

Kelly, Liz (1987) 'The Continuum of Sexual Violence', in Jalna Hanmer and Mary Maynard (eds) *Women, Violence and Social Control*, London: Macmillan Press.

—— and Radford, Jill (1996) '"Nothing Really Happened": The Invalidation of Women's Experiences of Sexual Violence', in Mariannne Hester, Liz Kelly and Jill Radford (eds) *Women, Violence and Male Power: Feminist Activism, Research and Practice*, Buckingham: Open University Press.

——, Burton, Sheila and Regan, Linda (1996) 'Beyond Victim or Survivor: Sexual Violence, Identity and Feminist Theory and Practice', in Lisa Adkins and Vicki

Merchant (eds) *Sexualizing the Social: Power and the Organization of Sexuality*, London: Macmillan.

Kenzo, Moriguchi (1999) 'Time Running out for "Knock" as Opinion Turns Against Him', *The Japan Times*, 20 December.

Kersten, Joachim (1996) 'Culture, Masculinities and Violence Against Women', *British Journal of Criminology* 36(3): 381–395.

Khor, Diana (1999) 'Organizing For Change: Women's Grassroots Activism in Japan', *Feminist Studies* 25(3): 633–661.

Kinjō, Kiyoko (1990) 'Seiteki Jiyū no Hoshō to Gōkanzai' (Rape and the Guarantee of Sexual Freedom), *Hōgaku Seminā* 35(10): 32–35.

—— (1991) *Hōjoseigaku: Sono Kōchiku to Kadai*, Tokyo: Nihon Hyōronsha.

Kondo, Dorinne K. (1990) *Crafting Selves: Power, Gender, and Discourses of Identity in a Japanese Workplace*, Chicago: University of Chicago Press.

Konradi, Amanda (1996) 'Preparing to Testify: Rape Survivors Negotiating the Criminal Justice Process', *Gender and Society* 10(4): 404–432.

Koshi, George M. (1970) *The Japanese Legal Advisor: Crimes and Punishments*, Tokyo: Charles E. Tuttle.

Koss, Mary P. (1998) 'Hidden Rape: Sexual Aggression and Victimization in a National Sample of Students in Higher Education', in Mary E. Odem and Jody Clay-Warner (eds) *Confronting Rape and Sexual Assault*, Wilmington: Scholarly Resources.

Kumagai, Fumie and O'Donoghue, Gearoid (1978) 'Conjugal Power and Conjugal Violence in Japan and the U.S.A.', *Journal of Comparative Family Studies* 9(2): 211–229.

Lacey, Nicola (1998) *unspeakable subjects: feminist essays in legal and social theory*, Oxford: Hart Publishing.

Larimer, Tim (1999) 'Japan's Shame', *Time Magazine*, 19 April: 60–61.

Lebra, Takie Sugiyama (1976) *Japanese Patterns of Behaviour*, Honolulu: University of Hawaii Press.

—— (1984) *Japanese Women: Constraint and Fulfillment*, Honolulu: University of Hawaii Press.

Lees, Sue (1993) 'Judicial Rape', *Women's Studies International Forum* 16(1): 11–36.

—— (1997) *Ruling Passions: Sexual Violence, Reputation and the Law*, Buckingham: Open University Press.

LeGrand, Camille E. (1973) 'Rape and Rape Laws: Sexism in Society and Law', *California Law Review* 61(3): 919–941.

Levin, Mark (1998) 'Applicants and Acceptance Statistics for Japan's Legal Training and Research Institute: 1949–1998'. Online, available at: www.tuj.ac.jp/newsite/main/law/lawresources/TUJonline/Japan'sLegalProfession/lrtistajJapanBarPassStats.html (accessed 1 November 2003).

Lock, Margaret (1987) 'Protests of a Good Wife and Wise Mother: The Medicalization of Distress in Japan', in Edward Norbeck and Margaret Lock (eds) *Health, Illness and Medical Care in Japan*, Honolulu: University of Hawaii Press.

L'Orange, Helen and Egger, Suzanne (1987) 'Adult Victims of Sexual Assault: An Evaluation of the Reforms', *Sexual Assault Law Reform in the 1980s: To Where From Now?*, Sydney: Institute of Criminology, Sydney University Law School.

Los, Maria (1992) 'Feminism and Rape Law Reform', in Loraine Gelsthorpe and Allison Morris (eds) *Feminist Perspectives in Criminology*, Milton Keynes: Open University Press.

McBarnet, Doreen J. (1981) *Conviction: Law, the State and the Construction of Justice*, London: Macmillan.

Mackie, Vera (1997) *Creating Socialist Women in Japan: Gender, Labour and Activism, 1900–1937*, Cambridge: Cambridge University Press.

—— (2003) *Feminism in Modern Japan: Citizenship, Embodiment and Sexuality*, Cambridge: Cambridge University Press.

MacKinnon, Catharine A. (1983) 'Feminism, Marxism, Method, and the State: Toward Feminist Jurisprudence', *Signs* 8(2): 635–658.

—— (1987) *Feminism Unmodified: Discourses on Life and Law*, Cambridge, MA: Harvard University Press.

McLeer, Anne (1998) 'Saving the Victim: Recuperating the Language of the Victim and Reassessing Global Feminism', *Hypatia* 13(1): 41–55.

McVeigh, Brian J. (1997) *Life in a Japanese Women's College: Learning to be Ladylike*, London: Routledge.

Manderson, Lenore and Linda Rae Bennett (eds) (2003) *Violence Against Women in Asian Societies*, London and New York: RoutledgeCurzon.

Marcus, Sharon (1992) 'Fighting Bodies, Fighting Words: A Theory and Politics of Rape Prevention', in Judith Butler and Joan W. Scott (eds) *Feminists Theorize the Political*, New York: Routledge.

Mayer, Cynthia (1984) 'Japan: Behind the Myth of Japanese Justice', *The American Lawyer* (July/August): 113–124.

Mikazuki, Akira (1976) 'Saibansho Seido' (Judicial System), in Tanaka Hideo (ed.) *The Japanese Legal System: Introductory Cases and Materials*, Tokyo: University of Tokyo Press.

Miller, Laura (1998) '"Bad Girls": Representations of Unsuitable, Unfit, and Unsatisfactory Women in Magazines', *U.S.–Japan Women's Journal* (English Supplement) 15: 31–51.

Ministry of Justice (1996) *Summary of White Paper on Crime 1996*, Tokyo.

—— 'A Guide to Court Procedures'. Online, available at: www.courts.go.jp/english/procedure/keiji2_e.html (accessed 7 November 2003).

Miya, Yōko (1995) 'Twenty-Eight and Single; Occupation: Secret', *Law in Japan* 25: 125–134.

Miya, Yoshiko (1984) *Dokyumento Seibōryoku/Reipu*, Tokyo: San Maku Shuppan.

—— (1989) *Sekushuaru Harasumento*, Tokyo: Kyōiku Shiryō Shuppankai.

Miyazawa, Setsuo (1991) 'Administrative Control of Japanese Judges', *Kobe University Law Review*, International Edition 25: 45–61.

—— (1992) *Policing in Japan: A Study on Making Crime*, Albany: State University of New York Press.

—— (2000) 'Legal Education and the Reproduction of the Elite in Japan', *Asian-Pacific Law and Policy Journal*. Online, available at: www.hawaii.edu/aplpj (accessed 5 December 2003).

Monbushō (1974) *Shishunki ni okeru Seito Shidōjō no Shomondai: Kōtō gakkō hen*, Tokyo.

Mossman, Mary Jane (1998) 'Achieving Gender Equality: Legal Principles and Social Arrangements', *Kobe University Law Review*, International Edition 32: 21–43.

Naffine, Ngaire (1995) 'Sexing the Subject (of Law)', in Margaret Thornton (ed.) *Public and Private: Feminist Legal Debates*, London: Oxford University Press.

—— (1997) *Feminism and Criminology*, St Leonards, NSW: Allen and Unwin.

Naftulin, Lois J. (1980) 'Women's Status Under Japanese Law', *Feminist International* 2: 13–16.

Nakamori, Yoshihiko (1988) 'Otto ni tsuki Tsuma ni Taisuru Gōkanzai no Seiritsu o Mitometa Jitsurei', *Hanrei Hyōron* 348, (in *Hanrei Jihō*1256, 1 February): 216–218.

Nakayama, Ken-ichi Inui (1990) 'The Legal Control of Prostitution in Japan', *EuroCriminology*, 3: 213–220.

National Police Agency (1995) *White Paper on Police 1995 (Excerpt)*, Tokyo.

Nolte, Sharon H. and Hastings, Sally Ann (1991) 'The Meiji State's Policy Toward Women, 1890–1910', in Gail Lee Bernstein (ed.) *Recreating Japanese Women, 1600–1945*, Berkeley: University of California Press.

Noonan, Sheila (1996) 'Battered Woman Syndrome: Shifting the Parameters of Criminal Law Defences (or (Re)Inscribing the Familiar?)', in Anne Bottomley (ed.) *Feminist Perspectives on the Foundational Subjects of Law*, London: Cavendish Publishing.

NSW Department for Women (1996) *Heroines of Fortitude: the Experiences of Women in Court as Victims of Sexual Assault*, Sydney.

Obuchi, Tetsuya (1987) 'Role of the Court in the Process of Informal Dispute Resolution in Japan: Traditional and Modern Aspects, With Special Emphasis on In-Court Compromise', *Law In Japan* 20: 74–101.

Office for Gender Equality (1997–2000) *Women in Japan Today*, Prime Minister's Office, Tokyo. Online, available at: www.gender.go.jp/index2.html (accessed 7 November 2003).

Olson, Susan M. and Batjer, Christina (1999) 'Competing Narratives in a Judicial Retention Election: Feminism versus Judicial Independence', *Law and Society Review* 33(1): 123–160.

Omatsu, Maryka (1997) 'The Fiction of Judicial Impartiality', *Canadian Journal of Women and the Law/Revue Femmes et Droit* 9(1): 1–16.

Otto Kara no Bōryoku' (D.V.) Chōsa Kenkyū Kai (1993) '"Otto (Aijin) kara no Bōryoku" ni tsuite no Chōsa Kenkyū', *D.V. Tsūshin* 3 (5 October).

Pateman, Carole (1988) *The Sexual Contract*, Stanford: Stanford University Press.

Perkins, Roberta (1991) *Working Girls: Prostitutes, Their Life and Social Control*, Canberra: Australian Institute of Criminology.

Pflugfelder, Gregory M. (1999) *Cartographies of Desire: Male-Male Sexuality in Japanese Discourse, 1600–1950*, Berkeley: University of California Press.

Pringle, Rosemay (1992) 'Absolute Sex? Unpacking the Sexuality/Gender Relationship', in R.W. Connell and G.W. Dowsett (eds) *Rethinking Sex: Social Theory and Sexuality Research*, Melbourne: Melbourne University Press.

Puren, Nina (1995) 'Hymeneal Acts: Interrogating the Hegemony of Rape and Romance', *The Australian Feminist Law Journal* 5: 15–26.

Rastam, Alina (ed.) (2002) *The Rape Report: An Overview of Rape in Malaysia*, Petaling Jaya: All Women's Action Society and Strategic Info Research Development.

Rhode, Deborah (1993) 'Feminist Critical Theories', in Patricia Smith (ed.) *Feminist Jurisprudence*, London: Oxford University Press.

Rich, Adrienne (1980) 'Compulsory Heterosexuality and Lesbian Existence', *Signs: Journal of Women in Culture and Society* 5: 631–660.

Roberts, Janine (1994) *Tales and Transformations: Stories in Families and Family Therapy*, New York: W.W. Norton.

Robertson, Jennifer (1991) 'The Shingaku Woman: Straight from the Heart', in Gail Lee Bernstein (ed.) *Recreating Japanese Women, 1600–1945*, Berkeley: University of California Press.

—— (1999) 'Dying to Tell: Sexuality and Suicide in Imperial Japan', *Signs: Journal of Women in Culture and Society* 25(1): 5–35.

Roden, Donald (1990) 'Taishō Culture and the Problem of Gender Ambivalence', in Thomas Rimer (ed.) *Culture and Identity: Japanese Intellectuals during the Interwar Years*, Princeton: Princeton University Press.

Rohlen, Thomas P. (1974) *For Harmony and Strength: Japanese White-Collar Organization in Anthropological Perspective*, Berkeley: University of California Press.

Roth, Louise Marie (1999) 'The Right to Privacy Is Political: Power, the Boundary Between Public and Private, and Sexual Harassment', *Law and Social Inquiry* 24(1): 45–71.

Russell, John G. (1998) 'Consuming Passions: Spectacle, Self-Transformation, and the Commodification of Blackness in Japan', *positions: East Asia cultures critique* 6(1): 113–177.

Saitō, Toyoji (1992) 'Preventive Detention in Japan', in Stanislaw Frankowski and Dinah Shelton (eds) *Preventive Detention: A Comparative and International Law Perspective*, London: Martinus Nijhoff Publishers.

Sasaki, Masahito (1989) 'Stress and Coping Among Divorced Single Women Living in Homes for Single Mothers and Children in Japan: A Descriptive Study', unpublished PhD book, Columbia University, UMI Dissertation Services.

Scheppele, Kim Lane (1987) 'The Re-vision of Rape Law', *The University of Chicago Law Review* 54(3): 1095–1116.

—— (1989) 'Foreword: Telling Stories', *Michigan Law Review* 87(8): 2073–2098.

—— (1991) 'Facing Facts in Legal Interpretation', in Robert Post (ed.) *Law and the Order of Culture*, Berkeley: University of California Press.

Scherdin, Lill (1994) 'The Creation of "Strangers" and Punishment in Japan', *Social Justice* 21(2): 204–236.

Schultz, Ulrike (2003) 'Introduction: Women in the World's Legal Professions: Overview and Synthesis', in Ulrike Shultz and Gisela Shaw (eds) *Women in the World's Legal Professions*, Oxford and Portland: Hart Publishing.

Scutt, Jocelynne A. (1990) *Women and the Law: Commentary and Materials*, Sydney: The Law Book Company.

—— (1992) 'The Incredible Woman: A Recurring Character in Criminal Law', *Women's Studies International Forum* 15(4): 441–460.

—— (1994a) *The Sexual Gerrymander*, North Melbourne: Spinifex.

—— (1994b) 'Judicial Vision: Rape, Prostitution, and the "Chaste Woman"', *Women's Studies International Forum* 17(4): 345–356.

Shibata, Tomo (1999) 'Japan's Wartime Mass-Rape Camps and Continuing Sexual Human-Rights Violations', *U.S.–Japan Women's Journal* (English Supplement) 16: 48–86.

Shigematsu, Setsu (1996) '"The Law of the Same" and Other (Non)-Perversions: Women's Body as a "Use-Me/Rape-Me" Signifier', *U.S.–Japan Women's Journal* (English Supplement) 12: 154–177.

Smart, Carol (1989) *Feminism and the Power of Law*, London: Routledge.

—— (1990) 'Law's Truth/Women's Experience', in Regina Graycar (ed.) *Dissenting Opinions: Feminist Explorations in Law and Society*, St Leonards, NSW: Allen and Unwin.

—— (1995) *Law, Crime and Sexuality: Essays in Feminism*, London: Sage.

—— (1996) 'Collusion, Collaboration and Confession: On Moving Beyond the Heterosexuality Debate', in Diane Richardson (ed.) *Theorising Heterosexuality: Telling it Straight*, Buckingham: Open University Press.

Smith, Robert J. (1987) 'Gender Inequality in Contemporary Japan', *Journal of Japanese Studies* 13(1): 1–25.

Sōmuchō Tokeikyoku (1991) *Nihon Tōkei Nenpō 3 nen* 411, Tokyo.

Sterling, Alinor C. (1995) 'Undressing the Victim: The Intersection of Evidentiary and Semiotic Meanings of Women's Clothing in Rape Trials', *Yale Journal of Law and Feminism* 7(1): 87–132.

Stetz, Margaret and Oh, Bonnie B.C. (eds) (2001) *Legacies of the Comfort Women of World War II*, New York: M.E. Sharpe.

Tanaka, Hideo (1980) 'Legal Equality Among Family Members in Japan – The Impact of the Japanese Constitution of 1946 on the Traditional Family System', *South Carolina Law Review* 53(2): 611–644.

Tanaka, Kazuko (1995) 'The New Feminist Movement in Japan, 1970–1990', in Kumiko Fujimura-Fanselow and Atsuko Kameda (eds) *Japanese Women: New Feminist Perspectives on the Past, Present and Future*, New York: The Feminist Press.

Tanaka, Yuki (1995) *Rape and War: The Japanese Experience*, Melbourne: Japanese Studies Centre, Monash University.

Taniguchi, Masataka (1970) 'Gōkanzai ni okeru Bōkō, Kyōhaku no Teido', *Hanrei Hyōron* 27, (in *Hanrei Jihō* 220, 11 April): 5–9.

Taylor, Veronica (1988) 'Prostitution Law and the Family: Japan and Victoria', *Law in Context* 6(1): 99–114.

Terrill, Richard (ed.) (1992) *World Criminal Justice Systems: A Survey*, 2nd edn, Cincinnati: Anderson Publishing.

Thornton, Margaret (1989) 'Hegemonic Masculinity and the Academy', *International Journal of the Sociology of Law* 17(2): 115–130.

—— (1991) 'Feminism and the Contradictions of Law Reform', *International Journal of the Sociology of Law* 19(4): 453–474.

—— (1995) 'The Cartography of Public and Private', in Margaret Thornton (ed.) *Public and Private: Feminist Legal Debates*, London: Oxford University Press.

—— (1998) 'Authority and Corporeality: The Conundrum for Women in Law', *Feminist Legal Studies* 6(2): 147–170.

Tokyo Gōkan Kyūen Sentā (1990) *Reipu Kuraishisu: Kono mijika na kiki*, Tokyo: Gakuyō Shōbō.

—— (1993) *Tokyo Gōkan Kyūen Sentā Nyūsu* (24 May).

Tokyo Metropolitan Government (1983) *Stride By Stride, Women's Issues in Tokyo: The Current Situation*, Tokyo: Tokyo Colony Printing.

Townsend, Kathleen (1996) 'Sexual Assault Law: A Fair Trial or Advantage to the Accused?', paper presented at the National Conference on Sexual Assault, 'Balancing the Scales', Freeway Hotel, Perth, 20–21 June.

Tsunoda, Yukiko (1990) 'Higaisha no gawa kara Mita Minji Saiban', *Hōgaku Seminā* 35(10): 44–47.

—— (1991) *Sei no Hōritsugaku*, Tokyo: Yūhikaku Sensho.

—— (1997) 'Sexual Harassment and Domestic Violence in Japan'. Online, available at: www.tuj.ac.jp/law/tsunoda.html (accessed 31 March 2000).

Ueno, Chizuko (1987a) 'The Position of Japanese Women Reconsidered', *Current Anthropology* 28(4): 75–84.

—— (1987b) 'Genesis of the Urban Housewife', *Japan Quarterly* 34(2): 130–142.
United Nations Asia and Far East Institute for the Prevention of Crime and Treatment of Offenders (1990) *Crime and Justice in Asia and the Pacific: A Report on the Third United Nations Survey of Crime Trends, Operations of Criminal Justice Systems and Crime Prevention Strategies, 1980–1986*, Canberra: Australian Institute of Criminology.
Uno, Kathleen S. (1991) 'Women and Changes in the Household Division of Labour', in Gail Lee Bernstein (ed.) *Recreating Japanese Women, 1600–1945*, Berkeley: University of California Press.
Uno, Sumie (1998) 'The First Large-Scale Survey on Domestic Violence in Japan: One-Third of Women are Victims!'. Online, available at: www.dawncenter.or.jp/english/publication/edawn/9811/column.html (accessed 3 November 2003).
Upham, Frank (1987) *Law and Social Change in Postwar Japan*, Cambridge: Harvard University Press.
Vaughn, Michael S. and Tomita, Nobuho (1990) 'A Longitudinal Analysis of Japanese Crime from 1926 to 1987: The Pre-War, War, and Post-War Eras', *International Journal of Comparative and Applied Criminal Justice* 14(2): 145–169.
Vogelman, Lloyd (1990) *The Sexual Face of Violence: Rapists on Rape*, Johannesburg: Ravan Press.
Wagatsuma, Hiroshi and Rosett, Arthur (1986) 'The Implications of Apology: Law and Culture in Japan and the United States', *Law and Society Review* 20(4): 461–498.
Weatherfield, Allison (1995a) 'Amerikajin Bengoshi no mita Nihon no Sekushuaru Harasumento (jō)', *Jurisuto* 1079 (15 November): 31–41.
—— (1995b) 'Amerikajin Bengoshi no mita Nihon no Sekushuaru Harasumento (ge)', *Jurisuto* 1080 (1 December): 75–81.
West, Robin (1996) 'A Comment on Consent, Sex, and Rape', *Legal Theory* 2: 233–251.
Whitford, Margaret (1991) *Luce Irigary: Philosophy in the Feminine*, London: Routledge.
Wolff, Leon (1996) 'Eastern Twists on Western Concepts: Equality Jurisprudence and Sexual Harassment in Japan', *Pacific Rim Law and Policy Journal* 5(3): 509–535.
Yamada, Shōzō (1999a) 'Shokuba ni okeru Sekushuaru Harasumento o Meguru Saiban Rei no Bunseki (1)', *Hōgaku Shinpō* 105(12): 41–83.
—— (1999b) 'Shokuba ni okeru Sekushuaru Harasumento o Meguru Saiban Rei no Bunseki (kan)', *Hōgaku Shinpō* 106(12): 89–146.
Yamazaki, Tomoko (1975) 'Sandakan No. 8 Brothel', *Bulletin of Concerned Asian Scholars* 7(5): 52–60.
Yasaki, Mitsukuni (1982) 'Law and Shakai-Tsūnen as a Legal Form of Consensus Idea', *Osaka University Law Review* 29: 1–10.
Yokohama Josei Fōramu (ed.) (1991) *Onna no Nettowākingu*, Tokyo: Gakuyō Shobō.
Yokoyama, Minoru (1993) 'Emergence of Anti-Prostitution Law In Japan – Analysis from Sociology of Criminal Law', *International Journal of Comparative and Applied Criminal Justice* 17(2): 211–218.
Young, Alison (1998) 'The Wasteland of the Law, the Wordless Song of the Rape Victim', *Melbourne University Law Review* 22: 442–465.
Young, Iris Marion (1990) *Throwing Like a Girl and Other Essays in Feminist Philosophy and Social Theory*, Bloomington: Indiana University Press.

Yunomae, Tomoko (1989) '"Ikebukuro-Baishun Dansei Shibō Jiken" Kara Mietekitamono', *Nihon Fujin Mondai Konwakai Kaihō* 48: 45–53.
—— (1990) 'Seibōryoku o Meguru Onna no Undō', in Kanai Yoshiko and Kanō Mikiyo (eds) *Onnatachi no Shisen: Ikiruba no Feminizumu*, Tokyo: Shakai Hyōronsha.
Yurchesyn, Kathaleen A., Keith, Ann and K. Edward Renner (1992) 'Contrasting Perspectives on the Nature of Sexual Assault Provided by a Service for Sexual Assault Victims and by the Law Courts', *Canadian Journal of Behavioural Science*, 24(1): 71–85.

Additional legal cases cited

Case of murder, Tokyo District Court, 1987 SH62 (wa) No. 67, Judgment 18 December 1987, *Hanrei Jihō* 1275, 11 July 1988: 41–45.
Case of murder, Tokyo High Court, 1988 SH63 (u) no. 155, Judgment 9 June 1988, *Hanrei Jihō* 1283, 9 June 1989: 54–58.
Case of rape resulting in death, murder, Tokyo High Court, 1981 SH56 (u) No. 625, Judgment 25 January 1984, *Hanrei Jihō* 1125, 21 October 1984: 166–174.
Case of break and entry, rape, habitual theft, murder, abandoning a corpse, Tokyo High Court, 1987 SH62 (u) No. 555, Appeal Judgment 23 April 1991, *Hanrei Jihō* 1395, 11 November 1991: 19–33.
Case of murder, rape resulting in death, attempted blackmail, Osaka High Court 1991 H3 (u) No. 822, Appeal Judgment 11 May 1994, *Hanrei Jihō* 1511, 21 January 1995: 153–171.
Case of break and entry, robbery and attempted rape, Tokyo High Court, 1993 H5 (u) No. 507, *Hanrei Jihō* 1495, 11 August 1994: 143–146.
Case of break and entry, larceny, attempted rape, rape, robbery, Osaka High Court, 1987 SH62 (u) No. 233, *Hanrei Jihō* 1297, 1 March 1989: 145–148.

Index